LOVE IN THE LEAD

The Miracle of the Seeing Eye Dog

Second Edition

Peter Brock Putnam

Peter Putnam

University Press of America,® Inc.
Lanham • New York • Oxford

Copyright © 1997 by
University Press of America,® Inc.
4720 Boston Way
Lanham, Maryland 20706

12 Hid's Copse Rd.
Cummor Hill, Oxford OX2 9JJ

Library of Congress Cataloging-in-Publication Data

Putnam, Peter
Love in the lead : the miracle of the seeing eye dog / Peter Brock
Putnam - 2nd ed.
p.   cm.
Includes index.
1. Seeing Eye, Inc.—History. 2. Guide dog schools—United
States—History. 3. Guide dogs—Training—United States—History.
I. Title.
HV1780.6U6P87 1997   636.7'088'6—dc21   97-15322 CIP

ISBN 0-7618-0777-2 (pbk: alk. ppr.)

♾™ The paper used in this publication meets the minimum
requirements of American National Standard for information
Sciences—Permanence of Paper for Printed Library Materials,
ANSI Z39.48—1984

Behind the human personalities of the Seeing Eye, there are dogs and behind both dogs and humans are another group of humans, the instructors of the Seeing Eye. They are tough and tender, sensible and sensitive, hard-headed, good-humored, and great-hearted. They have steel nerves, iron constitutions, and hair-trigger reflexes. They give of themselves cheerfully and without stint. They are like their dogs. I know of no class of human beings that I admire more.

With affection, admiration, and respect, this book is dedicated to the men and women instructors of the Seeing Eye—past, present, and future.

Contents

v

Book IV: SECOND GROWTH

Acknowledgments

This is the story of the Seeing Eye, the first school for the education of guide dogs and blind humans in the United States. Its development was a uniquely cooperative venture depending on the right combination of human ingredients at every stage in the process. As Morris Frank, one of its founders, used to insist, "If you know anything about the founding of the Seeing Eye, you have to believe in the Good Lord even if you're a damned atheist."

Hyperbole was Morris's style, but it is easy to agree with him here. Especially in the early days, the evolution of the Seeing Eye depended on such an extraordinary assortment of personalities and took so many unexpected twists and turns that serendipity seems too pale a concept to explain it. It may be simpler to account for it by a benevolent divinity forever intervening with just the right person or circumstance at the critical moment.

Besides the main actors, there were many other characters who played significant or crucial roles for longer or shorter periods. I have known most of them, though some only glancingly. I have received much help from them in writing this book. I am very much indebted to both Stuart Grout and his successors as president of the Seeing Eye, Dennis Murphy and Kenneth Rosenthal, for giving me access to the school's files and for refusing to exert even a hint of censorship. Significant assistance of different kinds has

Acknowledgments

come from all of the following, Jean Bernat, C. Warren Bledsoe, Adelaide Clifford Byers, Rosemary Carroll, G. William Debetaz, Edith Doudge De Heller, Judy Deuschle, Joseph Funke, Morris and Lois Frank, Alfreda Galt, Dr. Dolores Holle, George Humphrey, Elizabeth Hutchinson, Marian Jobson, Joan Jones, Margaret Kibbee, Dr. Robert Kirk, David Loux, Edward Myrose, Douglas Roberts, W. Sydnor Settle, Roger Taylor, George Werntz, Jr., Robert Whitstock, and Walter Abbot Wood III. Their universal eagerness to be helpful is a tribute to the school.

I have concentrated on the early history, because the early years were the formative years. They witnessed the development of the methods, the goals, and the philosophy that guided the later period. Cinderella becomes less interesting after she marries the prince, but the first edition of this book was published in 1979; this history would be incomplete without an account of the very significant and progressive changes in breeding, puppy raising, health care, training techniques, and physical facilities that have occurred since then.

Ever since 1941 I have been experiencing the extraordinary partnership of dog and human that is at the heart of the Seeing Eye, and I think I understand in my bones the leadership role the dogs played in the formulation of Seeing Eye philosophy. The dogs were leaders in more than the literal sense, and what gave the human leaders their direction was their ability to read the dogs' language.

In conclusion, I must acknowledge my tremendous debt to two people who spent many hundreds of hours poring over letters, clippings, articles, reports, pamphlets, and books. Both plunged into dull and painstaking research. Both made valuable suggestions for improving the style and structure of this book. They are my good friend and reader, Peggy Waldron, and my indispensable friend and wife, Durinda Dobbins Putnam.

Publication of this edition was made possible by funding from Mr. Audley Blackburn and *Augie*, the Dolfinger-McMahon Foundation, and Mr. and Mrs. Robert G. Scott.

Introduction: Partnership

"Is she really any good to you?"

The question came from a veterinary doctor, and the "she" referred to was Minnie, my first Seeing Eye dog, whom he had just returned to me at my Princeton dormitory room. A week before, prior to critical surgery, she had been on the verge of death, but except for the taped bandage that circled her middle, there was no sign of it now. In her joy at coming home, she wiggled into my lap, licked my face, and nipped my hands. Then she made a circular dash around the room, slipped on a throw rug, scrambled to her feet, sneezed, and, to cover her embarrassment at my laughter, began to chew on one arm of the sofa. It was an exhibition of thoroughly random behavior, and it is no wonder that there was a hint of genuine skepticism beneath the doctor's smiling question.

I cannot recall my reply. Even to me, the transformation of Minnie, the irresponsible schoolgirl, into Minerva, the trustworthy guide, was always a miracle. Miracles are better demonstrated than described, and my best answer would have been to pick up her harness. She always dove into it eagerly without waiting for me to slip it over her head, and instantly she became a new person—serious, self-possessed, and intent on her work.

Outside, she would tug me along across the campus at

1

four miles an hour, ignoring the tempting squirrels scampering across the grass, but dutifully mindful of the many steps along the walk, threading her way carefully through the moving crowd of students, but impatiently nudging aside the slower walkers by nosing them in the calves, hurrying across streets that were deserted, but stopping short in the face of oncoming traffic. All these things she would do, and yet they would have provided only a partial answer to the doctor's question.

The relationship between a Seeing Eye dog and its master is as complex as that between a child and its parent. Indeed, acquiring a dog is not unlike adopting a child. The weeks each applicant must spend at the Seeing Eye's school in Morristown, New Jersey, are a kind of character examination, and graduation, like the certificate of adoption, is not the end, but the beginning of a long emotional adjustment. There are many irritations as well as gratifications, but in the end the successful dog and master arrive at a working partnership whose balance is equaled in few human families.

Even during my first days at the school, I discovered that, while my "adopted child" was already perfectly educated in the partnership, I still had everything to learn. Unprepared for her sudden, precise stops, I might slip over curbs or stumble up steps, and more often than I care to think my awkwardness in following her turns cost her a bruised paw. However, basic coordination was much easier to master than orientation. It was Minnie's duty to guide me around obstacles as we walked, but it was I who had to direct her by word and gesture along the route I wished to travel. In total darkness I had to know where I was, where I was going, and how to get there in a series of lefts, rights, and forwards.

Perhaps I was unusually backward, but I found this a tremendous strain. Sweating with concentration, I would suddenly go blank as to the number of blocks to the next turn and fall instant prey to all the anxieties of a lost child.

Even back at Princeton, whose terrain ought to have been so familiar from my sighted years, I often misjudged distances or angles on the diagonally intersecting walks, steps, and archways on the campus. My uncertainty was fully as nerve-racking for Minerva as for me, but each problem had its resolution. To illustrate both I can find no better anecdote than one from the life of my second dog, Wick.

We were walking down a country road one evening when a recent acquaintance, pulling up in his car, asked me to stop by for a drink. I agreed, but suggested that I continue on foot for the exercise. The road was new to me and without curbs or sidewalks to act as landmarks, but I knew his house to be some distance ahead on the left-hand side and I assumed that he would hail me as I came up. Five hundred yards farther on I discarded this assumption, but there was no one to ask. I turned back. Up and down that road we went, trying tentative rights and lefts, and the more impatient my gestures became, the more uncertain and hesitant Wick grew. Nearly an hour later, having passed the proper driveway fully a dozen times, we finally turned into it and I made it all up to a much relieved Wick with a shower of pats and praises.

The climax was yet to come. Over a month later when for the first time we passed that way again, Wick, remembering the anxieties of that afternoon, paused before the elusive driveway as if to inquire whether I wanted to go in, and in all the years since then, he has never failed to hesitate at that same spot.

It was less my impatience while lost than the pats and "Atta good boys" which followed that had impressed the driveway on Wick's memory. This sort of reward is the motivating mainspring of every Seeing Eye dog. His pleasure in his master's praise seems sufficient compensation for every hardship. An aggressive terrier whom we were forced to pass almost daily used to persecute Wick with menacing sorties on our flanks for nearly a hundred yards, all the while screaming canine insults in a high staccato bark. I managed to congratulate Wick so warmly after each running of the gauntlet that he seemed almost to look forward to the ordeal, only quickening his pace a little to have it behind him. Then he would jump up on me joyously, saying plainer than any words could tell, "Oh, what a good boy am I!"

And so, through a thousand little episodes and adjustments, the child and the parent become full partners. The rigid mechanics of command and obey dissolve into a cooperation as instinctive and a coordination as spontaneous as those of ballroom dancers. I vividly recall the thrill of a moment when Wick and I were walking home from the post office one afternoon. As we passed a grocery store where I often stopped, Wick hesitated. For one split second we were suspended on the doubt of Wick's implied question. At the slightest sign from me, we could have turned into the store in perfect unison. Upon my negative uh-uh, we resumed the steady flow of our direction without breaking stride. The communication had been perfectly clear, and yet the whole movement was so smooth that I believe neither Wick's question nor my answer could have been detected by any but a trained observer. Such harmony of motion is a consequence of long practice, but it is derived from a deeper level of communion.

The most valuable lesson a Seeing Eye master can learn is also the simplest. He must understand that he is blind and that his dog can see. This adds up to a human limitation and a canine potentiality. On the other hand, he has the power of reason, while his dog has certain powerfully irrational instincts, and this adds up to a human potentiality and a canine limitation. Both have the power to love, which can alone make possible the patience, the concentration, and the self-discipline necessary to weld the two, the man animal and the dog animal, into a corporate unit. Through love, they learn to recognize and to forgive both their own and each other's limitations and therefore to realize their joint potentialities.

The discovery of this concept of joint self-realization opened a new world for me. Before blindness, having recognized the existence of no limitations, my life was confined to potentialities. Seven months after blindness, the acquisition of Minnie helped me to realize that the only way to overcome a limitation is to understand and accept it. Together, Minnie and I could do anything, and I felt a greater confidence and appetite for life than I had ever known.

Returning to Princeton, I found that my academic activities could not fully satisfy this appetite. In response to a secret yearning, I took piano lessons for the first time. To work off steam, I swam seventy to a hundred laps daily in the gym pool. Fulfilling a freshman dream, I ran for and was elected to the presidency of the Princeton Triangle Club, whose musical comedy I helped to write and direct. Dwarfing everything else, I met and fell in love with the girl I was to marry, Durinda.

Minnie was with me through all of it—in the lecture halls and classrooms, in the piano studios, beside the pool, on the stage in the theater, and on the floor of the trains swaying off to New York or Northampton for weekends with Durinda. All these things demanded varying degrees of sacrifice from the undeviating Minnie. I could demand it from Minnie then, as I could demand it from Wick later, not because I regarded either of them as a tool, but because I did not.

Any attempt to define a Seeing Eye dog as a tool, a guiding instrument for a blind man, breaks down on the love that alone enables that instrument to function. This love can no more make the dog the tool of the master than it can make the master the tool of the dog. It forges a bond of sympathy so strong that their happiness becomes interdependent.

It is so with my dog today, but it was from Minnie, my first dog, that I learned it first. My very love for her compelled me to force my will upon her in the knowledge that my every success would be her justification, that my every failure would imply her betrayal, and that my happiness would include her own. Humans find this same dynamic inspiration in the love of their own kind, but there is a sense in which a dog strikes closer to the heart, because a dog seems to understand organically without benefit of reasoned explanation. Minnie could have no understanding of the sounds of the piano, of the words of the lectures, or of the splashings in the pool, and yet she seemed to understand better than anyone their deeper meaning for my, and therefore for her, happiness. And to answer the doctor's question at last, it was in this compelling love and understanding that I realized the full and true measure of Minnie's good to me.

I
BIRTH BY SERENDIPITY

1
Fortunate Fields

The Seeing Eye's official birthday is January 29, 1929, but its origin goes back much further. We could trace it all the way back to the moment, some 20,000 years ago, when human beings first domesticated the ancestor of the dog. For our purposes here, we may prefer the day in 1914 when Dorothy Harrison Wood returned from Europe with a German shepherd named Hans von Saarbrücken. That event combined three elements essential for the later development of the organization called The Seeing Eye: Hans was a shepherd. He was an extraordinary specimen of the breed. Finally, his mistress was as remarkable as he was.

Dorothy Leib Harrison was born on May 30, 1886, into an old Philadelphia family. Her father, Charles Custis Harrison, a one-time provost of the University of Pennsylvania, owned a prosperous sugar refining company. With three brothers and two sisters, Dorothy was the youngest of six children. Educated at the Agnes Irwin School in Philadelphia and the Rathbowie School in Eastbourne, England, she was raised a blue blood who became, as a matter of course, a member of the Daughters of the American Revolution, the Colonial Dames of America, the Descendants of the Signers of the Declaration of Independence, and the Society of Magna Carta Dames. In 1906, at the age of twenty, she was married to Walter Abbot Wood, Jr.

Walter Wood was considerably older than Dorothy. A New York state senator, he owned a mowing and reaping machine company in Hoosick Falls. Walter and Dorothy had two sons, Walter III, born in 1907, and Harrison, in

1914. Living on the Wood estate, Dorothy interested herself in the selective breeding of cattle to increase milk productivity. She was an aristocrat imbued with the work ethic. She was also extremely observant, and from the time she acquired her dog, Hans, her keen eyes and mind took him in.

A German shepherd, Hans belonged to a breed that had been herding sheep in Central Europe for two centuries. Throughout history the vast majority of dogs have been workers. They have been employed to hunt, track, and retrieve game; to haul carts or sleds; to guard homes or farms; to rescue lost travelers or track fugitives; to dig truffles; to kill rats; or to herd flocks. Even when their work involved such barbarous amusements as bull baiting or dog fighting, they had the dignity of a job to do. It is only in the last century or more that many breeds of dog have been reduced from the status of working partners to that of unemployed pets.

In 1899, the German Shepherd Society was founded, and its members began breeding shepherds for the show ring. The result was to damage the working qualities of the breed. More interested in aesthetics than in utility, in appearance than in temperament, show breeders produced a shepherd that was elegant to behold, but lacking in the strength, stamina, and mental qualities of a good working dog. Hans von Saarbrücken was not one of this new breed. He lacked the refined lines and extreme angulation of the hind legs that appealed to show breeders, but he possessed in abundance all the physical and mental characteristics of the worker. Dorothy retained her appreciation of these qualities in spite of the changes in her life that followed fast on her acquisition of Hans.

The death of Walter in 1915 made her a widow in her twenties. She continued to live in Hoosick Falls for two years before moving back to Radnor on Philadelphia's Main Line. There, in 1923, she married George Eustis of Aiken, South Carolina.

George was closer in age to young Walter than to Dorothy, but age was not their sole discrepancy. George was tall and carelessly handsome. Dorothy was petite, neat, and plain except for humorous brown eyes and an engaging directness of manner. She was a born worker. George lived to play. She had the joy of life and an exceptionally merry laugh, but she was driven by a strong sense of purpose. He was full of animal spirits. One friend described him as "an utterly charming, utterly attractive rascal." Young Walter suggested that his mother's awareness of the lack of purpose in her new husband may have prompted an important decision.

George Eustis's stepfather was the celebrated concert pianist Josef Hofmann, and Hofmann owned a spectacular chalet on Mt. Pelerin, overlooking Vevey, Switzerland. Dorothy proposed to rent the chalet and there to establish a breeding and training kennel to breed back into the German shepherd the working qualities she so valued in Hans. Soon after the wedding in 1923, she moved with her husband, her sons, and her Hans to Mt. Pelerin where she set up the kennels she named Fortunate Fields. Walter commented, "I think Mother thought it would give George something to do."

The chalet resembled a small hotel. One wing had three stories; the other, four. Both were surrounded with balconies and outside staircases having breathtaking views of the lake and mountains. The drawing room had two concert grand pianos with space for half a dozen. A visitor wrote, "The house bulges with people, people that work and guests that play." George Eustis loved parties and people. His wife's wealth and his stepfather's chalet offered splendid opportunities for entertaining. Following World War I, Europe became a stomping ground for American expatriates and travelers on the Grand Tour. E. H. Sothern and Julia Marlowe, the Broadway matinee idols of their day, had settled nearby. Josef Hofmann was often in residence. There were streams of visitors of the sort that might today be labeled the "beautiful people."

Like her husband, Dorothy enjoyed "heaps of guests," and, like Dorothy, George worked at the breeding and training, but there was a difference. For George it was a kind of game, a game that he enjoyed and that he played hard and well. Dorothy's commitment had a religious dimension. During their first year of marriage, she was drawn to Christian Science, and George became a connoisseur of good wine.

Early in 1924, Dorothy read some articles on the genetics and breeding of German shepherds in the *Shepherd Dog Review*. The author was Elliott S. Humphrey, and she began to correspond with him. Humphrey tried to answer the questions with which her letters teemed, but it soon became clear that he could not tell her what she wanted to know without first inspecting her dogs. She offered to pay his way to Switzerland, and he arranged a leave of absence from his job breeding Arabian horses in Berlin, New Hampshire. He arrived on Mt. Pelerin for the first time in August of 1924.

Jack, as Humphrey was generally known, was thirty-four, below medium height, and with the wiry, muscular build and bow legs of a cowboy, which for a time he had been. His ears stuck out, and the snuff that he habitually carried between gum and upper lip had won him the nickname of "the cowboy with a weeping lip." He reminded people of Will Rogers. There was a leathery charm to his looks. His eyes were gray blue, and his face was alight with intelligence.

Jack's upbringing had been the opposite of that of the "lady boss." He was born in Saratoga Springs, New York, where he had worked as an apprentice jockey during the racing season. In his teens, he went West where he drove mules, punched cattle, and broke horses. He worked as a barker on a sight-seeing bus in Los Angeles and entertained visitors to Catalina by diving for abalone shells. At one point he had trained lions and tigers for Diamond Billy Hall, who sold animal acts to circuses, and he once had taught a camel to walk backward for seventeen steps. It was an incredible feat that had gained him instant oblivion until the writer Alexander Woollcott resurrected it in a *New Yorker* "Profile" twenty-five years later. During the war he had joined the Cavalry Remount Service, purchasing, caring for, and shipping horses. Afterward, he was hired to breed and train Arabians for a millionaire paper-maker in New Hampshire. Three times he rode in and finished the army's grueling three-hundred-mile endurance race, and once he won it.

Jack Humphrey's brain was as active as his body. He compensated for his lack of formal education by becoming an omnivorous reader and an acute observer of what went on about him. He had a prodigious memory for what he read and saw. From the study of horse breeding in New Hampshire, he turned to an analysis of the genetics of the German shepherd. The publication of his findings in the *Shepherd Dog Review* brought the Philadelphia blue blood and the cowboy with the weeping lip together.

For all the differences in their backgrounds, Dorothy Eustis and Jack Humphrey had much in common. Both were strong-willed. Both had keen, active, and analytical minds. Both were hard workers and were strongly attracted to the idea of breeding good working qualities into the shepherd dog. Not long after Jack's arrival at Fortunate Fields, they agreed to enter into a working partnership for this purpose. Along with his wife, Nettie, and two-year-old son, George, Jack was installed in an apartment in one wing of the chalet, and the experiment at Fortunate Fields began to assume significant shape.

The breeding and training program at Fortunate Fields was unique in three ways. The first was its purpose. To Dorothy, the shepherd dog population represented a virtual Niagara of energy going to waste because breeders were aiming for beauty instead of utility. Their efforts seemed to her as misguided as converting Niagara Falls into decorative fountain displays instead of harnessing its hydroelectric power. Fortunate Fields was not indifferent to beauty, but it sought to combine it with the temperament, intelligence, endurance, and strength that would make dogs useful citizens. Although the German army had employed 48,000 working dogs by the end of the war, Fortunate Fields was the first systematic attempt to breed for working qualities as well as for conformation.

A second peculiar feature was made possible by Dorothy's wealth. Unlike breeders who depended on the sale of their stock to underwrite their operations, she was financially independent. She did not need to compromise her standards by breeding the kind of dog that would appeal to the commercial market. She was not interested in selling her dogs.

Jack Humphrey contributed the third unique feature of the program: the use of scientific method. He began with a systematic analysis of the evidence. Since 1899, the German Shepherd Dog Society had recognized 97 show ring champions and 38 working champions. Jack traced and compared the genealogies of all 135 dogs to identify any ancestors common to both types. He found pitifully few. The commercial incentive to breed for the show ring had virtually eliminated working strains. No breeding stock that combined good working qualities with conformation was available. He would have to begin at the very beginning. He first had to define the qualities of the ideal dog that Fortunate Fields was seeking and then try to breed for those qualities.

Point by point, Jack defined 35 distinct mental and physical characteristics. He assigned each a numerical value based on its desirability and difficulty of attainment. Teachability and endurance rated the highest. He devised a method of compiling a numerical score for each dog's temperament and conformation. The two were then combined into a single number. According to Jack's system, the ideal dog would score 6,720 points.

Jack's ideal dog differed significantly from the standard shepherd of that day. The large size desired in the show ring tended to weaken endurance. Jack preferred a somewhat smaller dog endowed with sufficient strength for its work. The show ring put a high value on extreme angulation of the hind legs, but Jack found that it tended to be coupled with poor shoulder structure. He preferred sound shoulders. He discovered an apparent correlation between the gene for light eyes and that for intelligence. The show ring vogue called for dark eyes. If he was right, breeding for dark eyes would be tantamount to breeding out intelligence. But Jack was a good pragmatist. He did not permit his theory to blind him to reality. When a dog whose paws he had scored low was able to run almost continuously for twenty-four hours without becoming footsore, he realized his scoring was at fault.

Jack believed that the fine working qualities of shepherds like Hans had been lost through the practices of line breeding and inbreeding. Line breeding paired offspring of the same line. Inbreeding was an intensification of line breeding. It mated father with daughter, mother with son, or brother with sister to accentuate certain desirable characteristics. Jack proposed the reverse approach. He would open up blood lines by breeding dogs that were only distantly related. He sought out and purchased breeding stock of six distinct strains. These, he believed, offered sufficient genetic variety to provide all the characteristics for his ideal dog.

Breeding was only half the program. The puppies must then be raised, trained, and put to work. Unlike the puppies raised by most breeders, those whelped at Fortunate Fields were not confined indefinitely to kennel runs where they could learn nothing. When they had been weaned, they were farmed out to peasant families to grow up with the human contact that is so congenial and important for dogs. At four, six, nine, twelve, and fifteen months, they were visited in their foster homes and scored by the Humphrey method. Meticulous records for each dog were updated and carefully filed in the home office. When they attained the proper age, dogs were brought back to Fortunate Fields and trained to work. This was the only way of measuring the success of the breeding program. Ultimately they were graduated into police work, trailing, border patrol, prison duty, military communications, or Red Cross rescue work, but the breeding rights were retained for Fortunate Fields.

Jack was already an experienced trainer. George Eustis showed considerable natural ability, and he honed his skills by becoming one of the first civilians to take the full four-month course at the Prussian Police Dog Center at Grünheide. A German Swiss named Mueller who had police dog experience was quartered on the grounds. Dorothy was too small for hard attack work, but she was active in other phases of the training, and together they graduated a number of dogs and masters into the police force of the Canton de Vaud.

Police dogs must have some instinct for aggression, but it goes against the grain of many mentally balanced dogs to attack the human beings who have been their traditional allies for 20,000 years. Often they must be taught to attack. The trainer begins by fluttering a piece of gunny sacking in the dog's face. The dog wants to please, but may not be able to figure out what the trainer wants. There may be a long delay before the worried animal snaps at the sacking in sheer exasperation. Immediately the trainer showers it with praise. When a dog has learned to attack the sacking on command, the sacking is wrapped around the arm of another man, who wears a padded suit, and the training continues.

The desire to please a human master is uniquely canine. In testing intelligence, psychologists must motivate all other animals with rewards of food. Dogs will attempt to solve a puzzle set for them simply because master was silly enough to want them to do it. In *Working Dogs*, a brilliant book that he later wrote with Lucian Warner, Humphrey concluded that although dogs are probably more intelligent than any other animal below the primates, it is not their intelligence but their desire to please that makes them so teachable.

Their sensory acuity is advantageous in certain types of work. Dogs are color blind and cannot see as far or as clearly as humans. If unaided by sound or smell, they may fail to recognize their own masters at a short distance, but dogs perceive motion far better than we do. Their hearing is much keener than ours, and their sense of smell is so far superior as to defy comparison. With their noses they distinguish as many shades and nuances of scent as our eyes detect in the colors of the rainbow.

Among Fortunate Fields dogs certain traits seemed genetically linked to gender. Males were significantly more aggressive than females, while females were significantly more intelligent than males. At one point Jack thought he detected an inherited reluctance to jump barriers. Since this is an exercise in which dogs generally delight, he was curious and took slow-motion pictures of reluctant dogs jumping. It turned out that dogs whose forelegs had too straight an angulation could not break the force of a steep descent and therefore bumped their noses when they landed. Their dislike of jumping was due to a structural, not a behavioral, flaw. Willingness seemed inheritable. Wigger von Blasienberg, an outstanding trailer purchased in Germany, passed on his trail-willingness to twenty of his progeny.

An interesting genetic phenomenon appears when dogs who trail silently are crossed with those that bay on the scent. The baying gene is dominant, and all the progeny will trail in cry, but they will take their voice from the mute parent. A litter bred from a bloodhound and a German shepherd will trail in cry like bloodhounds, barking like shepherds.

Wigger's trailing feats with the Swiss police became
legendary. In his time he tracked down more than fifty
criminals. He endeared himself to the local peasantry by
tracking down a dog who had been working carnage on the
domesticated chinchillas of neighboring farms. On another
occasion, a peasant discovered that he had lost a wallet con-
taining valuable papers while plowing a two-acre field.
Wigger was called in and set to sniffing methodically along
the furrows. In less than a half hour he stopped, dug down
six inches, and unearthed the wallet. There had been no
way to inform Wigger that he was supposed to find a wallet. He simply sniffed along until his scent identified something unusual.

With the constant flow of guests through the chalet on
Mt. Pelerin, tales of Wigger's prowess crossed the Atlantic.
When they reached the ear of an alert editor in Philadelphia, she asked Dorothy Eustis to write an article for the
Saturday Evening Post. As Jack recalled, "This request probably had in mind the story of the work being done at Fortunate Fields. To have written such a story would at that time
have caused a lot of inquiries to buy Fortunate Fields dogs
when none were for sale, as they were being trained, put to
work, and breeding rights retained for future breeding use.
To have sold them to come to the States could have resulted
in a loss of animals that would later be needed for our
breeding program. As a result, Dorothy decided on the
story of what the Germans had done for their war blind."

With her deepening involvement with Christian Science, Dorothy chose her title from the Bible. A verse from
Proverbs reads: "The hearing ear and the seeing eye, the
Lord hath made even both of them." She titled her article
"The Seeing Eye." She chose her subject to deflect publicity
from Fortunate Fields and to avoid nuisance mail from
American shepherd breeders. She succeeded in her immediate object, but the *Post* article had other, wholly unfore-
seen consequences.

2
The Seeing Eye

In 1927, guide dogs for the blind were nothing new. A blind Germanic king was supposed to have had a guide dog in 100 B.C. A wall painting in Pompeii depicts what seems to be a blind man whose dog is leading him through the marketplace. The blind St. Herve is said to have been led throughout Brittany by a small white dog in the sixth century. A thirteenth-century Chinese scroll shows a dog leading its blind master, and there are manuscript references to guide dogs in Western Europe at the same period.

From the fifteenth century on, there were a great many drawings and paintings of blind men with dogs, including those by Tintoretto, Rembrandt, and Gainsborough. They have many features in common. The dogs are too small to pull their masters out of danger. They guide with flexible leashes that could have indicated only a general direction. The masters carry long staffs or canes. All are men and all are apparently wandering beggars or musicians. The general impression is depressing and the guidance is ineffective. Occasionally a dog is shown leading its master into a ditch or looking on as he falls off a bridge. Presumably all these dogs were trained by their blind masters.

In 1819 Father Johann Klein, a Viennese priest, first proposed that guide dogs should be trained by sighted instructors. He pointed out that a rigid leading stick attached to the dog's harness would give its master a much more accurate sense of the dog's movements than a flexible leash. He added a brief description of how the dogs might be trained and recommended shepherds and poodles for the work. Yet so far as we know, there was no attempt to establish a systematic school for guide dogs until nearly a century after Father Klein's suggestion.

In 1916, the German Shepherd Dog Society proposed a school to provide guides for the mounting number of Germany's blind war veterans. A training school was begun at Oldenburg, and its success led to a second school at Württemberg. Following the war, schools to train dogs to guide the civilian blind were established at Potsdam and Munich. By the time Dorothy's article appeared, an estimated 4,000 Germans were using guide dogs.

Dorothy had known of the work in Germany for several years. Too often the story has been told as if the discovery of the Potsdam school had come as a dazzling revelation that she immediately sought to share with the American public. In January of 1924, a certain Herr Schwanatus had written George a detailed account of German guide dogs. In that same year, Dorothy had made an offer to the American Red Cross to pay for the cost of bringing a German dog and trainer to the United States. She and George had visited the Potsdam school in 1925 and again in 1926. Moreover, the German work had been brought to the attention of American workers for the blind long before Dorothy's *Post* article was published. In 1923, the American Association of Workers for the Blind had heard a lecture on guide dog schooling by a German trainer. In 1925, the Potsdam school offered to provide Robert Irwin of the American Foundation for the Blind with both dogs and trainers for a fee. John L. Synikin, a Minneapolis dog breeder, studied the work in Germany and returned to establish the Master Eye Foundation. He imported a German-trained dog that he retrained for Senator Schall of Minnesota in 1927. At about the same time, Josef Weber, who had worked with both police dogs and guide dogs in his native Germany, was setting up a training kennel outside Princeton, New Jersey.

Strangely, none of these early efforts interested American workers for the blind. Apparently they conceived of guiding work very much as depicted in the paintings of earlier centuries. Edward Allen, head of the prestigious Perkins School for the Blind, wrote of "a dirty little cur dragging a blind man along at the end of a string, the very index of incompetence and beggary." Robert Irwin at the American Foundation announced that he "would not be caught with one of the blooming things." The preconceptions of such professionals distorted their understanding of the very different image presented in Dorothy Eustis's article, but the article was addressed to the general public, not to professionals in the field. The professionals had convinced themselves that guide dogs would not work. The public had an open mind. Readers were gripped by the article's opening lines:

> To everyone, I think, there is always something particularly pathetic about a blind man. Shorn of his strength and his independence, he is prey to all the sensitiveness of his position, and he is at the mercy of all with whom he comes in contact. The sensitiveness above all is an almost insuperable obstacle to cope with in his fight for a new life, for life goes on, willy-nilly, and the new conditions must be reckoned with. In darkness and uncertainty he must start again, wholly dependent on outside help for every move. His other senses may rally to his aid, but they cannot replace his eyesight. To man's never failing friend has been accorded this special privilege. Gentleman, I give you the German shepherd dog!
>
> Because of their extraordinary intelligence and fidelity, Germany has chosen her own breed of shepherd dogs to help her in the rehabilitation of her war blind, and in the lovely city of Potsdam, she has established a very simple and business-like school for training her dogs as blind leaders.
>
> Enclosed with a high board fence, the school consists of dormitories for the blind, kennels for the dogs, and quarters for the teachers, the different buildings framing a large park laid out in sidewalks, in roads with curbs, steps, brid-

ges and obstacles of all kinds, such as scaffoldings, barriers, telephone poles and ditches, everything, in fact, that a blind man has to cope with in everyday life.

The article then described the various stages in guide dog education over a four-month period. The total cost of a dog fully trained and ready to leave the school was only $60. The guide was able to transmit signals to its blind master through a semirigid U-shaped handle attached to the harness. The dog learned to pull back before curbs until the master could find the edge with his cane, to stop before approaching traffic, and to swerve around trees or pedestrians. Up to this point in the article readers must have been interested but incredulous. Dorothy Eustis anticipated their skepticism by proclaiming her own:

I had seen so many so-called trained dogs which, put to the test, did mediocre work accompanied by many excuses that I was more or less prepared to hear reasons for poor work. I had expected possibly to see an instructor with eyes bandaged give an exhibition with one special dog to the running accompaniment of He's off his work today—didn't eat this morning; he was not exercised yesterday; that's funny, he usually does that perfectly; there must be something distracting him and so on. I had read of the blind man who crosses the Potsdamer Platz in Berlin with his dog twice a day, going to and from work, and had seen a photograph of him there, but knowing how much the Potsdamer Platz would resemble Fifth Avenue and Forty-Second Street if all the traffic were allowed to circulate at the same time, I put it down to a good story and a better photograph. Consequently, I was not prepared to have one little incident open wide the door to my conversion.

She described a class of blind men shuffling and groping uncertainly down a path to a gate where they called their dogs for harnessing.

I shall never forget the change that came over one man as he turned away from that gate. It was as though a complete transformation had taken place before my eyes. One moment it was an uncertain, shuffling blind man, tapping with a cane. The next, it was an assured person with his dog firmly in hand and his head up, who walked toward us quickly and firmly, giving his orders in a low, confident voice. That one quick glimpse of the crying need for guidance and companionship in the lonely, all-enveloping darkness stood out clearly before my swimming eyes. To think that one small dog could stand for so much in the life of a human being, not only with his usual role of companion, but as his eyes, sword, shield and buckler! How many humans could fill those roles with the same uncomplaining devotion and untiring fidelity? Darned few, I think!

As I followed him, it seemed impossible to believe that the man wasn't taking the dog for a walk and stopping for traffic on his own accord. Not once during the whole hour that I followed them did that dog's attention wander. The walk lay through the crowded shopping street with all the traffic of a big city, its noises, distractions, its scents and stray dogs on mischief or pleasure bent.

As he threaded his way along the street, and the pair went much more quickly without interference than I, who continually bumped into people in my attempt to keep up, I was amazed at the pace; I had started by walking briskly, but I found the distance ever widening and the need to make it up every so often at a jog trot.

The most critical test came when the man and dog entered a path which had barriers constructed to keep out cyclists. The bicycle barriers were broken here and there by narrow openings to admit pedestrians. Since the barriers were waist-high, it would be easy for the dog to walk beneath the bar that would catch his master in the midriff.

A couple strolling ahead had dropped a coat directly in the path, but the blind man and dog skirted, and the dog immediately came back to a line that would lead him between the barriers, although for him it would have been simpler and shorter to go under.

There was a big catch in my throat as I saw them turn into the school grounds with other pairs coming from different directions, and I knew that I was converted.

It had not been a particular exhibition staged for my special benefit, but just one of the many dogs turned out every month with its blind master. There were no fireworks, no display, no excuses, no muddling, but honest work done by honest dogs, and my hat was off to those who had worked out and perfected such a method of sympathetic training.

After describing a meeting with another blind man who had had his dog for three whole years without bumping into anything except once when it was the master's fault, Dorothy Eustis concluded with a fanfare:

The future of all blind men can be the same, however blinded. No longer dependent on a member of the family, a friend, or a paid attendant, the blind can once more take up their normal lives as nearly as possible where they left them off, and each can begin or go back to a wage-earning occupation, secure in the knowledge that he can get to and from his work safely and without cost; that crowds and traffic have no longer any terrors for him and that his evenings can be spent among friends without responsibility or burden to them; and last but far from least, that long healthful walks are now possible to exercise off the unhealthy fat of inactivity and so keep the body strong and fit. Gentlemen, again, without reservation, I give you the shepherd dog!

Dorothy had written the article, sent it to America, and forgotten about it. Toward the end of the summer of 1927, she and George, her sons, Walter, now twenty, and Harrison, thirteen, and her orphaned niece and ward, Esther Rowland, had enjoyed a holiday in Venice. On their return to Fortunate Fields, they were joined by Jack Humphrey, who had been in the States winding up his final obligations to his former employer in New Hampshire. He was now free of all concerns but the management of Fortunate Fields. Both he and Dorothy were looking forward eagerly to the work ahead. A rude shock awaited them.

The *Post* published "The Seeing Eye" on November 5. The reaction was rapid and unexpected. As Jack put it, "What had not been thought of was the fact that it would be read to the blind. Soon, bundles of letters came to Dorothy from the Curtis Publishing Company, letters from the blind, mostly on one theme: Is this story true? If it is true, where can I get a dog? I am blind."

Dorothy had written about Potsdam to divert the attention of dog fanciers from Fortunate Fields, but the strategy had backfired. Jack walked into the big room one day to find his lady boss in tears. When he asked what was wrong, she said, "Jack, what have I done! I have shown the American blind there is a way to liberty and raised their hopes when there is no way they can have the liberty we have shown them."

She had brought Jack Humphrey to Fortunate Fields to make its breeding program a scientific experiment. Now humanitarian demands were intruding. Was science deaf to humanity? Were the two incompatible?

As Dorothy Eustis debated these questions, her attention was drawn to a letter written on the stationery of the National Life and Accident Insurance Company, Incorporated, Nashville, Tennessee. It was addressed to the Curtis Publishing Company and dated November 9, 1927. The opening paragraphs follow, precisely as written.

My dear Mrs. Eustis,

In reference to your article, "The All Seeing Eye," which appeared in the *Saturday Evening Post* of November 5th, is of great interest to me so that is the reason why I take the liberty to address this letter to you.

I have often thought of this solution for the blind but I have never heard of it being put to a practical use before, of course, there are a few cases throughout the United States realizing that if handled in the proper manner and supervised correctly this would be quite a help to the blind of our country. I would appreciate very much if you would be kind enough to give me more information upon this matter and if you would give me the address of this school in Germany, or of any trainer in this country who might have anything similar as I should like very much to forward this work in this country, as three and a half years ago at the age of sixteen I was deprived of my sight and know from practical experience what rehabilitation means and what it means to be dependent upon a paid helper who are unsympathetic and not interested in their work and do not appreciate kindness as shown to them and as you well know that there are many throughout the land who not even have paid attendants.

The letter was signed Morris S. Frank. As the reader can see, it is rambling and almost without punctuation. It gives the wrong title for Dorothy Eustis's article. Although the writer states that he "should like very much to forward this work in this country," that could hardly be considered a firm commitment, especially in the context of a structureless sentence. Yet for some reason Dorothy Eustis, a stickler for clarity of expression, sensed something special in the garbled message of a nineteen-year-old youth from Nashville. Was it intuition? Dumb luck? Divine Providence? Whatever it was, it is certain that, of all the people who had written her, no one was so well equipped for the role he would play in The Seeing Eye as Morris S. Frank.

3
Southern Rebel

Morris Frank was born in Nashville on March 23, 1908, the third and much the youngest son of well-to-do parents. John Frank was the stereotypical Southern gentleman: soft-spoken, suave, courteous. Jessie Hirsch Frank was a fighter imbued by her Jewish heritage with a passion for social reform. She had lost the sight of one eye when it hemorrhaged as she was giving birth to her first son. Some fifteen years later, on the Fourth of July, she was riding horseback when a boy threw a firecracker beneath her horse. She was thrown and stunned. When she returned to consciousness, she was totally blind.

Blindness did not deaden her social conscience. Every day of her life, Morris recalled, she had made three baby nightgowns for distribution through the settlement house she helped to found in Nashville. She knew personally the leading social workers in Chicago's Hull House and New York's Henry Street Settlement. She was active in the Council of Jewish Women. She was an ardent supporter of Margaret Sanger and birth control. Morris could remember sitting with George Washington Carver at the family dinner table at a time when interracial dining was taboo. Other houseguests were the prison reformer and warden of Sing Sing, Thomas Mott Osborne, and such advocates of work for the blind as Edward Van Cleve of the New York Institute of the Blind, Edward Allen of the Perkins School, and Olin Burritt of the Philadelphia School for the Blind.

As far back as Morris could remember, his mother had been blind and he had been her helper. When he was only

six, he had been her sole traveling companion and guide on
a trip to Maine. He had already lost one eye to an overhanging limb while riding horseback. At sixteen, he was spar-
ring with friends on the school playground when a fist
caught him squarely in the other eye. He never saw again.

His early apprenticeship with his mother had prepared
him for some aspects of blindness. Its conspicuousness did
not bother him in the least, but he was active and impatient
by nature, and he resented his lack of freedom. In 1924,
services for the blind were meager. There were no classes
in the use of a cane for travel; there would be no scientific
attempt to develop cane technique until World War II. What
Morris learned about the use of a cane he taught himself.
Following World War I, the white cane was introduced in
France. It later spread to England, but it was almost unknown in America. The first city ordinance to grant users of
a white cane the right of way was passed in Peoria, Illinois,
in 1930.

The education of blind children was well established
by 1924. The Perkins School had been chartered by the Massachusetts legislature in 1829 and Charles Dickens had described it in his *American Notes*. The New York Institute and
Philadelphia School came soon after, but all these schools
isolated blind children from the sighted world. Perkins had
been founded as the "New England Asylum for the Blind,"
and when Morris lost his sight, many schools were still
called asylums. Louis Braille had invented the code that
bears his name in 1829, but there had been so many attempts to improve on it that they created a sort of Babel in
embossed type. Up until 1917, when an international conference agreed on a single system, books for the blind were
coded in five different alphabets. There was a small federal
subsidy for embossing texts for schoolchildren, but there
was no subsidy for embossing adult books until 1931. Talking Book records were still further in the future.

In 1924, the American Foundation for the Blind was
only three years old and had developed few special aids

and devices. There were no braille watches, for example. Morris acquired a pocket repeater bought in Europe. Repeaters were invented in the nineteenth century to enable sighted people to tell time in the dark. When the owner pressed a spring, the watch chimed the hours, quarter hours, and minutes. The mechanism was cunning, but far beyond the financial means of the average blind person, and counting chimes was less efficient than feeling the face of a watch with braille numbers.

Work for the adult blind had begun around the turn of the century. States established commissions for the blind that employed itinerant instructors to give braille lessons in the homes of clients. Sheltered workshops offered blind men and women a means of earning money instead of begging, singing on street corners, or depending on their families. But segregation breeds its own poison, and charity could become despotic. Mrs. Quinan, who directed a sheltered workshop in San Francisco, was so jealous of her domain that she refused permission to blind and deaf Helen Keller to set foot inside it. Helen Keller declared, "Not blindness, but the attitude of the seeing to the blind is the hardest burden to bear."

At the time Morris lost his sight, agencies for the blind regarded their clients as helpless. The phrase "for the blind" in so many agency titles implied helplessness. Blindness was so terrible a handicap that it wiped out all individual distinctions in those it "afflicted." There were no blind individuals. "The blind" were homogenized, a class reduced to its lowest common denominator.

Mervyn Sinclair graduated from Princeton and spent nearly twenty years in the family business before being blinded in a hunting accident at age thirty-nine. When he consulted an agency for the blind for guidance, he found that his education and executive experience counted for nothing. He was blind. "The blind" make brooms. Sinclair was offered a job in the broom shop.

Morris had been exposed to many leaders in work for

the blind, but he did not share the prevailing philosophy. He did not consider blind people helpless, and he was far too full of himself to accept classification as one of "the blind." He was a rebel with the courage of his impetuous convictions. Offered a job making brooms, he decided to sell insurance instead. He also enrolled in Vanderbilt University. Several months before, he had given up studying braille with a home teacher. Finding that he needed it for business and college, he taught it to himself.

Looking back in later life, Morris felt that he was blessed in having a loyal group of school friends who included him in their social activities without patronizing and who refused to let him exploit his handicap. One night at a country club dance, he had too much to drink and got into an argument with a boy who did not know he was blind. Morris challenged him to a fight. One of his friends intervened, but afterward, Morris recalled, "The boys took me out on the green and beat the hell out of me for getting drunk and acting like a son of a bitch." At Vanderbilt, "every time I came out of a class, there was always a friend who just happened to be going where I was going. It wasn't until years later that it finally dawned on me that those wonderful bastards had worked it out between themselves without letting me catch on."

He was not so lucky with paid guides. He was attending the university part-time. For his business he hired young blacks to lead him. They were often late and sometimes failed to show up at all. One boy demanded a raise when they were out on the street. When Morris refused, his guide abandoned him in the business district. This was what Morris meant when he wrote to Dorothy Eustis that he knew "what it means to be dependent on a paid helper." The freedom of movement a guide dog would offer fired his imagination.

He wrote to a number of his mother's connections among work for the blind to ask their opinions of guide dogs. The responses were universally discouraging, but

Morris refused to be discouraged. His hopes soared when he heard from Mrs. Eustis at last.

She explained that she was a Philadelphian living in Switzerland. Although her kennel had produced many working dogs, it had never trained a dog to lead a blind man. However, she had a man who might be able to train one for Morris. She would be home in Philadelphia for the Christmas holidays and would be in touch with him again.

Morris answered at once. He began, "I have some good news for you. Senator Smutz of Minnesota [he meant Senator Schall] has purchased a dog from Munich, which was trained in German, but is now being retrained in English and is proving absolutely satisfactory to our sightless senator, taking him all over Washington. I believe that in a month after I have the dog, I can train it to take me anywhere in the United States. Now if it would be possible for you to bring one of these dogs with you already trained, I should be very glad to send you either a banker's check or money by the American Express or any way you so desire, because I hope in the winter to make my eastern trip, and then I will be able to get in touch with the leaders of the blind work in the United States. I have the honor and privilege, through my mother, of being personally acquainted with Charles Campbell, who is head of the blind soldiers at Evergreen, the United States Hospital for blind soldiers."

He added that he was also acquainted with Allen at Perkins, Van Cleve at the New York Institute, "and many other notable leaders of this great work, and I believe we can show them where this is feasible." If there was any red tape about importing the dog, he begged her to let him know "so that I may be able to bring to bear any political influence that my family may be able to have." Dorothy Harrison Eustis must have smiled at this offer of political influence from a lad of nineteen, but she admired both his altruism and his initiative. He wanted a dog not only for himself, but also for all his fellow blind Americans, and he was willing to work for it. She cabled him that there was no possibility of bringing a dog on this trip and followed up with a letter of explanation.

Morris accepted the delay with the thought that "there is absolutely no use in rushing our work." The "our" assumed his belief that they had already entered into partnership. He added that Senator Schall had not done nearly so well with his dog as he had at first supposed. In fact, his difficulties had hurt the guide dog cause among workers for the blind. "Of course, you and I know that this is as much the Senator's fault as the dog's, but I am confident that with good demonstration, this objection can be quickly overruled."

When she arrived in the States, Dorothy made her own contacts with leaders for the blind. For all Morris's claims of friendship, Charles Campbell, now with the Detroit League for the Blind, could not recall Mrs. Frank. A letter from the National Society for the Prevention of Blindness acknowledged Mrs. Frank's work with the Council of Jewish Women, but regretted that, since the society dealt only with prevention, "we cannot give you any guidance." Mr. Allen at Perkins portrayed Mrs. Frank as "a lady whose delight seems to be in social service" and Morris as "a fine young fellow," but he volunteered no assistance. Olin Burritt at the Philadelphia, later the Overbrook, School was distinctly cool.

The New York Lighthouse sidestepped Dorothy's approach by referring her to the American Foundation for the Blind. She called on Robert Irwin and promised that if the foundation would sponsor a guide dog program, she and George would bring a string of dogs from Fortunate Fields and spend four months training the dogs, teaching a pair of instructors and supervising the adjustment of a class of blind people and dogs. She would do all this at her own expense, provided the foundation would carry on the program from there. She estimated that a pair of instructors working full-time could turn out from sixty to seventy dogs and masters annually at a cost of no more than $150 per unit.

Irwin agreed to put her proposal before the executive committee late in January. If he had presented the plan with his enthusiastic approval, the committee might have accepted, and the guide dog movement in America would have taken a different direction. But Irwin had already rejected two earlier offers from the Potsdam school, and he had personal reasons for distrusting guide dogs. Irwin had a first-rate mind, but physically he was described by a colleague as "the blindest man I ever saw." Aware that he lacked the coordination and orientation to work a guide dog himself, he probably projected his own limitations upon the blind population as a whole.

A cultural bias may also have played a part. As a people, Germans understood, appreciated, and trusted the working capacities of dogs. Americans did not. With the exception of the hunting breeds, most American dogs were pampered, undisciplined house pets, far from the useful citizens trained at Fortunate Fields. People who were unfamiliar with responsible working dogs would naturally be wary of delivering blind people to their care. In some quarters, too, German shepherds had a bad reputation. Following World War I, shepherds had been imported from Germany, and a number that had been trained for police or guard work had become the property of inexperienced masters. A dog with attack training in the hands of a novice is potentially as dangerous as a loaded revolver in the hands of a child. Some ugly incidents had resulted, and German shepherds gained an undeserved reputation for viciousness.

In fairness to Irwin, Dorothy's proposal involved a financial commitment. Generous as was her offer, she was expecting the foundation to assume a highly experimental program that she estimated to cost roughly $10,000 a year. That was a lot of money in 1928. In any case, Irwin did not

endorse her proposal to the foundation's executive committee, and it was politely declined.

Dorothy Eustis set her small jaw. She had spent an entire month trying to interest American agencies in the virtues of the guide dog, and everywhere she had encountered
the dead weight of inertia. That a man as physically blind
and groping as Robert Irwin should refuse the opportunity
to experience the confidence and security she had seen and
described in Potsdam was galling. His negativism was in
sharp contrast to the ebullient affirmation of the brash
young man in Nashville.

On the night of February 9, she placed a long-distance
call to Morris. He listened in rising excitement to her cultivated Philadelphia accent. She offered to pay his fare to
Switzerland and to train him there with a dog. "Would you
be willing to travel all the way to Switzerland for a dog?"

Morris nearly shouted his answer into the mouthpiece:
"Mrs. Eustis, to get my independence back, I'd go to hell."

The following morning, he wrote her a long letter. "I
can arrange to leave at any time that is convenient for you
and, naturally, under any conditions you think best, but as
I am accustomed to traveling alone, I would really prefer
it." He outlined his preparations, asked for any books on
dogs or dog training she would recommend, and expressed
his confidence in the future success of the guide dog movement in a burst of cliché. "I believe this work can be put
over by good hard work, for my motto is and always has
been A winner never quits, and a quitter never wins."

Dorothy's original plan had been to buy from the Potsdam School two trained dogs that Jack and her husband
would then polish and turn over to Morris Frank and another blind American, Howard Buchanan of Monmouth, Illinois. Buchanan had gone blind several years before while
working as a missionary doctor in the Sudan. Dorothy liked
having a second string to her bow, and she thought Dr.
Buchanan could supply the maturity and experience that
young Morris lacked.

The plan did not materialize. Potsdam refused to sell her the dogs. Jack and George were forced to find time in their crowded schedules to teach guiding to a pair of Fortunate Fields dogs. Both had seen enough of German schools to have a grasp of basic principles, and Jack was a genius with animals. Nevertheless they had to feel their way, and they had less than the three months that the Germans customarily allotted for preparing a dog. A second difficulty arose when Dr. Buchanan was forced to cancel his trip to Switzerland on account of illness. Temporarily at least, Dorothy would have to consign the fate of the American guide dog movement into the sole care of the young rebel from Nashville. She delegated travel arrangements for Morris to her personal secretary, Gretchen Green. Of the whole cast of characters involved in the origins of The Seeing Eye, Gretchen Green was the most implausible. Both picturesque and picaresque, she was a sort of feminine Don Quixote, but she was the opposite of melancholy and so extraordinarily resourceful that her adventures seemed always to end in triumph. She was nearly six feet tall with sloping shoulders and an unnaturally sunken chest as the result of a crippling childhood accident. She walked with the lope of a camel, dressed floridly with long loops of showy beads, and always wore the bishop's ring she had inherited from her grandfather.

She had been raised as the daughter of a clergyman with pulpits in Alabama, Missouri, Kansas, Tennessee, and Maine. She began adult life as a social worker in Philadelphia. Her later peregrinations took her to five continents, and she made herself completely at home wherever she went. She was a Big Sister in New York and the director of a woman's clinic at the University of Tagore in India. As an advance agent for the sculptress Malvina Hoffman, she traveled throughout the Orient in search of racial types. During World War II, she ran a camel corps canteen for the British in North Africa.

Without pretensions to wealth, social position or

beauty, she commanded immense influence by her charm, humor, energy or just plain goodness. People who knew her were likely to recall her with a warm smile and one of three opening remarks: "Gretchen knew *everybody!*" "Gretchen could do *anything!*" "Gretchen would do *anything* for *anybody!*" She would arrange to have your daughter presented at the Court of St. James, but her generosity ignored class distinctions. She could "walk with kings, nor lose the common touch." In Paris, where she saw Lindbergh land, she had a chance encounter with a gendarme. Discovering, as only she would have, that he was trying to improve his English, she contrived, as only she knew how, to have him transferred to a quarter with many English and American residents. Once, staying in a Chinese hotel, she had a call from a man who had recognized her name on the hotel register. He was studying to be a Buddhist monk, but had last seen Gretchen many years before in Boise, Idaho, where he was being held in the lockup and Gretchen was a policewoman.

When Dorothy Eustis met her, Gretchen was running a tea house in Venice. As a favor to the former British ambassador to Turkey, Gretchen agreed to find a tenant for his palazzo. Dorothy became the tenant. It was the summer of 1927. Walter recalled, "Mother and Gretchen were as different as day and night, but they got on famously." When Dorothy and her family returned to Mt. Pelerin in the fall, Gretchen went along as her personal secretary and good right hand.

Gretchen's solution for a blind man traveling alone from New York to Vevey had the simplicity of genius. She shipped him by American Express. That solved Gretchen's problem, but not Morris Frank's.

The Cunard Line steward who took him in charge for the crossing treated him like a precious pet dog. He led him to the dining room for feeding at breakfast, lunch, and dinner, trotted him around the deck for exercise, and sat him in a deck chair. He would probably have liked to strap him in, for if Morris dared to leave his chair to meet and mingle with the other passengers, his hawk-eyed guardian seized him by the elbow and firmly returned him to his place. After dinner, he was permitted to socialize briefly in the lounge, where he met a delightful English girl, but at nine o'clock sharp he was led off to his cabin and locked in for the night.

As consolation for his blindness, John Milton wrote, "They also serve who only stand and wait." The words were no consolation to Morris when he landed at Le Havre. He was told to stand and wait in the customs shed until he was fetched to the Paris train. He stood and waited. Listening to the voices on all sides shouting meaningless sounds, he was seized with panic. In this strange land where he could neither speak nor understand the language, he was not only blind, but deaf and dumb as well. He dared not move for fear of being run down by the clattering baggage barrows of hurrying porters. "I never had felt so helpless in my life."

After what seemed an eternity of waiting, a representative of American Express boarded him on the train for the city of wine, women, and song. For Morris, Paris provided one woman and one bottle of wine. The woman, a French employee of American Express, guided him to a hotel room, showed him a bottle of wine, and locked him in. "Throughout this trip to gain my freedom, I was a closely guarded prisoner. I drank the wine and lay down on the bed." Hours later, American Express shook him awake to catch the midnight train to Vevey. He arrived on the morning of April 25, 1928.

Mrs. Eustis and Jack Humphrey met him at the station. They had seen a portrait photograph of a dark, handsome young face with even features and a mouth that seemed ready to smile, but they were more concerned with his physique and coordination. They scanned him closely. He was a six-footer of medium build. When they spoke, he looked directly at them and would not have appeared blind except for his posture. During the years of groping and straining to hear, he had developed a forward thrust of his head. They had seen the similarly hanging heads of the new students at Potsdam—they soon straightened up after receiving their dogs. This young man walked better than most, picking up his feet, and he showed good orientation as he climbed into the back of the Rolls Royce.

Morris was equally curious about Mrs. Eustis and Jack. He noted her small, firm hand and Jack's strong, hard one, her clear low voice and Jack's big laugh. Jack was adept at guiding him to the limousine, and he noticed that they didn't raise their voices to him as so many people did, as if he were deaf as well as blind. Mrs. Eustis was direct and friendly, but he sensed something formidable about her. When she spoke to the chauffeur in French, her voice carried a quiet tone of command. "I could tell she was a dame who liked to have her own way." It was good to hear American, even with Yankee accents, but as they neared the chalet, his hostess embarrassed him. On the gates of the property, she said, was a sign that read, "Prenez garde aux chiens, et s'addressez à la ferme vis-à-vis." One guest had translated this as "Take care of the dogs and address them with a firm face." Morris was quick, and he joined in the laughter, but he had no idea what she was talking about.

During the next five weeks Morris would experience a series of emotions and sensations that would be repeated with variations literally thousands of times by those who followed him. They ranged from uncertainty to confidence, from anxiety to exhilaration, from depression to exasperation, from fear, anger, and panic to love, laughter, and triumph. Uncertainty came first. On arrival, the vastness of the chalet was bewildering. The dining room was on the second floor. Below it, the huge drawing room was entered hazardously down three steps. Although the Eustises and Humphreys spoke English, their conversation referred to so many things outside his experience that it was difficult to follow. He was travel weary, and it was a relief to retreat to the safety of his bedroom for a good night's sleep.

When he had gone, Jack and George conferred. Because Dr. Buchanan had postponed his trip, they had two dogs to choose from, Gala and Kiss. Both were good and willing workers. Kiss was imperturbable as well. The dog who pioneered the way across America with Morris would need nerves of steel. Kiss had them. They decided on her. When they told Morris at breakfast the following morning, the name horrified him. Kiss! Imagine what the gang at Vanderbilt would say! Kiss! He would be the laughingstock of the campus.

The meeting came right after breakfast. Jack took Morris to his room and explained that the first thing he must do was to make friends with his dog. Pat her. Talk to her. Play with her. Make it a pleasure for her to be with him. Then he gave Morris a piece of raw meat to give her as a friendship offering and went off to fetch her from the kennels. Morris sat in a chair with the raw meat in his palm and waited. The minutes dragged by. Then he heard Jack's footsteps and the jingle of a chain collar. The door opened.

"Here, girl!" Morris called. His tone was warm and coaxing, but he refused to use the awful name. Claws clicked across the floor. He opened his hand. A cool nose sniffed. Then he felt the lap of a warm, wet tongue, and she began eating daintily. He ran his free hand over her warm fur, the contours of her head and shoulders, from the erect velvet ears down to a busy tail that swooped in a graceful S curve. She was beautiful. The tail waved slightly.

"Kiss!" he growled under his breath. "That's a hell of a name for a dog. I'm going to call you Buddy."

When the introduction was over, Jack showed Morris a leash and a harness and explained their use. The leash was a thin leather strap about four feet long with a metal clip at either end. He let Morris feel it. One clip was for the dog's collar. The other could be doubled over and snapped to a ring at the dog's end to make a short leash. If it were snapped to a ring a foot from the master's end, it formed a convenient loop for the master's hand and made a long leash. Jack had Morris change from short to long leash several times before he showed him the harness.

The harness consisted of three straps. The vertical strap ran over Buddy's shoulders and buckled under her rib cage. It was sewn at the shoulders to a horizontal strap running across her chest. From the center of the chest strap, a third strap, or martingale, ran between her front legs and ended in a loop through which the first strap had to be passed before buckling. As an experienced horseman, Morris was familiar with a martingale, but when Jack asked him to harness and unharness Buddy, it proved not as simple as he had imagined. If he miscalculated the position of her head, he could catch the chest strap on her nose, pinch her ear, or put a finger in her eye. By means of metal clips, a loop of heavy leather was attached to the harness at Buddy's shoulders. To work Buddy, he must hold this loop in his left hand. Since it was twenty inches long, it positioned Buddy well in front of him. In addition to the harness handle in his palm, his left hand would have the short leash looped around his middle and ring fingers. If he were to drop the harness handle for any reason, he would still have Buddy on short leash in his left hand. He would hold a cane in his right hand.

Morris wanted to try it at once, but Jack told him he would have to wait. A guide dog works for the praise of the master it loves. It would take time for Morris to win Buddy's affection, and for the first twenty-four hours, he must give her a chance to get used to him. When he moved around, he must keep Buddy at heel on short leash. Today and from now on, he must feed Buddy personally twice a day and take her out to empty four times daily. A staircase from the balcony adjoining Morris's bedroom led to a stretch of lawn for this purpose. Even at meals, he must keep Buddy on leash, lying out of the way under the table.

His foot should be over the long leash close to her. The other end of the leash should be over his knee.

Being leashed to Buddy every waking moment restricted Morris's freedom of movement, and his attempts to make friends with her were frustrating. He had pictured himself with a devoted and fun-loving Rin-Tin-Tin, a dog whose tail would wag furiously at a word from him, who would be eager to lick his hands and face, always ready for a roughhouse. This Buddy was beautiful, but aloof. She tolerated his caresses, but the only times she showed genuine enthusiasm was when George or Jack appeared. Then she jumped to her feet and her tail thumped hard against his leg. When he got in bed that night, feeling the cool alpine air pouring in through the window, he called Buddy up on the bed. That was more like it. He dropped off to sleep, aware of her warm, furry bulk beside him.

The next morning Morris had his first direct experience of what having a guide dog could mean. To anyone trying it for the first time, following a guide dog is a thrilling new form of locomotion. It seems as different from ordinary walking as skiing, skating, or riding a bicycle. It requires a new set of physical responses. There is a fluid quality to it. The harness handle seems alive, vibrant with the rhythm of the dog's shoulders. The sensation of speed is intense. You feel half uncertain, half triumphant. Wendy may have felt something like it when Peter Pan taught her to fly. Morris felt it with Buddy on that April morning on Mt. Pelerin.

Buddy was trained to walk much faster and pull much harder than the guide dogs of today. The rigid U-shaped harness handle that was introduced a few years later indicated a dog's position accurately even when it was standing still. The flexible strap attached to Buddy's harness required a hard pull to give a clear sense of direction. She tugged Morris along at four miles an hour. He had never walked so fast. His stride lengthened. His spine straightened. He was flying. A radiant smile spread across his face.

But this was work, not play. Jack followed close behind with a running fire of instructions.

"Don't grip the harness handle so tight. Let your thumb hang free." A moment later, "Follow your dog. She's trying to lead you left. Your harness handle is riding forward. Straighten up." A few moments of silence. "In a few steps she's going to stop. Be ready to stop with her. Good! Reward your dog. You're at a curb. Feel with your cane. Is it a step up or down?"

There was a right and a wrong way to do everything. Morris had to learn not only the right way, but also the reason why it was right. The commands of "left" and "right" were to be accompanied by precise hand signals and body movements. At curbs, Morris was to position himself with his right foot on the edge and the left foot back. At the command, "Buddy, right," he was to gesture right with his right hand while turning his body 90 degrees to the right and moving his right foot back to offer Buddy free passage. Commands were to be given in a clear, firm voice, and every command obeyed, every service performed must be promptly and unfailingly rewarded with the words "Atta *good* girl!" And because dogs understand inflections far better than words, this reward must be spoken in tones of rapture.

Twice a day, either Jack Humphrey or George Eustis escorted Morris and Buddy on a walk. From the chalet, they went down to the station from which the funicular railway descended the mountain to Vevey. There they worked over the chosen route. Morris enjoyed the challenge, but it was hard work both mentally and physically. The harness handle rubbed blisters on his left hand. His left shoulder ached. The muscles of his calves and thighs stiffened. There were a hundred things to remember, and in addition to the walks, Morris had to put Buddy through obedience exercises daily, brush and curry her daily, feed, water, and take her out to empty four times a day. He must do these things himself, so that Buddy would come to depend on him, as he depended on her. When he fixed her food pan, he mixed the meat and meal with a bare hand, so that Buddy would associate his scent with the pleasure of eating. If he forgot anything, Jack, George, or Dorothy was sure to catch him up.

After a week, Jack announced that Morris was ready for a solo, a trip to Vevey and back without any comments or intervention or help.

"I'll be right behind you," Jack said, "but I'm not going to say a word unless you're in actual danger."

The walk to the funicular seemed strange without the usual running commentary. Jack was wearing rubber soles, so Morris could hear no footsteps. The sounds he could hear and even the feel of the road seemed unfamiliar. He had thought he knew it so well. They should have reached the station before this. Had he taken a wrong turn somehow? Buddy stopped suddenly, and before Morris knew it, he had stumbled up the concrete steps leading to the station. Damn! He'd bruised his shins, but at least he knew where he was.

Seating himself in the cable car, he felt his shins instead of positioning Buddy under his knees as he should have. She let out a yelp. Some son of a bitch had stepped on her. Jack would give him hell for that. In Vevey he missed one turn and lost his way until a tapping hammer in a cobbler's shop provided a landmark. Was Jack letting him get lost on purpose? He followed the route correctly after that, but tripped at two curbs, bumped a passerby, and forgot to reward Buddy promptly a half-dozen times. He climbed the hill to the chalet angry with Jack, himself, and the world.

"How did you make out?" Jack greeted him at the chalet entrance.

"You mean you weren't with me?"

Jack laughed. "Who do you think stepped on Buddy's paw?"

Morris took a deep breath. "You son of a bitch!"

Dorothy Eustis's voice spoke close to his right shoulder. "Wasn't this a lovely day for a walk?" she inquired sweetly. Morris recovered quickly.

"Oh, yes, Madame," he agreed. "Lovely."

One afternoon in Vevey, Jack directed Morris and Buddy over an unfamiliar route. When Buddy stopped for a curb, Morris identified a down step with his cane. Jack asked, "How far down?"

Morris leaned forward, nearly losing his balance until Jack grabbed him around the waist. Something was dragging at his cane. Water! Jack had maneuvered him to the bank of the river.

"Let that teach you never to step off a curb ahead of your dog."

Morris exploded, and this time Dorothy Eustis was not there to stop him. Jack waited until he was through, then spoke seriously.

"Look, boy, as long as you're here, you've got me or George to look out for you. When you go back to America, you will have no one to depend on but Buddy. I want to make damned sure you do."

Both during work and apart from it, Morris was feeling closer to Buddy every day. Currying and brushing her made him familiar with every contour of her beautiful body. At meals her head rested on his foot under the table. At night she slept up on the bed beside him. Her warm tongue licking his face woke him in the morning.

Before he left Vevey, two experiences completed his conversion to a religious faith in Buddy. The first occurred on a sunken road leading up from the funicular to Fortunate Fields. Ahead of him he heard galloping hooves and clattering wheels bearing down at a breakneck speed. For just an instant, Buddy paused, then wheeled right and pulled him off the road up a steep embankment. The harness handle seemed to be rising nearly over his head, but he hung on tight and stumbled up after her. He reached the top only moments before a pair of runaway horses dragging a heavy peasant cart thundered by. Jack Humphrey, who saw it all, was too far behind to come to the rescue. Buddy had done it all on her own.

The second experience was far less dramatic, even prosaic. Morris was sitting in the drawing room before lunch, listening to Mrs. Eustis play one of the grand pianos.

"I need a haircut," he mused, fingering the hair above his ears. "Do you think Mr. Eustis could take me down to the barber shop this afternoon?"

The piano paused. "You have Buddy, Morris," Mrs. Eustis suggested. "Why don't you go with her?"

Why didn't he go with her? The thought was staggering. It was a long moment before he could take it in. He could go with Buddy. He didn't have to depend on a human guide, wait until it suited his convenience, and feel obligated for the favor afterward. He could go with Buddy, who would ask for no thanks beyond the "Atta *good* girls" that were becoming second nature and who would feel proud and happy at the opportunity to work.

After lunch, Morris harnessed Buddy and headed for the funicular. In Vevey they threaded their way to the barber shop and returned. The trip had none of the thrill of a narrow escape from runaway horses, but its meaning was far more exciting to Morris. A runaway team comes once in a lifetime. Haircuts come every few weeks. Nothing could be more ordinary. That is the reason why it is so hard to get a human guide to take a blind man for a haircut. Family and friends will be generous on special occasions. It is the ordinary, prosaic little chores, the trips to the barber shop or post office, the purchase of shoelaces or toothpaste that can be most frustrating by reason of their very simplicity.

Late that afternoon, sitting alone on the terrace overlooking the lake, Morris ran one hand over his new haircut and began to laugh. He couldn't stop. The more he tried, the harder he laughed. Mrs. Eustis overheard him and came out to find him alone, laughing as she had never heard him laugh before.

"What in the world is the matter?"

It took Morris a moment to control himself. Then he explained. "At home in Nashville getting my hair cut was a major event. Some days Father would drop me off at the barber shop on his way to work and leave me there until he could pick me up on his way home to lunch. Today Buddy took me to get my hair cut. For the first time in four years, I'm free. That's why I'm laughing. Because I'm free, by God. I'm free!"

4
Incorporation

Morris was made over. He was scarcely recognizable as the pale youth with hanging head and drooping shoulders who had stepped off the night train from Paris a month before. He walked with head erect, chest out and shoulders squared. In time he would develop an almost military bearing. His voice rang with new confidence and his smile was radiant. He felt he had signed his personal declaration of independence, and he was eager to share it with others.

Both Dorothy Eustis and Jack Humphrey wanted to help. In his youth Jack had had a younger brother, Leslie, who was born blind. He had been Leslie's guide until his premature death. Dorothy had shed tears over the letters she had received from blind Americans after the publication of the *Post* article. She would assist Morris with advice and financial support, and both Dorothy and Jack promised to help him find a trainer, but the school was to be his project. Their main interest was in the program of Fortunate Fields. Its aim was scientific, not humanitarian. Its focus was working shepherds, not blind people. The responsibility for the founding of a guide dog school in the United States was to be Morris's alone. He decided to name it after Dorothy's *Post* article, "The Seeing Eye."

They discussed Morris's plans with him. The first thing he must do on his return was to test Buddy in American traffic. He must expose her to the most congested areas of New York and other large cities he passed through on his way back to Nashville. He must prove that she was every bit as safe as a human guide and he must demonstrate that

47

to the press and the public. Once that had been accomplished, they would send him a trainer.

Morris and Buddy made a triumphant ocean crossing. Buddy was the hit of the Cunard liner *Tuscania* and was given free passage as a compliment to the work Morris planned. At one point, having cashed a traveler's check with the purser, Morris returned to his cabin for a nap. He was just stretching out on his bunk when Buddy put up her paws and dropped something on his chest. It was his wallet. He had dropped it on the floor in the purser's office. Neither man had noticed, but Buddy had picked it up and carried it half the length of the ship to his cabin.

On June 11, 1928, the *Tuscania* docked in New York. There Morris was met by Walter Wood and a crowd of reporters assigned to cover ship arrivals. Morris gave an interview in which the cockiness of his claims for Buddy got under one reporter's skin.

"You say that dog can take you anywhere?"

"Anywhere."

"Could she take you across West Street?"

"Show me to it, brother, and Buddy will take me across it."

What Morris did not know was that West Street was popularly called Death Street—and with good reason. Its vast cobblestone expanse churned with the horse-drawn and motor-driven trucks of the waterfront, unregulated by stoplights. Confident in his ignorance, Morris accompanied the reporter to the curb outside the dock entrance. When he had located the edge with his right foot, he commanded, "Buddy, forward."

Morris later recalled the next few minutes as the longest in his life. Clashing gears and roaring motors mingled with the clop of horses' hooves and metal rims whining against cobblestones. Horns blew. Brakes squealed. Voices shouted. After perhaps a dozen steps, Buddy backed hard to pull Morris away from a lumbering truck, then moved forward cautiously. Through the harness handle, he could feel her head jerking alertly from side to side, sizing up the situation. As she threaded this way and that, paused, backed and moved forward, Morris lost all sense of direction. For all he knew, they could be describing a figure eight, but there was only one thing to do: depend on Buddy. If he stepped out in front of her, if she lost her nerve or her judgment, their public failure would discredit his dream of a guide dog school in America within an hour of their landing. But Buddy had nerves of steel, and Morris had learned Jack's lesson at the river edge. Pulling Morris around a waiting taxi, Buddy stopped at the opposite curb at last. Nothing in Switzerland had prepared them for this. Buddy had made the transition from the peaceful routine of shipboard life to the din and turmoil of Death Street without a qualm. It was a magnificent feat.

That evening after dinner, Morris tested Buddy on Broadway. As he described it later, "The theater hour was in full swing. Crowds were hurrying here and there on the sidewalk. Automobiles crowded the thoroughfares, but Buddy was as much at home in the seething mob as if she had been on the quiet streets of Vevey. Not once did she falter, and not once did I bump into a soul."

The next day Morris arranged to call on Robert Irwin at the American Foundation for the Blind. Irwin described the visit in his memoirs, contrasting it sharply with the call Morris had paid on his way to Vevey. Then, Irwin wrote, Morris had been "appalled by the terrors of New York traffic." On his return trip, Morris telephoned from the same hotel two miles away and made an appointment to come to the foundation an hour later. "Accompanied only by his dog, Frank traveled across the city on foot to the foundation offices and after a chat of an hour or so, returned alone with his dog to his hotel." Morris wrote to Dorothy Eustis, "Mr. Irwin of the American Foundation wants a dog, so I need not say how my interview there was."

When he met the steamer, Walter had informed Morris that it had been arranged for him to give a network radio speech the following evening. But the talk was postponed, so Morris left for Washington where he met Paul McNutt and Frank Miller, who would prove powerful allies in the federal bureaucracy in years to come. On his return to New York, he discovered that his radio speech had been postponed again. He had written the speech out, so he gave the script to Walter to read and started home. The speech began with a magniloquent reference to the Declaration of Independence and its self-evident truth that all men are created equal. The blind man, Morris said, was excluded from his American birthright by his dependence on family or friends to guide him on the most trivial errands. "I have signed my Declaration of Independence and enjoy it to the fullest with my dog, Buddy." The speech then described Buddy's performance in the Broadway theater rush and went on to stress two important points. The first was that it was just as important for the master to be trained in the use of his guide as for the dog to be taught to guide. The second was that he planned to open a nonprofit school, because he did not want to see the work falling into the hands of commercial breeders or trainers as a money-making proposition.

Even before Walter had read this speech on the radio, Morris had returned to Nashville, but en route he stopped for a visit with his Aunt Selma in Cincinnati. Selma, Mrs. Leo Schwartz, had been president of the National Council of Jewish Women and was able to provide Morris with introductions to the leaders of the Jewish community throughout the United States. His visit also offered him the opportunity to test Buddy in downtown Cincinnati.

On June 20, only nine days after landing in New York, he wrote the Eustises triumphantly: "I am the happiest boy in all the world today, for I have gone all over Nashville or, I should say, the business part of Nashville today, visiting all my friends and having a marvelous feeling. I have had two long-distance calls, God knows how many letters and how many people wanting to reserve dogs. It is like a stampede of people who have been locked up in a dark cell for

many years rushing for the light." He was flushed with
confidence in future success. "Things are much easier than
I anticipated." A few days later, he wrote again, enclosing
newspaper clippings. The *New Outlook*, a publication of the
American Foundation for the Blind, had requested a three-
thousand word article from him. He was expecting to have
a trolley car pass for Buddy in a day or two. He proposed
incorporating The Seeing Eye.

Late in July, he received his first response from Dorothy Eustis since leaving Vevey. She had been totally ab-
sorbed in training communications dogs for the Swiss
army, a project that had followed hard on the heels of a
police course. George had managed to turn over the Rolls
Royce, putting himself and two passengers in the hospital.
However, she assured Morris, "I think I have found just the
man to handle the training for you." By the time Morris
had gotten this letter, he had received inquiries from blind
people in all forty-eight states and had been offered enough
dogs "to run my school for a year. For the first fifty dogs I
will not have to go out of my state. I have also been promised a lot in a convenient location, enough lumber to build
my kennels with, and wire offered me at cost. I believe
within a year or two, when our school is finally established,
we will be able to turn over a small endowment to the
American Foundation for the Blind, that they will add quite
a sum to it and make The Seeing Eye a permanent organization. Mr. Irwin was quite enthusiastic over this idea." It
seemed to Morris that he had everything ready to go. He
had the blind applicants, the dogs, the kennel site, and the
potential backing of the American Foundation. All he
needed was the trainer Dorothy Eustis and Jack Humphrey
had promised. He could not have imagined that he would
not hear from Mrs. Eustis for nearly two months.

Gretchen Green's word picture of life at Mt. Pelerin
that summer would suggest that Dorothy was simply too
busy to look for a trainer:

A course of liaison dogs is in training with Dorothy Eustis doing the actual training herself. Fortunate Fields is under military discipline. No one is allowed to enter during working hours without permission. Mrs. Theodore Roosevelt wrote from Lausanne to ask if she might come up with Ethel and her children. She did come, staunch exquisite little lady, standing hours to watch dogs and men.

It is fun running according to schedule. A bugle sounds *Reveille* at six. Breakfast follows and obedience exercises, the latter for dogs, not guests, then training throughout the day and, sometimes, during the night. The dogs were being the communications for the army, carrying telephone wires, messages in tin capsules, and carrier pigeons in baskets on their backs.

In need of a hostile force, the household is drafted, the guests enlisted for vanguard. Some days there are forced marches three miles over the mountain. A cart equipped with food drives on before, the hostile force following in the rear. The heat is terrific. Army and foe bivouac at noon under the trees, fortifying themselves with goat cheese and milk. Night raids are startling. As the dogs run between trenches, the enemy hurls giant crackers for bombs, all to accustom them to the gentle art of war. Dorothy, dogs, and soldiers train for six weeks and set out for maneuvers tomorrow.

Dorothy's preoccupation was not the real reason for the delay in finding Morris a trainer. She and Jack had been overconfident about securing a German trainer. Those who worked for the government were guaranteed liberal pension benefits that they would forfeit if they went to the United States. The compensation they asked in return made them too expensive. There were a few trainers not under government contract, but selecting the right one was not easy. Dorothy's first choice, Herr Stiersdorfer, had fractured his skull in the automobile accident with George Eustis. Another candidate, a certain Knapp, lacked initiative.

The disruption of Dorothy's private life was another cause for delay. For some time she had been aware of her basic incompatibility with George. He was too much the playboy, impulsive, reckless. The accident with the Rolls Royce was the last straw. He had been driving too fast because he had not allowed sufficient time to catch a train. It was careless. Worse, it was stupid. Dorothy hated to accept defeat on anything, but she had to admit that her marriage to George was a mistake. They were hopelessly mismatched. Having made up her mind to that, she did not hesitate. She began divorce proceedings while George was still in the hospital.

Because George lacked her single-minded interest and commitment, Dorothy tended to minimize his contributions to Fortunate Fields. Jack Humphrey was more generous. He said of George, "In the early stages he was a great help, due to his facility with various languages and a natural training ability. He worked equally with me on the first two dogs, Kiss and Gala, and worked equally with me on teaching Morris to work with Buddy." Although George Eustis's contribution to The Seeing Eye was so brief, it was real, and his talents were missed. If the marriage had lasted another year, it is not unlikely that George would have come to the United States to train the first class or two.

As the summer wore to a close, Dorothy's thoughts again returned to Stiersdorfer. She wrote Morris, "Thanks to his good health and habits, he is well on the road to recovery. I am going to Karlsruhe to see the dogs he has trained there. If everything meets with my approval, he is ready to come in January." Still ignorant of the impending divorce, Morris was firing off one letter after another. He had investigated the immigration quota. It posed no problem for a trainer as he could remain in America five years on a visa. Morris was ready to choose his board and apply for a charter, but he had received no answers to his letters, and his anxiety grew. On October 15, he wrote, "My dear Mr. and Mrs. Eustis, since it has been five weeks since I have had any communication from you, I am forced to stop work on The Seeing Eye." He could go no further without information on the raising of the money, the choice of a trainer, the number of dogs he could train, his salary, and his country of origin. He was discovering problems. "Americans were afraid of shepherds and seemed to consider Buddy a wild lion. Even those who accept Buddy at face value express doubts that dogs like her could be put out in numbers. Oh, if I only had you here to sit down and talk these things over quickly. The slow mails cramp my style of work."

Within a few days, Morris had a letter. "Yesterday I was granted my divorce from Mr. Eustis, which I expect explains a number of things to you." She was optimistic about Stiersdorfer. Mr. Humphrey had looked over the dogs he had trained at Karlsruhe and they seemed sound, but she wanted Stiersdorfer to go to Potsdam with Humphrey for three weeks. Then she wanted him to spend a month or so at Fortunate Fields, so that she could be absolutely sure of his work.

In the same letter, she gave Morris some advice that would be repeated often: "You must educate the public to the fact that Buddy is a working instrument first and a dog second. No one should pat her or touch her. It will double the difficulty of the work she has to do." With the tart humor that occasionally spiced her letters, she appealed to his "common sense, of which, every now and then, I get a glimpse." She promised Morris that she would come to Nashville in January, but even as he was reading this news, she was having misgivings about Stiersdorfer. There was something about him she did not trust. Her thoughts turned to another possibility.

In June, her ward, Esther Roland, had been married to Henry Clifford at Fortunate Fields, and a member of the wedding party had been Henry's younger sister, Adelaide. At eighteen, Adelaide Clifford was a handsome, talented, and athletic girl uncertain what to do with her life. Her father had died soon after she was born, and her mother had remarried, but the marriage had ended in divorce. Adelaide had spent five years in a Swiss boarding school in Mon-treux before returning to the States to graduate properly from finishing school. Except for her passionate attachment to the family summer place in Maine, she lacked emotional roots. She had meant to spend only a few days at Fortunate Fields, but she felt very much at home in French Switzer-land, and she was fascinated by the work with the dogs. Under Jack Humphrey's tutelage, she was soon helping with the training and showed a real talent for it. She found it far more exciting than the life of a New York debutante, and both Jack and Nettie Humphrey encouraged her to take it seriously. Nearly fifty years later, Adelaide recalled, "I got into pants and big boots and loved it. Hell, I was the first hippie."

She had been working with guide dogs for months now and could work a dog under blindfold around Vevey. Dorothy asked Jack whether Adelaide could be trusted as the trainer for The Seeing Eye in Nashville. Jack said that she had trained dogs all right, but she had yet to train a blind person. Until she had, she would need the supervi-sion of someone more experienced. Dorothy pondered. Morris had blind students lined up and waiting. Nearly six months ago she had promised to find him a trainer, and she had to make good on that promise. Reluctantly she came to a decision. Jack must go to Nashville with Adelaide to train the first class.

Jack was incensed. He had come to Switzerland to do scientific research. Four long years of selective breeding, thorough training, and painstaking analysis were just be-ginning to produce data with potential significance for the whole field of genetics. Now Dorothy was asking him to interrupt his research and leave his wife and son for months to help a cocky kid barely out of his teens in Nashville.

Both Dorothy Eustis and Jack Humphrey had wills of steel. Neither was accustomed to taking orders. Their con-tract wisely took their characters into account. It provided that, in case of a conflict, they would each hold their peace for two weeks. If, at the end of that time, they were still unreconciled, they could dissolve the partnership. Jack fumed in silence for fourteen days. Then he wrote out his resignation and placed it on the tray that would be carried up to Mrs. Eustis with her breakfast the following morning.

As Alexander Woollcott wrote years later in the *New Yorker*, "Mrs. Eustis never got that letter, for in the hours before dawn, Humphrey, waking from a troubled sleep, sneaked down and tore it up. For the first time in years, he had dreamed of his brother, Leslie. He had heard the remembered little voice calling to him as it always used to do, calling to him for help." The years since he had run away from home in his teens had been so eventful that Humphrey's memories of his childhood in Saratoga Springs were buried deep, but young Leslie had been an important part of that world. Jack had been his constant guide. He had even taken him along to school, so that he could look after him during classes. Leslie's death had lifted a burden of responsibility from young Jack. It also left a tender memory slumbering below the hard-boiled exterior of the grown man. And so the development of The Seeing Eye was rescued by the coincidence that the self-taught genius who managed Fortunate Fields happened to have had a younger brother who was blind. Jack could refuse to obey the orders of Dorothy Eustis, but he could not resist the voice of Leslie. He agreed to go to Nashville.

Dorothy wrote Morris, "So as not to disappoint you, I am disrupting my whole organization and sending you Jack Humphrey for two or three months to get things established and organized and to train the first batch of dogs for you. He will bring over at least three trained dogs, and I hope to send to Nashville with him an assistant trainer, Miss Adelaide Clifford, who has been working with me for the last three months and is a natural born trainer." Morris was ecstatic. "Mr. Humphrey is just the man to get The Seeing Eye rolling. With his personality, there will be no trouble."

Dorothy assigned Morris a number of tasks. She wanted kennels ready for eight dogs as near the route they were to work as possible. This route should take about forty minutes, and it should include busy streets, trolley cars, and crossings, both the kind controlled by policemen and those regulated by lights. If students were to come from out of town, they would need a place to stay. Also there should be a meeting room near the kennels where the class could listen to Mr. Humphrey's lectures, rest after work, and study braille maps of the route. She was having a Fortunate Fields dog trained for Mr. Howard Buchanan in the first class. A second Fortunate Fields dog was very beautiful and should go to "as well-to-do a person as possible." A third and possibly a fourth dog "will not be of our breeding and therefore more ordinary. I tell you this so that you can fit the people to them." Ordinary dogs were for ordinary people. Beautiful dogs were for the well-to-do, who were not, it seemed, ordinary. She expected to get the third and fourth dogs from Potsdam where Jack had gone for three weeks' brushup and where he would "at the same time study the question of a trainer to take his place when he comes back, but you don't have to worry about that part of the question, you lucky dog."

Morris answered, "I may be a lucky dog not having to find a trainer, but this preparing things over here is nobody's joke." After enumerating his difficulties, he proudly profiled the people he had selected for his board, but even before Dorothy received the letter, she wrote to express her concern that the board be representative. Huger Jervey, Dean of the Columbia Law School, who had been staying at Fortunate Fields, had given her letters of introduction to some important people in Memphis and Nashville. Since Miss Adelaide Clifford was a member of the Junior League, the Nashville chapter might be involved. Regarding her forthcoming trip, she stated that, since most of her time in the States would be devoted to fund-raising in New York and Philadelphia, she would stay in Nashville only three days. "Much as I would like to stop with you and your mother, I think it would really be better to put up at some hotel. I will have so many people to see and so many calls to make that I think it would be best." Of the banquet Morris had proposed, she wrote, "If the banquet is a Dutch treat, I'll come with pleasure, but I'd hate like fury to have it given at the expense of friends of The Seeing Eye."

Morris replied politely, but beneath the surface we feel him bristling at Mrs. Eustis's condescending attitude. So she has letters to some important people in Nashville, does she! He replied: "My board, with no credit to myself, is one of the most representative that could be formed in this part of the country: Governor and Mrs. Horton, Mr. Roger S. Caldwell, one of the South's biggest financiers, Mr. Lee J. Lowenthal, one of the biggest social workers in the city, Chancellor Kirkland of Vanderbilt University, Dr. Payne of Peabody College for Teachers, Mr. J. P. W. Brown, head of the local railroad and light company, Mr. C. A. Craig, president of the largest life insurance company in the South," and so forth. The Nashville chapter of the Junior League was too deeply involved with crippled children to be of any assistance, but Frances Dudley Brown, the national president of the Junior League, was a neighbor and had agreed to serve on the board.

> Of course, you do what is convenient for you, although I believe you will find it most convenient to stay at my home, as it is quiet and only fifteen minutes from the city. You will have a private bedroom, bath and sitting room. Miss Freeman, my mother's secretary, aids her in looking after the house. A car will be at your disposal the entire time you are in the city. We have decided not to have a banquet, but instead to have a buffet supper. My mother and father will do this in your honor. It would cost The Seeing Eye nothing.

Morris may have been tempted to add, "We know how to do things right even if we weren't born on the Main

Line," but having vented his pique, he closed with a rush of enthusiasm: "I am much more excited over your coming than I was over my going to Europe."

Differences in their age, temperament, and upbringing would continue to be a source of friction between Morris and Dorothy Eustis throughout their association, but these always melted in the ardor of their mutual devotion to the guide dog movement. Yet even here there was a difference in their perspective. The American Seeing Eye filled Morris's whole horizon. He expressed his commitment in religious terms. "This work shall not fail, and by the God that made me, I shall leave no stone unturned until The Seeing Eye is on a firm running basis."

Dorothy Eustis was behind the American school four-square. She was sending over Jack Humphrey and she promised financial backing, but she saw America as only part of the picture. If Morris were right, The Seeing Eye would be taken over in a year or two as a division of the American Foundation for the Blind. Her contribution to the guide dog movement should be international. Already she had conceived the idea of an international training school for guide dog instructors. It would require substantial resources. At least at the outset, Fortunate Fields could supply the dogs, but the school would need apprentice instructors, their blind students, and a building in which to house instructors, students, and dogs. Dorothy could not afford to underwrite the project alone, but Gretchen Green had a friend who might help (she always did). She invited Margery Chadbourne, just then in Paris, to come for a visit.

Mrs. Chadbourne stayed for some days and seemed much interested in watching Adelaide Clifford and Jack Humphrey working the dogs, but left without making any commitment. Not long afterward, there was a visit from Huger Jervey. Margery Chadbourne had asked his advice on the project, and when he approved, she agreed to back it. An international school was planned. It would be called

L'Oeil qui Voit. With the exception of Jack Humphrey's salary, it was to be underwritten entirely by Mrs. Chadbourne.

When Dorothy, Gretchen, Adelaide, and two Fortunate Fields dogs docked in New York in December, 1928, the newspapers carried the story. Adelaide, described as "having deserted the ranks of society for the equally exhausting life of dog trainer," was quoted on plans for an international school. It would be directed by Captain George Balsiger, who had worked with Mrs. Eustis on the liaison course that summer. A cavalry veterinarian, he had agreed to rent his house and kennels in Lausanne for school headquarters. Thus, even as her liner steamed for New York, Dorothy was planning for another Seeing Eye on the other side of the Atlantic.

It had been settled that Jack would precede her to Nashville. She would arrive on January 5. Gretchen Green had scheduled her for speaking dates or dinners including appearances at the New York Lighthouse, the Colony Club, and the Cosmopolitan Club on January 2, 12, 15, 16, and 18. She would sail for Europe on January 19.

The results of Dorothy's whirlwind visit to Nashville were summed up in a memorandum she prepared the day before she sailed. It reported that she had raised $7,500 to cover the 1929 budget. Of this, $3,500 was for administration, including a salary of $1,500 for Morris as managing director, a secretary, office equipment, and incidental expenses. Morris was to recruit blind people who wanted guide dogs. He would also administer a revolving fund of $4,500 to underwrite the purchase and training of the dogs. The fund was to be renewed with the money paid by blind students who could afford it or with scholarships contributed by individuals or groups.

Mrs. Eustis's visit was a social success as well. The buffet at the Franks was festive, and the movies shown of the training at Vevey were greeted enthusiastically. It must have been balm to Morris's ego when the Philadelphia blue blood who had tried to evade his invitation wrote, "Will you please thank your mother for her charming hospitality and tell her that I have never stayed in a household so cheerful and sunny as hers."

On January 29, 1929, The Seeing Eye was issued its certificate of incorporation. On February 1, Morris reported to Mrs. Eustis that he had rented an office in the Fourth and First National Bank Building for $15 a month and had bought a typewriter desk, a plain desk, four chairs, and a coat tree for another $15. "How's that for putting the Scotch trick on them!"

He was managing director of The Seeing Eye, Incorporated, with a board, a budget, an office, a trainer, and, best of all, a class about to begin. But the woman who had made it possible was back in Switzerland preparing to give a two-month course to Mussolini's police in Rome. She and Morris would not meet face to face for nearly a year, and The Seeing Eye would experience many vicissitudes in the interim.

II
WANDERING ADOLESCENCE

5

The Nashville Classes

On his way to Nashville from Fortunate Fields, Jack Humphrey stopped off for a few days to visit his friends Willi and Florence Ebeling at Lake Openaka in Dover, New Jersey. Willi had met Jack five years before in Boston, where he had heard Jack lecture on the breeding of German shepherds. They had been drawn to each other from the start. The Ebelings were breeders of shepherds with a keen appreciation of their working qualities. They were acquainted with Dorothy Eustis and had been following the progress of the Fortunate Fields experiment with the greatest interest.

Willi was then forty-six, dapper, and slight of stature, with piercing gray eyes and a quizzical smile habitually playing around the corners of his mouth. He had been born Willi Heinrich Karl Louis Ebeling in a tiny German village not far from Bremen. He had come to America in 1904 as the representative of a Bremen firm of importers. Three years later, he became engaged to Florence Evans, the daughter of an American importer, and they were married in 1908. Following World War I, Ebeling retired from his own prosperous firm to become a gentleman farmer at Lake Openaka. The house overlooking their private lake had originally been a swimming club, which the Ebelings adapted to their own uses. When the difficulty of hiring labor made farming impractical, they converted their henhouses into kennels and began breeding German shepherds.

Willi Ebeling delighted in good conversation, and over

billiards or sipping brandy in the paneled living room, Jack regaled him with stories of the work at Fortunate Fields. Before he was through, Jack had so fired Willi with enthusiasm that he volunteered to come to Nashville at his own expense to take instruction in guide dog technique from Jack. The Ebelings were childless and although Willi was about to become editor of the *Shepherd Dog Review*, he was unencumbered and ready for a lark. He little suspected that it would lead to a second career far more challenging than his first.

Through Willi, Jack heard of Josef Weber, a German who had opened a training kennel outside Princeton, New Jersey. Weber had trained dogs for the Berlin police and was familiar with the guide dog work at Potsdam. Willi and Jack drove over in Willi's seven-passenger Packard to interview him. At Jack's suggestion Weber agreed to come to Nashville to learn Jack's modifications of the Potsdam technique. The Seeing Eye would pay his expenses and it was understood that, if all went well, Weber would contract to train dogs for the school. Since Adelaide was also coming to Nashville, Jack hoped that by the time he returned to Switzerland, he would leave behind three people schooled in the basics of guide dog instruction.

Jack went ahead to Nashville to look over the kennels of which Morris had written and the dogs of which he had boasted. To his disgust, he found that the kennels existed only in Morris's imagination and that all the dogs were puppies too young for training. With his customary energy he found an old building to rent and had it equipped with fencing and stalls for the dogs. Combing Nashville and environs, he could find only three dogs, and two of them were of uncertain temperament. He appealed to Willi Ebeling, who arranged a shipment of six bitches of his own breeding. A seventh came from a woman in Wellesley, Massachusetts. One of the Ebeling dogs was questionable, but Jack kept the three uncertain dogs to illustrate to his apprentices what made them undesirable. Weber could not leave

Princeton until late in February, but Adelaide and Willi Ebeling showed up promptly. Jack assigned Adelaide three dogs to train on her own, so that he could devote full time to Willi Ebeling. The teenage girl in pants and boots, the bowlegged cowboy with snuff under his lip, and the retired importer in voluminous plus fours and flashy argyle stockings were a daily sight working their dogs on the streets of Nashville.

By February 2, Jack had tuned up Gala and Tartar for the two students of the first American class. Jack had trained both dogs personally at Fortunate Fields, although letters from representatives of the Potsdam School to Robert Irwin and the Shepherd Dog Club of America claimed he had not. When Mrs. Eustis had asked permission for Humphrey to spend three weeks in Potsdam, they said they had suspected her of commercial motives and had therefore allowed Humphrey to see only dogs that were already fully trained so that he would be able to learn nothing. Later, when she had asked to buy two trained dogs for America, the Potsdam representatives claimed they had "refused categorically Mrs. E.'s demand. Unfortunately, Mrs. E. succeeded to get two trained dogs from another school of training and took them with her. These dogs were never trained by Mr. H. himself."

This was patent poppycock, if not a barefaced lie. With George Eustis, Jack had trained Gala at Fortunate Fields nearly a year before. She had been intended for Dr. Buchanan of Monmouth, Illinois; although illness had forced him to cancel his trip to Switzerland then, she was paired with him now in Nashville. Tartar was the beautiful Fortunate Fields dog that Mrs. Eustis had recommended to be paired with "as well-to-do a person as possible." Morris had chosen another doctor, R. V. Harris of Savannah, Georgia.

Both doctors were active, intelligent men in their middle years, and the class began well. Morris's chief worry was not with their work, but their lodging, "because we could not get rooms for them anywhere near the kennels. Buchanan was staying at the YMCA and the more affluent Harris at the Andrew Jackson Hotel.

"It is not at all satisfactory for either students, dogs or trainers," Morris wrote Dorothy. "There are at least twenty-four boarding houses within a few blocks, but after personally calling on them, I was all but thrown out as soon as I told them I wanted a place for two blind men and their dogs. Therefore, The Seeing Eye will be forced to either rent or buy a house."

This was typical of Morris's impetuous thought processes. He went on to describe a house for which he recommended a year's lease with option to buy and the expenditure of about $1,000 in furniture and improvements, "even though it will be vacant for nine months."

Morris had not bothered to consult either Jack Humphrey or Willi Ebeling about this scheme, and Dorothy Eustis's response was predictably cool. She reminded Morris that The Seeing Eye was still in an experimental stage. She did not want to spend money "until we see what we are doing. You want to gauge what there is to do next year in a factual way before launching yourself high and wide." But Morris's mood continued high and wide. In the growing enthusiasm of Dr. Buchanan and Harris, he relived the excitement of his own emancipation with Buddy, and he shared in the triumphant mood of their graduation. It provided proof to the skeptics that Buddy was not an isolated phenomenon and that The Seeing Eye could turn out competent guides in numbers. His optimism was buttressed by a letter Buchanan wrote from his home: "Gala is doing fine. I go everywhere alone, getting into places I want, sometimes with a little trouble, but generally without trouble and always get home safe and thankful to God that I did it without having to ask some member of my family or friend to go with me. I do not have to stay at home now, because I hate to ask my wife to stop her work or my daughter to stop her play to go with me."

Preparations for the second class were going forward. Morris wrote Dorothy, "Mr. Weber came Saturday night, and I liked him very much. The rest of the gang are grumbling about our weather, snow fifteen inches deep, the first in eleven years. Mr. Humphrey is out of snuff and can't get the same brand in town, so you can imagine what a pleasant lunch we had today."

Two weeks later, he announced that he had lined up seven students for the March 28 class, five of them from Nashville, three paid for by scholarships. The biggest news was that he had arranged to have Adelaide Clifford turn over a dog to Herbert Immeln in New York in May.

Herbert Immeln was the highly respected director of the Lighthouse, which had been founded as the New York Association of the Blind in 1905. The Lighthouse was well endowed, and although it was not a national organization, it performed all the functions of the New York State Commission for the Blind within the city. It also operated an assortment of recreational, social, cultural, and artistic programs. Dorothy Eustis had spoken there in January shortly before her return to Europe, and apparently her remarks had been sufficiently persuasive to prompt Immeln to go to Nashville to see for himself. His decision to apply for a dog was a major breakthrough in the wall of prejudice surrounding workers for the blind. Both Morris and Dorothy had also been delighted to learn of Edward Allen's announcement the previous January: "I am a convert to the modern guidance of man by a dog, because it is so totally different from the ancient and medieval way." But if Allen's words carried weight, Immeln's example would be far more telling.

Curiously, Dorothy did not mention Immeln in her reply to Morris. Perhaps she was skeptical. She advised Morris not to invest too much of himself in the job of managing director, since it was "a work that will never take up a man's whole time." Meanwhile, the executive committee in Nashville confirmed his arrangements for two future classes. Adelaide Clifford would be paid $50 each for turning over dogs to Immeln and a Mr. Hedrick of Norfolk, Virginia, in May. Weber would be paid $170 each for both training and turning over three dogs in New York City in July. Adelaide would be brought down from Maine at Seeing Eye expense to pass on the safety of Weber's dogs before the end of the class.

Meanwhile, although one of the Nashville students had dropped out at the last moment, the March 28 class had gotten off to a spirited start, thanks to a telegram from Dr. Harris. It read in part: "You are about to start the most enjoyable journey of your darkness. My experience assures you that you may place implicit confidence in your instructors and confidence and faith in your dogs. Life's pathway is strewn with many pitfalls and dangers, but your dog will successfully negotiate for you all of these and protect you at all times. Let your watchwords be courage and perseverance. Thank God, the Great Master, for The Seeing Eye, and your instructors."

Four of the six students were from Nashville: E. A. Rogers, Sidney Sweeney, Matt Alexander, and Earl Pendleton. Young Pendleton was in his last year at the Tennessee School for the Blind, and because authorities there were anxious about a dog's behavior in the crowded dining hall, corridors, and classrooms, his application had been approved only after considerable discussion. The two remaining students were from out of state, Mrs. Elford Eddy of Berkeley, California, the first woman student, and Dr. R. A. Blair, a clergyman from Parnassus, Pennsylvania. He had been a missionary in China three years before when his retinas detached.

Blair's letter of inquiry to Morris indicated that he was exactly the sort of man The Seeing Eye wanted. It showed not a trace of self-pity: "I can read braille and write on the typewriter, as I am doing now, but I cannot visit my flock. My wife, who took me on calls at first, is now an invalid, bedridden for a year and a half. My daughter is a cripple with infantile paralysis, so cannot help me to get around. If I had a dog to take me about the parish, that would overcome about the only handicap I now suffer from blindness." They were brave words, but when faced with the reality of working a dog in a strange city, the confidence and courage reflected in this letter deserted Blair. In his nervous agitation and confusion, he was forever giving the wrong commands and pulling against his dog instead of following her. By the end of a week, she was so bewildered by his incomprehensible behavior that she refused to work for him at all.

E. A. Rogers with Pal, Sidney Sweeney with Anitra, and Earl Pendleton with Muddles were all coming along nicely, but Alexander was proving a problem. He was sixty-three, feeble and so rheumatic that he ought never to have been admitted to a class. If his dog moved with any haste, as she would surely have to do sometimes working in traffic, he lost his balance. After a week, Jack Humphrey decided that he would never make part of a safe man-dog unit and dropped him from the class. This enabled him to substitute Dot for the dog Dr. Blair had spoiled and to give the clergyman a second chance.

Mrs. Eddy posed a different sort of problem. Her husband had accompanied her on the long train trip from California, and his constant presence, not only in the hotel, but also on the street, confused her dog, Beta. She seemed uncertain as to which of the Eddys was her master. Mr. Eddy was also a distraction to his wife. Aware of his proximity as a potential protector from harm, Mrs. Eddy subconsciously withheld full confidence in her instructor, Willi Ebeling, and more important, in Beta. Jack and Willi discussed the problem. Jack took Mr. Eddy aside, and Willi Ebeling directed Mrs. Eddy and Beta down a congested street without her husband hovering in the background. Later she recalled this as the crucial moment in her adjustment. As she was following Beta through the crowd, she heard Willi Ebeling calling her to stop. She obeyed, and he came up breathless with excitement to tell her that Beta had just taken her around an open manhole. "Mr. Ebeling's excitement was contagious, and my heart started to pound. This incident established my confidence in the dog and The Seeing Eye and engendered an everlasting devotion to Mr. Ebeling."

The moment may have been equally memorable for Ebeling. The retired importer had come to Nashville on a lark, but the work engrossed his interest more each day. Under Jack's instruction, he had taught guide work to Beta, a dog of his own breeding. Taking and passing a blindfold test with her had been a thrill, but still as part of a game. He had watched with alarm the consequences of Mrs. Eddy's failure to place full faith in Beta. Canine intuition told her that part of her mistress was hanging back. Then had come this moment, a sudden fusing of human and dog into a smoothly functioning unit as Beta guided her around a yawning manhole. This was no longer a game. This was reality, a miracle for which he could take no credit, but for which he had served as a catalyst. It was a moment of supreme excitement.

Meanwhile, under the tutelage of Herr Weber, Blair was beginning to acquire confidence in Dot, and he, too, had a revelation. It happened one morning when Weber lost a trouser button midway on the route. There was a tailor shop across the street, and Weber told Blair to wait while he had the button sewn on. While Weber was in the shop, the foreman of a demolition crew came up to Blair. He was about to set off a charge of dynamite, he said, and he asked Blair to move to the end of the block. Inside the shop, where he had given his pants to the tailor, Weber saw Blair and Dot moving off. In his shorts, he rushed into the street, yelling to Blair to stop. The minister was hugely delighted by the episode, which somehow demonstrated that he and Dot had a joint independent existence apart from their instructor. It was a turning point.

On his return to Parnassus, he wrote Morris, "Dot and I go out walking every morning and walk between fifteen and seventeen blocks and then go calling in the afternoon and evening. She took me to church sabbath morning, and lay at my feet in the pulpit while I preached."

Mrs. Eddy was the last member of the class to graduate, and Jack Humphrey accompanied the Eddys to the railroad station to see them off. While Mr. Eddy took Beta to the baggage car, Mrs. Eddy tried to express her gratitude to Jack. He put her off with a grunt. She began again, but as she was still speaking, he turned and walked away without a word. At that moment, Mr. Eddy returned from the baggage car, and she described Humphrey's rudeness. Mr. Eddy, who had seen Jack's departure, said he couldn't talk.

"Why not?" she asked.

"Well, you see, my dear, he was crying."

6

Wawasee and Astoria

For the first four months of 1929, Seeing Eye activities had been centered in Nashville, but the climate was far too hot for year-round training, and after the second class was over there was a general exodus. Weber returned to Princeton and Willi Ebeling to Openaka. Before he returned to Switzerland, Jack spent a few days with the Ebelings. Adelaide, too, moved into Openaka to put the finishing touches on Bella and Betty for her May class. From his office in Nashville, the managing director reported that things were mighty quiet. Adelaide wrote him, "We all took Jack to the boat last Friday, and believe me, I was never so sorry to see anybody go before. It almost feels as if the bottom of everything had dropped out." But she was soon driving her dogs into nearby Morristown for work, and she reported to Morris, "Saw Weber. He had got three dandy dogs to train. Willi and I tested them out for temperament."

Willi Ebeling was beginning to assume an important role. In the absence of Jack Humphrey, he was deputized to pass on the safety of man-dog units before they were graduated. This was a crucial function that no blind man could perform. He also undertook the acquisition of dogs suitable for guide work. His own stock, his knowledge of fellow breeders, his editorship of *Shepherd Dog Review*, and his apprenticeship in Nashville qualified him uniquely for this job. Finally, Dorothy Eustis and Jack Humphrey counted on him to advise Morris on business matters. The effect was to divide power and authority among Nashville,

Openaka, and Fortunate Fields, and the inevitable result was tension.

Some of the irritation was petty. Morris's custody of the equipment in Nashville was awkward, especially as most of it had come originally from Switzerland. Before her May 9 class, Morris mailed Adelaide two harnesses, leashes, muzzles, curry combs, and brushes, but only one feed pan. "Why you didn't send two feed pans is beyond me," she protested, and Willi Ebeling told Morris the muzzles he sent were too large. He had bought proper ones and was sending the others back. Later Adelaide returned some leashes. "For crying out loud, the next time you get leashes, get good ones like ours."

Expense accounts were another source of friction. Adelaide felt Morris's payments were made grudgingly, and she accompanied her accounting with the assurance, "I've only spent what was absolutely necessary." During the class, she would live with her mother in Manhattan. Immeln lived in Astoria. "The first week we shall work in Astoria, as it is quieter for the beginning. Therefore, I shall have to spend carfare between my house and Astoria. I take it for granted you will pay my expenses. Am I right?" Since she had to ask, she could not really take it for granted, and there was something absurd about a New York debutante haggling with The Seeing Eye's managing director over carfare.

Willi Ebeling's complaints could also be trivial. The laundry in Nashville had shrunk a prized pair of golf stockings, and several exchanges dealt with Morris's unsuccessful attempts to have them brought up to size. Occasionally Willi could be astringent. If Morris had not already done so, he hoped that he would write letters of thanks to Jack, Adelaide, and Mrs. Eustis and make sure that "the nice things you will say are not spoiled by the customary little dirty digs." At other times, Willi dwelt on fundamental differences of opinion. When they were in Nashville together, Morris had wired Charles Campbell and Edward Van Cleve for advice. This seemed perfectly natural to Morris. The Seeing Eye was an agency for the blind. He was consulting the heads of other agencies for the blind who were known to his mother. To Jack and Willi, the opinions of workers for the blind had no bearing on Seeing Eye affairs, where the knowledge of dogs was what mattered. Campbell, Van Cleve, and their ilk knew nothing about dogs and their opinions were therefore worthless. Willi wrote, "You still seem to have a habit of asking opinions. Stop asking opinions. Work to turn out a product that is so good that it will form the opinion, and then you will know that the opinion of the world is with you. I thought we drove that lesson home to you when we were in Nashville."

He said that Morris had missed the chance of a lifetime by not having Jack Humphrey talk to the Nashville Lions Club. Morris promptly went before the Lions himself. He reported triumphantly that the Nashville chapter would propose a resolution to the International Lions meeting in Louisville on June 18. It would ask that the work of The Seeing Eye be adopted in the program of work for the blind by every chapter in the United States and that they lend their support and cooperation by forming classes and giving scholarships.

He sent Willi Ebeling the draft of a pamphlet he wished to take to Louisville and asked for revision. Willi made a number of improvements, and Morris acknowledged that "all corrections are splendid." Willi Ebeling's feeling for the precise meaning and nuance of language was to prove invaluable.

Meanwhile, Adelaide had started her adjustment of Immeln and Hedrick with Bella and Betty. "Immeln is doing a great piece of work with his dog, and everything is tic-tac, so I am very pleased." Hedrick was showing improvement, but "is the clumsiest fellow I ever saw, forever stepping on the bitch." A few days later she comments:

> Immeln is doing now what he should be doing in his third week, he is so far advanced. Bella, although in heat, is work-

ing tic-tac with him, and you would think they had been working for five years together. He has a broad grin on his face when he is working. His only fear appears to be the elevated trains overhead, which deafen him when crossing the street. This, however, has been good practice for him, as he has had to depend on his dog. Bella is a changed girl. She took him over in two or three days. She is in perfect condition with the slickest coat you ever saw. I understand from Mrs. Immeln that Immeln spends a half hour every morning cleaning her, and at night the two are so slushy, she can hardly sit in the same room with them.

Hedrick, too, was working much better. His main fault was his failure to reward his dog "in a laughing enough manner." He managed to graduate and went home with Betty to Norfolk, but Immeln was the real star. On May 30 "we took Immeln down to 42nd Street and Fifth Avenue to work his dog before the president of the New York Association for the Blind and the police commissioner, who directed traffic for twenty minutes. There were a lot of reporters and people to take pictures." Willi Ebeling exulted, "Immeln was the brightest star we have hit to this day. Fox Movietone took talking pictures with Immeln speaking, which will be shown all over the world."

This was good news Morris sorely needed, because he had just received a letter from Mrs. Eustis that raked him over the coals for a number of lapses in his letters and his administration of Seeing Eye affairs:

You are not accurate either in your work or in your statements, and in each case it brings discredit on The Seeing Eye. You do not weigh conditions and therefore you come to conclusions unsupported by facts or reason. Your secretary is careless in her typing. Your administrative work is under inspection because of your amateur methods. Your excuse that you are young is no reason for your not learning by experience. As I have told you, it is pardonable to make a mistake the first time, but to make it again is just plain

dumb. Your indiscriminate use of telegrams with their attendant expense is deplorable. You need to temper your statements with facts and remember always that you are a very
small cog in a very big wheel. I would like to have from you
in concrete form your plans for 1930, not what you think or
hope, but what, after careful study and discussion with your
board, can really be carried out.

On top of this, she opposed his attendance at the meeting of the American Association of Workers for the Blind
(AAWB) at Wawasee, Indiana, and her reasons dealt a blow
to his pride. "Where you work your dog for exhibition,
your tendency is to show off, and it makes such a bad impression that the effect on a stranger is zero. You make so
many inaccurate statements that the public would be in no
way benefited." She suggested that either Dr. Buchanan or
Dr. Blair could represent The Seeing Eye far more effectively than Morris.

Jack's analysis of the Nashville classes was less personal, but equally unflattering. It threw serious doubts on
"the business of Mr. Frank." It recommended that much
greater care be exercised in the selection of blind applicants
for training. Not only should students be physically fit, as
Mr. Alexander was not, but the school should be certain
that the applicant needs the dog as a working helper and
not as a plaything. This latter referred to Dr. Harris and
Tartar. When Adelaide Clifford had gone north by way of
Savannah to check on him, she found, "He plays too much
with the dog and uses him very little as, having two automobiles and a chauffeur, he has no actual need for a dog
other than as a companion." Jack Humphrey delivered the
crowning insult by concluding that whenever a demonstration was necessary, Mr. Rogers and Pal be used in preference to Morris and Buddy. In an accompanying letter to
Morris, Dorothy stressed her agreement: "You have let
Buddy become so careless and inexact in her work that she
is no longer an exhibition dog. I'm sorry, but it is true."

Morris was careful not to hurry his answer to Dorothy. He took more than a week to craft a careful reply. He began humbly. "I deeply appreciate your advice and checkup on my shortcomings. I am sorry that you have taken this attitude toward my attending the convention of the workers for the blind in Wawasee. I feel it is a big mistake not to have The Seeing Eye represented." He understood that Immeln would be the only one with a dog attending, and he would represent, not The Seeing Eye, but the Lighthouse. He responded to her criticisms carefully, one by one, clarifying misunderstandings, but avoiding "dirty digs" or counteroffensives. The letter was faultlessly typed.

In fairness to Morris, neither Dorothy nor Jack appreciated the magnitude of his problem in trying to recruit classes. Despite inquires from every state in the union and a massive correspondence, it was impossible to find more than one or two candidates in any given city. Even in his hometown of Nashville, where he could meet applicants face to face, he had been able to muster only four students, including the rheumatic and overage Alexander. He was convinced that it was essential to enlist the cooperation of workers for the blind to recruit classes, and Wawasee was the place to do it. There would not be another convention of the American Association of Workers for the Blind until 1931, and The Seeing Eye could not afford to wait.

At the last minute Dorothy Eustis relented and cabled her approval of Morris's attendance at Wawasee, but he was not in Nashville to receive her cable. Apparently he had decided to go with or without her permission. He was already off on a trip that would take him to Cincinnati, Louisville, and Wawasee.

The first fruits of this trip were coincidental. Morris was driven by a college classmate, Mike Martin, and they devised a stratagem for getting Buddy into restaurants over the objections of headwaiters. Morris had arguments to overcome objections. Buddy was his eyes. You wouldn't ask a customer to check his eyes before entering the dining room. Buddy was as essential to his mobility as an artificial leg is for an amputee. You would not ask a customer to check his wooden leg in the cloak room. But such arguments did not count with a headwaiter who was afraid of dogs or who feared that his customers were afraid of dogs, so Morris and Mike worked out an alternative plan. Buddy knew Mike as a good friend. She would naturally seek him out in a crowd of strangers. Therefore, Mike went into the dining room alone and was seated at a table before Morris and Buddy came in. Without consultation with the headwaiter, Morris and Buddy made for Mike, circling any obstacles, including waiters. Once Morris was seated with Buddy tucked out of sight underneath the table, he had the advantage. It was easier to serve him than to risk a row before the other customers.

The youth and brashness that were such a handicap in administrative matters were a great advantage in breaking down the barriers against dogs in public places, and breaking down those barriers was essential if guide dogs were to succeed. Morris was a fighter. He was not afraid of being conspicuous and he did not care what means he used to gain his ends. Sweet reason and old-fashioned courtesy were of no use in this sort of battle. The Doctors Buchanan, Blair, and Harris were too conventional for such methods, and even Morris's critics agree that there was no one in work for the blind at the time who could have done what he did.

Morris always acknowledged his debt to uninhibited college friends like Mike Martin. They were invaluable allies, because they regarded the integration of guide dogs in public places as both a challenge and a game. Morris recalled one episode in which he and a dozen friends entered an all-night diner in the small hours. When the manager objected to Buddy, one of the boys turned to another. "I don't object to the dog, do you?" The question was relayed around the circle, eliciting one negative response after the other. Morris claimed that, when it became clear that the manager was the only one who objected to the dog, the boys picked the manager up and carried him out.

In Cincinnati, Morris's Aunt Selma introduced him to Calvin Glover, president of the American Association of Workers for the Blind. From Glover, Morris learned that Thomas Sinykin, who had imported and trained Senator Schall's guide dog, was scheduled to speak to the convention and planned to ask for a resolution of support. Morris explained that The Seeing Eye was a nonprofit organization providing dogs at cost. Sinykin was a businessman seeking a substantial profit. In consequence, the invitation to Sinykin was rescinded and Morris was scheduled in his place. Luck and Morris saved the day for The Seeing Eye in the nick of time.

From Cincinnati Mike drove Morris to Louisville. When he and Buddy strode out on the stage before 7,000 Lions, they received a thunderous ovation. Buddy reacted with a chorus of barks, which put the audience in a good humor. Then Morris gave a short talk modeled on his radio speech in New York, but enriched by anecdotal material from the classes in Nashville and the successes of the new graduates. He was applauded enthusiastically. The Nashville resolution was proposed and passed. The Seeing Eye had a potential source of recruiters and supporters in every Lions Club from coast to coast.

In Wawasee, Morris and Buddy repeated this success. "You can talk about your other dogs, madame, but I must salute mine. The corridors were packed with sighted, semi-sighted and blind people. She has been stepped upon. She has been kicked, petted and in many ways annoyed, but at no time did she snap or bark or growl. I got through the crowds with less trouble than the sighted people."

Morris's talk described his training in Switzerland, his return trip through New York City, the establishment of The Seeing Eye in Nashville, and the success of the first two classes. When he was finished, a braille teacher from Berkeley, Kate Foley, rose to report a feat she had seen performed by Mrs. Eddy and Beta. The most recent issue of the *New Outlook* contained a complimentary article on The Seeing Eye, and the support of Allen and Van Cleve further boosted the movement. Morris reckoned, "The ones who were once on the fence are now in favor of it, and the 40% who did not favor it are either in favor or on the fence. I do not believe that anyone at the convention is actually opposed to it." Van Cleve wrote Jessie Frank, "We are all very proud of Morris and the splendid manner in which he put over his proposition."

Morris's informal contacts at the convention were as important as his public presentation. He met Mary Dranga Campbell, the former wife of Charles Campbell and executive secretary of the Missouri State Commission for the Blind. She had earlier written to Morris in Nashville to recommend an applicant for a dog. Only now did Morris realize that the applicant was Mervyn Sinclair, president of the Pennsylvania Council for the Blind, where Mary Campbell had previously worked. Sinclair would be as invaluable a convert as Herbert Immeln, and Morris reported, "I have offered him an opening in the class we are planning to hold in the last part of November in Birmingham, Alabama."

He had met Herbert Immeln, too. Immeln said the Lighthouse was thinking of building kennels, which would make it an ideal place for Adelaide to train six dogs for the Birmingham class. The July class under Weber and sponsored by the Lighthouse was about to begin, and it seemed to promise a pattern of cooperation for the future. As managing director of the Nashville headquarters, Morris would correspond with the appropriate local agency, which would line up a class of students in its city. From Lake Openaka Willi Ebeling would locate suitable dogs for Adelaide or Herr Weber to train, and they would then take the dogs to the city in question to hold a class.

Morris was well satisfied that his trip to Wawasee had won important gains. The savor of success was sweeter for his having won over the objections of Dorothy Eustis. He returned to Nashville flushed with confidence in the future, but the Lighthouse "plan" failed to take certain pitfalls into account. There was no clear division of authority and responsibility between the Lighthouse and The Seeing Eye. Willi Ebeling's role was not understood by Immeln, Weber, or even Morris. Weber was still an unknown quantity. There was the likelihood of serious trouble.

Even before the class began, relations between Willi Ebeling and Morris Frank were strained. Willi was finding his workload much heavier than he had anticipated. "I seem to have time for nothing but Seeing Eye business." In addition to advising Morris, he was responsible for analyzing and solving by letter the problems that graduates encountered in the field. Although she had been shown in Nashville, Mrs. Eddy did not know how to board a streetcar. Earl Pendleton's Muddles was becoming crowd-shy in the noise and confusion of the Tennessee School for the Blind. Letters to correct problems of this sort had to be explicit, tactful, and carefully composed.

Ebeling's search for suitable dogs entailed long automobile trips for which his expenses were inadequately reimbursed. He could afford the cost, but he was a stickler for precision, and Morris's lapses irritated him. "I want to help, Morris, but I am not going to do your work for you." From Immeln he learned that Morris had quoted him indiscreetly at Wawasee. "Put a padlock on your mouth and talk with your brain," Ebeling wrote him. Adelaide Clifford was also unhappy with Morris. She had enjoyed the New York class, but at different times Morris had asked her tentatively to take classes in Trenton, Pittsburgh, Cincinnati, Birmingham, Berkeley, and San Francisco, and nothing was definite.

Although Willi Ebeling had suggested Weber originally, the two Germans were not sympathetic. Willi drove over to Princeton with Adelaide to watch Weber take his blindfold tests. By the time he got to his third dog, Willi wrote, he "was staggering like a drunken man. We had a good laugh at his expense." Weber resented their supervision. He had been training dogs for twice as long as Willi Ebeling and Adelaide Clifford put together.

The truth was that Weber's years of experience were a handicap rather than an asset. They had been devoted to a type of training that inculcated prompt and precise obedience. Such obedience was unsuitable for a blind man's guide, which must have the freedom to disobey a dangerous command. Even when its blind master demanded it, his guide must not lead him forward into an open manhole, an overhanging branch, or a stream of moving cars. Teaching a dog to make decisions required a completely different approach than training it to obey.

This difference explained the necessity for the blindfold test. With their extraordinary sensory acuity, dogs learning to guide become keenly aware of the body language of their instructors. Approaching an obstacle he could see, an instructor might slacken his pace almost imperceptibly or shift his balance ever so slightly preparing to turn around it. The instructor might be entirely unaware of such a body signal, but to an alert dog it would signal a command as clear as the spoken word. Having obeyed the unspoken and unconscious command, the dog would be rewarded by the instructor's rapturous "Atta *good* girl!" and this would encourage it to do the same again when the opportunity presented. Under a blindfold, an instructor could not anticipate physical obstacles, and the dog would have to solve its guiding problems on its own initiative without benefit of body signals.

The Seeing Eye's educational philosophy applied even to the teaching of obedience exercises. The school did not want to inculcate conditioned reflexes; it did not teach instant obedience because, for a guide dog, every command must include an element of request. The dog must be allowed to think it over. "Forward" means "Forward, if you think it's a good idea." If you teach that "Down" means "Down! Right away! No matter what!" the dog may think that "Forward" means "Forward! Right away! No matter what!" even though a car is coming.

Educating according to principles of dog psychology was far more demanding than training by corporal punishment. It is easier to produce a conditioned reflex than a reasoned response. In Nashville, Jack Humphrey had tried to explain Seeing Eye methods to Weber in teaching obedience to Anitra and Betty, but, Jack recalled, "One day when I wasn't looking, he put on the spikes and spoiled everything." The spikes referred to a training collar with spikes on the inside used to enforce obedience. At the time, these cruel devices were quite common in other types of training, but anathema to The Seeing Eye. This incident probably explains why Jack was insistent that Weber's dogs be checked for safety by Willi Ebeling and Adelaide Clifford.

Immeln had lined up three men for Weber's class. They were a student at Harvard Law named Prendergast, Carl Wartenburg of Brooklyn, who caned chairs, and Peter Gillen of Astoria, who was unemployed. They had heard from Morris by letter, but their direct contact was with Lighthouse personnel and, during the early stages of the class, with Weber. The Seeing Eye was for them only a shadowy entity in the background.

Weber began the class on July 4. At the time the sale of fireworks was unrestricted, and firecrackers exploded everywhere. Willi Ebeling disapproved. "It is too risky to have strange dogs and strange people in a strange location on such a noisy day. One firecracker tied to a dog's tail, and he would never come home." On July 9, he drove three hours through the summer heat to inspect the class on the streets of Astoria. He found Prendergast paired with Gretel, Wartenburg with Blackie, and Gillen with Asta. His reaction to Weber was immediate, unequivocal, and negative. He announced, "I have come to the conclusion that we do not want him. I am not going to comment on his work, but he has an insubordinate character which does not fit into our plans. I had a disagreement with him. He had changed his schedule, and I had to make him work one dog a second time that afternoon. He was abusive, and I will have nothing further to do with him." Because the first student had worked before he arrived, Willi was justified in asking him to work again, and when Weber objected, he asserted his authority. Two Teutonic tempers sizzled in the July heat, but it was more than a matter of temperament. It was a matter of safety. Willi had seen evidence of unsound technique, but he did not attempt to describe it to Morris, who would not have understood the subtleties. Unfortunately he had said only, "I am not going to comment on his work," leaving Morris with the impression that it was only Weber's "insubordinate character" to which Willi objected. Weber's students were in the dark about the role of this stranger who had argued with their instructor.

Adelaide was due to come down from Maine for an inspection, and Willi's instinct was to remove Weber and turn the class over to her. It would cost something, but "the success of the class is more important than a few dollars." Having found Weber unsatisfactory, he did not want him to finish a class, because that would seem to confer The Seeing Eye's stamp of approval. He was certain that "Weber someday will be a competitor."

It was certainly to Weber's advantage to sever connections. The Seeing Eye was an infant organization operating on a shoestring. The Lighthouse was a flourishing and well-endowed institution with an operating budget of half a million dollars a year. Weber knew that Immeln was already raising money for a second class and would need an instructor. If he remained with The Seeing Eye, his work would be under the constant supervision of Willi Ebeling or Adelaide Clifford. With the Lighthouse, he could train as he pleased with no nonsense about blindfold tests.

Willi Ebeling postponed any decision until Adelaide Clifford had made her inspection. Probably at Weber's suggestion, Immeln, too, was present. Like Morris, he worked well with his own dog, and he probably believed that this gave him a knowledge of guide dog instruction. As he later described it to Morris, Prendergast worked Gretel on the sidewalk while Willi and Adelaide watched, "driving along in Mr. Ebeling's machine. The dog reached the corner and slanted to the other side. [That is, Gretel crossed the intersection diagonally]. Miss Clifford jumped from the machine and told Mr. Weber to make the dog do it over again. Mr. Weber said no, they would do it at the next corner."

Adelaide called Willi Ebeling from his car, and a heated argument ensued in front of Prendergast. Immeln reported, "Mr. Ebeling and Miss Clifford were handling Mr. Weber as if they were dealing with a low type of servant instead of a human being." He did not realize how very wrong Weber was. The diagonal crossing of an intersection is extremely dangerous in traffic, and even on a deserted street, it will confuse the master's orientation and cause him to lose his way. Far more important, the time to correct an error is at the moment it occurs. This is a fundamental and inflexible rule of guide dog education. A single wrong impression can spoil a dog. Weber's refusal to make the correction then and there was inexcusable. It is probable that he was using the argument to promote an open break between The Seeing Eye and the Lighthouse.

Willi Ebeling had the authority to discharge Weber and put the class under Adelaide, but there were two obstacles. The first was the confidence of the students. "Weber had poisoned the minds of the blind against us and tells them that we know nothing and he knows it all." The second was the division of authority between the Lighthouse and The Seeing Eye. Immeln repeatedly insisted that the class was under Lighthouse "supervision," a word to which Morris had consented. Willi wrote him, "When you use such a word, you must define what you mean. If you had used the word 'auspices,' you would have taken some of the authority away." Caught in an untenable position, Willi Ebeling compromised. After a three-hour conference with Immeln, he agreed to let Weber complete the class without supervision by Adelaide. In return, she was to have absolute authority to pass or fail each man-dog unit at the end of the class. This reserved to The Seeing Eye the all-important right to insist on safety.

Willi reported all this to Morris in a long letter and repeated earlier requests that Morris forward to him copies of any letters he had received from either Immeln or Weber. Morris had received a letter from Immeln, but instead of sending a copy to Willi Ebeling, he discussed it with two members of his board. He "didn't deem it wise" to send on Immeln's letter. He therefore withheld it and telephoned Immeln to mediate long-distance.

Morris was meddling where he had no business. This was a question of training, and in Jack Humphrey's absence, Willi Ebeling was responsible for all training matters. Morris had relapsed into his old habit of asking advice from people unqualified to give it. His board members, who knew nothing about training, advised him to telephone Immeln, who also knew nothing about training. Worse yet, he accepted Immeln's version of events rather than Willi Ebeling's. He wrote Dorothy, "I feel Herr Weber has received the most unfair treatment and that if he had received the proper cooperation, he could have finished the class." After talking to Immeln, Morris sent a wire, not to Willi Ebeling, but to Adelaide Clifford. "No mail since your arrival in New York. Send a report at once on working of dogs and blind masters, also suggestions on anything that is necessary. Take no action without first asking my approval. Situation delicate."

Willi Ebeling was outraged. The reference to "no mail" ignored his very detailed reports or implied that they were useless. Concerning the statement "Take no action without first asking my approval," Willi wired Morris: "My interpretation is that you disapprove of my action. As I have fulfilled my promise, my supervision is ended with the day." Morris was stricken by Willi's resignation, but he still was inclined to side with Immeln. He wrote Dorothy, "Mr.

Immeln said he felt very friendly toward me. Speaking for himself as well as his organization, as long as Mr. Ebeling is in any way connected, the Lighthouse will have nothing else to do with The Seeing Eye. Mr. Immeln also says that Herr Weber would train the next class."

Apparently Morris still felt some hope of a reconciliation. The prospect of cooperation was tempting, and flushed with his triumphs with the International Lions and the AAWB, he tried his hand at diplomacy. From his perspective, the hostility between Ebeling and Immeln looked more like a clash of temperament than of principle.

From Mt. Pelerin, Dorothy saw more clearly. She fully backed Willi Ebeling and Adelaide, who had rightly focused on The Seeing Eye's single overriding objective, the safety of the blind students. "That point must be kept in mind first, last and all the time." She concluded that neither Weber nor Immeln grasped the basic principle of guide dog education and should have no place in the school's future plans. If there were to be any cooperation with other agencies in the future, The Seeing Eye's absolute responsibility would have to be spelled out clearly.

Willi Ebeling compromised his resignation by sharing with Adelaide in judging the safety of the three students. They passed on all three, though somewhat reluctantly in the case of Gillen and Asta. Willi also agreed to make Openaka available to Adelaide for training her next string of dogs and even to put up a Swiss trainer from L'Oeil qui Voit, but he made his position with Morris clear in a letter dated August 4: "Now, Morris, life is too short for me to waste my time the way I have been wasting it with fruitless attempts at helping you. In another capacity I shall still continue to be some help to The Seeing Eye for a bit, but no more of this. You will have to find a better man than I am and one that you can trust more." Dorothy Eustis pinned Morris down with a string of embarrassing questions. "If you have cut yourself off from further assistance from Mr. Ebeling, will you let me know how you plan to collect your dogs: attend to the shipping, kennels, etc., how you plan to inspect the work, advise the men, etc., if you have not Mr. Ebeling as supervisor? I am afraid you have left yourself in a very unfortunate position." But at that moment, Willi Ebeling relented. He had been deeply hurt by Morris's lack of trust, his readiness to consult virtually anyone in preference to himself, but the six months he had devoted to The Seeing Eye had made a true believer of him. The Seeing Eye and Morris needed him, and he could not resist that need. On August 9, only five days after telling Morris to find someone else, he wrote again: "The Lighthouse is a dead issue with me." He went on for pages of minutely detailed advice for arranging classes in Berkeley and San Francisco in 1930. Willi Ebeling was hooked, and he knew it. The Seeing Eye would consume all his considerable talents and energy for the next twenty-five years.

7

L'Oeil qui Voit

"Quite naturally, people are asking me about The Seeing Eye, and I have been doing my level best to put them straight. The point is, however, I am stumped with the many questions I am asked." Writing Dorothy Eustis in September 1929, Adelaide Clifford poured out her perplexity about the confused affairs of The Seeing Eye. People were surprised, she wrote, because there seemed to be "no real head to make the movement go except a charming woman who is on a Swiss mountain top thousands of miles away. Funny that a new organization should be put in the hands of a young boy, twenty-one years old, and the organization has but one trainer to start the work here with and that trainer, at that, a young girl. Why hasn't there been more progress in the movement? Why doesn't The Seeing Eye find trainers in this country?" There followed a series of questions culminating in "the one big question, why you, the president of the organization, don't come over here and see that things are run the way they ought to be?"

Dorothy Eustis answered promptly with her usual candor. The Seeing Eye "was put in the hands of a blind boy of twenty-one because he was the only one who had the guts to touch it." The Red Cross, the American Foundation for the Blind, the Lighthouse, and the Philadelphia School for the Blind had all turned down her offer to bring guide dogs to America.

The reason there had not been more progress was the difficulty of finding trainers. If she had trained Americans, they would have demanded wages that would put the cost of a guide dog out of reach. She was aware that things were not being run properly, but there was no point in her coming to the United States and arousing interest until she had the trainers to make good on her promises. This work was for the betterment of the blind "and not to provide dinner conversation for the seeing."

Meanwhile, "the Swiss mountain top on which I am supposed to be sitting is the last place where anyone would find time to sit, and we are learning far more by having a Lausanne school developing under our noses than in a hundred trips to Germany."

The school in Lausanne had been going for four months. Dorothy had spent March and April in Rome, overseeing a course for Italian police. Jack Humphrey did not return from Nashville until May. In the interim, Captain Balsiger had prepared his house and kennels to quarter blind students, apprentices, and dogs. Through Gretchen Green, Dorothy negotiated with Italian and French authorities to supply both military and civilian blind for training, and L'Oeil qui Voit officially opened its doors on June 2.

In July, Dorothy and Jack attended the International Conference of the Blind in Vienna, and Dorothy was named chairman of a committee to study the use and practicability of dogs as leaders for the blind. The commission was to report to the next international conference in 1931. Another delegate to the conference was Robert Irwin of the American Foundation. During a visit to Fortunate Fields, Dorothy wrote, "Mr. Irwin went over every day to Lausanne to take a walk with one of the dogs in training. He is personally very much in favor of the work, but I do not think he is ready to give the endorsement of the American Foundation."

Balsiger was the administrative head of L'Oeil qui Voit, but Humphrey was its guiding genius. His restless mind was soon devising improvements on German technique. German dogs were taught to bark at pedestrians who blocked their path, but this would have intimidated Americans, and Jack's dogs were taught to work silently. At some stages in the training, German instructors used slaps to correct the dogs. Jack found such corporal punishment both unnecessary and undesirable. It might inculcate unthinking obedience. As time went on, Jack devised literally scores of further modifications.

Some interesting cultural problems emerged in the training of French and Italian war veterans. In a mixed class, they wasted so much time arguing about who had won the war that they were trained separately thereafter. Basic to training in any language was the necessity of rewarding a dog verbally for every desirable act and doing it with sufficient expression to convey meaning to the dog. French and Swiss students seemed to have no difficulty, but many Italians were listless in their praise. When reminded, they would shrug and say, "But a dog has no soul."

The Marchesa Cavalletti, a friend of Dorothy's, hit on the solution. Italians, she said, should be thought to think of their dogs in the context, not of theology, but of theater. All Italians understood the audience's obligation to applaud a fine performance, and their rewards for their guides soon rang with the gusto of curtain calls at La Scala.

The French objected to the use of German shepherds and insisted on sending the school a variety of French dogs, all of which proved unsuitable. "The poodles were the most interesting, as they were amazingly quick to learn, but oh so la-de-da! They were totally lacking in a feeling of responsibility for the person they were leading. If something caught their attention, they would go right over a curb or drop their trainer in a hole."

These were the comments of one more of the remarkable personalities whom Dorothy attracted to Fortunate Fields. She was Edith "Missy" Doudge, a strikingly attractive young horsewoman from Virginia who spoke both French and Italian fluently. Dorothy felt that she would be a natural with dogs and, against Jack's will, persuaded him to give her a try. Considering her "a slip of a young lady" without the stamina to take the physical strain, Jack put her through a rough blindfold test. "When I thought I had her discouraged with a trip under blindfold behind a strange and hard-pulling dog in the heaviest of Lausanne traffic for better than an hour, I told her to pull the blindfold and asked her, 'Well, what do you think?' She looked clear through me with her cold blue eyes and said, 'I think I like it.' To make a long story short, in a few months, she was in charge of the training and cut a big work load from my shoulders."

Jack summed up his philosophy in a letter to Adelaide Clifford. "You can learn something from each dog and each blind man you come in contact with. Keep your eyes and ears and mind open and learn, learn, learn. Your work will constantly get better, and you will constantly find the work more interesting. That is why I like the breeding and training of animals. Each mating, each animal is a new problem and offers something new to be learned."

What Jack was learning might have been lost but for a project triggered by Gretchen Green. One day, Dorothy told Jack she wanted him to go to Paris to see a woman named Helen Hubbard. "Just that," he recalled, "and not what to see her about." Helen Hubbard was another of Gretchen's wealthy friends. He went, saw Helen Hubbard, and answered questions. Then she announced that there was something she wished to finance. To guarantee that the knowledge Jack had accumulated should be preserved in permanent form, she (with an assist from Dorothy) would subsidize Jack in the writing of two scientific reports, "as time allows."

Both reports were written. The first, in collaboration with Lucien Warner, was published as a book, *Working Dogs*, in 1934. The second was completed in 1938. It was in the form of a series of lectures on 3,000 typewritten pages, illustrated with hundreds of photographs and collected in twenty notebooks. The Hubbard lectures constituted the

gospel according to Jack Humphrey on th
dogs, students, and instructors at The Seeing

Jack defined the qualities desired in a g
addition to good health and the appropriate siz   ength,
and stamina, a guide must have willingness and intelligence. Appearances could be deceiving. One dog seemed lacking in intelligence because he was playing dumb. Paired with a different instructor who put up with no nonsense, he proved highly intelligent. Jack warned that if an apprentice found his dog's intelligence rating going down during training, it was a sign that his dog was thinking faster than he was. When a stubborn dog was put under an instructor who disliked her, she soon refused to work at all. Under an instructor free from personal dislike, her willingness increased markedly. It became a rule that no instructor should work with a dog he disliked. Jack believed that the dog or horse or any other animal that was stubborn made much the better worker once that stubbornness was overcome than the animal who never gave any trouble. "I am always afraid of the future with any animal that does not set its will against mine for a while."

Shyness was the most undesirable trait. A guide must be absolutely gun-sure, not startled by sudden or loud noises or overly sensitive to physical pain. On the other hand, a dog with too low a sensitivity of either ear or body was difficult to reach. For best results a dog should be medium sensitive to both sound and touch. Too keen a sense of smell was a handicap. One dog so willing that she took fifteen different blind men for a walk in a single afternoon was so sensitive to the scent of pigeons that she would start to give chase to ones she could not see around a corner. A guide dog requires sufficient aggressiveness to lead its master through crowds and to stand its ground steadily between two lines of moving traffic, yet it must be willing to tolerate jostling and the unwelcome attention and caresses of strangers.

Working Dogs reported the case of Fortunate Fields dog

315. When its character was tested at twelve, fifteen, and eighteen months, it was found to lack sufficient aggressiveness for police work. As a guide, the dog worked well, but only until the apprentice put on a blindfold. It then headed for the shade of a tree and lay down. If a man under blindfold was being watched by a sighted instructor, dog 315 worked. When not under observation, it was back to the shade of the tree. Having failed as a guide, it was returned to Fortunate Fields for another chance at police work. By sheer accident, a trainer lying in ambush for a different dog mistakenly staged a mock attack on dog 315 and its trainer. To the surprise of all concerned, it sprang ferociously to the defense. The dog's entire character had changed in the interval between eighteen and thirty-three months. It was trained as a hard attack dog.

Jack believed that a dog's ability to learn is almost unlimited, if it can be made to understand what its master wants. For guide work, this required the instructor to get inside the dog's mind. In other types of training, the man imposed his will on the dog from above. In the education of a guide dog, the instructor must learn to understand the dog's point of view and work, not down from the man, but up from the dog.

After learning to pull in harness, a dog is taught to stop at curbs. A curb is not an obstacle for a dog, and it is natural for her to run right over it. To show her that this is wrong, the instructor pretends to stumble, tramples his feet noisily, and utters the worst word in a guide dog's vocabulary, "Pfui!" It is spoken with venom, and the dog is immediately aware that something is terribly wrong. The instructor steps backward onto the curb and calls the dog to come and sit on his left side. Her obedient response is rewarded with an "Atta *good* girl!" as joyous as the "pfui" was angry. The dog is reassured and pleased. Her instructor then commands, "Forward." The moment she moves, she receives another rapturous "Atta *good* girl," but just when she thinks everything is going swimmingly, she runs the curb on the opposite side of the street. Again, trampling feet and a terrible "Pfui!" Again, "come" and "sit" are rewarded with an ecstatic "Atta *good* girl!"

In a very few repetitions, the dog becomes aware that there is something potentially dangerous about a curb. She slows and stops warily, several feet away. The instructor commands, "Hopp, hopp." This German phrase is roughly translatable as "Go on. Keep going." It is spoken encouragingly and with a forward gesture of the right hand. If the dog does not understand, the instructor may swing his right foot around and nudge his guide gently in the hindquarters with his toe. This is not a kick or a correction, only a gentle physical reinforcement of a command she does not understand. The moment she moves forward, there is another "Atta *good* girl," and when she comes to a stop at the curb, this is repeated joyously and accompanied by a few pats. Timing, consistency, and total concentration on the dog are everything. When they fail, a dog can get the wrong idea of what is wanted.

One apprentice seemed to be working well with his dog. Jack noticed that whenever she stopped for curbs or obstacles, he rewarded her with "*Oui, il est beau*," the French equivalent of "Atta *good* girl." But when Jack took her for a test walk and rewarded her for swerving to avoid an oncoming pedestrian, the dog sat down. It developed that the apprentice had forgotten to reward her for any act except sitting at curbs or barriers. As a result, she came to think that "*Oui, il est beau*" meant sit. The mistake was inconsistency, the failure to reward every desired act, rather than those of a particular category.

Concentration on the dog's reactions is vital. An example of the failure to think first of the dog occurred years later in America. Here well meaning dog lovers with kind hearts, but no understanding of guide dog technique, sometimes proved troublesome. One apprentice working his dog up to a curb noticed two elderly women whom he imagined to be of the interfering type. When his dog ran the curb, he trampled his feet in the prescribed manner but stepped on her paw in the process. She yelped in pain, and to forestall any protest from the women bystanders, the instructor lavished her with undeserved praise and pats. He was so preoccupied with his effect on the human observers that he did not calculate his even deeper impression on his dog. When they reached the next down curb, she repeated the yelp of pain that had elicited such generous rewards at the previous corner. The association was so firmly established in her mind that she could not be broken of yelping at every curb and had to be retired from training.

A different sort of misunderstanding arose between a dog and an instructor who became overzealous in teaching her to avoid parking meters. When she failed to give sufficient clearance, he slapped the meter with his right hand and rewarded her with "Atta *good* girl" as soon as she moved left. This form of correction was possible for a blind master, but the instructor added a sort of positive reinforcement that was not. He rewarded his dog every time she passed a meter, though a blind master could not have known the meter was there. A blindfold test revealed the error of his ways. When the dog had passed three meters in a row without receiving her customary reward, she decided her instructor did not know where the meters were and proceeded to show him by bumping him into every remaining meter on the block.

Even under blindfold, it was possible for an instructor to give body cues that could cause problems for a blind student. One apprentice unconsciously encouraged a somewhat unwilling dog by giving a slight lift to the harness handle on the command of forward. The dog learned to respond, not to the verbal command but to the lift. When she was paired with a blind master, she would not budge on command.

Not all the problems were the fault of instructors. Sometimes trouble resulted from circumstances beyond their control. Fortunate Fields dog 270 tested as gun-sure and was paired successfully with a war veteran. Months later as they were waiting at a curb, a nearby truck backfired almost in the dog's face. The veteran, who had been shell-shocked, screamed, started backward, stepped on his dog's paw, and fell on her. The ear pain reinforced by the body pain and the contagion of her master's panic proved traumatic. Dog 270 became too sound-sensitive for safety and had to be replaced.

At L'Oeil qui Voit throughout 1929, Jack Humphrey was constantly discovering new nuances and subtleties of guide dog technique. He had something new to tell his lady boss almost every day. Therefore, although Dorothy was troubled by the slowness of progress in America and the questions Adelaide Clifford raised in September of 1929, she was confident that the work in L'Oeil qui Voit was laying the foundations of knowledge on which the American school would build. Her confidence was further buoyed by the knowledge that the Swiss school was about to graduate its first apprentice instructor and ship him across the Atlantic to The Seeing Eye.

8
On the Road—Harrisburg

Georges Guillaume Louis Debetaz was born in Lausanne on May 20, 1906. In the spring of 1929, with the College Scientifique and his military service behind him, he was looking for a job when an old friend of the family, Major Champod, told him about L'Oeil qui Voit. Champod was a police officer who had worked with Mrs. Eustis; he offered to recommend young Debetaz as an apprentice. Debetaz knew absolutely nothing about dogs and less about blind people, but one aspect of Champod's reports of L'Oeil qui Voit made him prick up his ears. An apprentice instructor was likely to be sent to the United States.

It was a time when many young Swiss emigrated to foreign countries in search of economic opportunities not available at home. Those who returned on vacation cut a wide swath. Debetaz recalled them "flashing their money all over creation." It was not a love of dogs or concern for blind people, but the lure of the Yankee dollar that prompted him to enroll in the school. He launched on a lifelong career without the faintest notion what it would entail.

Jack Humphrey was not impressed by the blond young man in the jaunty beret. His wiry physique seemed too frail and his temperament too anxious for him to be a trainer. Reminded of this judgment many years later, Debetaz laughed: "Anxious! When they order me into the box with the dog, I was not anxious. I was scared stiff." Jack Humphrey predicted he would not last a week, but of the scores of young men who enrolled in L'Oeil qui Voit, Debetaz was the first of only three who rose to the rank of instructor, and he lasted not a week but forty-three years.

With the exception of his command of English, Debetaz possessed in abundance all the qualities of the ideal instructor. Three of these qualities—intelligence, willingness, and physical stamina—were also qualities of the ideal guide dog. Physically, an instructor must have the strength to control a dog, but large size was not an advantage. If it interfered with quickness and agility, it was a handicap. The ideal instructor tended to be of middle height with a frame that carried no excess fat. Instructors must be willing workers. They worked from ten to twelve hours a day, six days a week. They walked ten miles a day at three-and-a-half miles per hour, training up to ten dogs in a string. Daily, these dogs must also be curried, fed, watered, and given obedience exercises. During classes, instructors were on call twenty-four hours a day for up to four weeks.

Training guide dogs required mental concentration of a high order, the imagination to see things from the dog's point of view, and the ability to communicate with a dog. Even those who possessed these qualities often failed for lack of the ability to communicate with blind humans. During class, the students were under a severe strain, and their anxiety made it hard for them to understand. Directions had to be clear and precise. A degree of sympathy was important, but too much patience was a failing. If they were allowed to make the same mistakes over and over, neither the dogs nor their masters learned as well as they did from a teacher who insisted on getting things right the first time.

Good nerves were another prerequisite. Instructors generally worked two students at a time. Keeping an eye on two novices working strange dogs around routes that combined pedestrian and automobile traffic with steps, barriers, and overhangs could be draining, and many instructors dropped out from nervous exhaustion. Dorothy and Jack reckoned that only 5 to 8 percent of all the apprentices in the German schools ever completed training.

Young Debetaz progressed remarkably. As early as August, Dorothy was writing to Morris of a Swiss she was preparing to send over to work under Adelaide. Morris hesitated. Bank failures in Birmingham had wiped out the savings both of the prospective students and of the agency sponsoring the class. He doubted he had enough work for a second instructor. Later, when Mervyn Sinclair and the Pennsylvania Council for the Blind were able to assemble a class in Harrisburg for November, Debetaz was sent for posthaste. He had just time for a ten-day course in English at the Berlitz School before he sailed. Jack wrote Adelaide, "You will not have trouble with him taking orders from anybody else, since he will not learn English until he gets over there, and you will be the only one who can really talk to him." In his native Lausanne, Debetaz had all the qualities of the ideal instructor. In his adopted country, he would have a language problem with his blind students.

On November 8, he saw the Statue of Liberty raising her lamp beside the Golden Door. He came to make his fortune on the eve of the worst depression in American history. Willi Ebeling met the young Swiss at the steamer and drove him back to Lake Openaka, where he was given lodging in "the help house," board, and $75 a month. In return, he worked a seventy-hour week. Every morning and afternoon, Adelaide Clifford, who lived with the Ebelings, drove him into Morristown in her cream-colored convertible with wire wheels, and the pair of them worked eight dogs through the streets. What with their other responsibilities in looking after the dogs, Adelaide wrote Morris, "I don't have time to write letters, even to my own mother."

Earlier in the fall, Adelaide had taken time out to make her debut in New York, but there was no time to spare now. A week after Debetaz's arrival, she sprained her foot giving a curb correction. Willi Ebeling instructed Morris to postpone the class for two weeks, but even this additional time was insufficient. Two of the dogs in Adelaide's string had been graduated before, Betty with Hedrick and Asta with

Gillen. Hedrick had returned Betty because his landlord objected to her. For submitting without a fight, Morris had
pronounced Hedrick "yellow to the core" and barred him
from admission to any class in the future. Gillen had
spoiled Asta by playing with her at home and failing to
reward her work on the streets. According to her perspective, Gillen loved her only at home, so that she sought to
keep him there and refused to work outside. Betty accepted
retraining, but toward the end of November Adelaide decided that the rehabilitation of Asta had failed. "I got her
to work well, but she is unsafe and won't work for anyone
but me, so I don't want to take chances."

Willi wired Morris that he would have to cut one of the
students from the Harrisburg class. Morris groaned. Having sold the virtues of the guide dog to the members of the
class, he now had to dash the hopes of one of them. Willi
suggested compensating the unlucky one with the offer of
a place in Morristown in February or March with one of
the two new dogs Debetaz was training. As a candidate for
Debetaz's second dog, Willi wrote Morris, "There is a local
blind man, a Negro, and someone wants to collect for getting him a dog. If he is a deserving Negro, what is to be
done about it?"

The young man who had met George Washington
Carver at the family dinner table knew exactly where he
stood on race. He answered, "Have him write to the office,
and put him through the same routine as the rest. We are
an organization to furnish dogs for the deserving blind, and
I do not think we can discriminate and still call ourselves a
non-profit organization." Willi responded, "I just wanted
to know whether the organization had drawn a color line. I
did not think so, but I wanted to be sure."

In this brief exchange in 1929, the Seeing Eye policy on
race was settled once and for all. By way of contrast, as late
as the 1950s, an association for the blind in a Southern city
was posting sighted monitors at the doors to its Christmas

party in order to segregate the blind guests who could not see each other's color.

Of the five students now scheduled for the Harrisburg class, Morris was particularly eager for success with three workers for the blind. They were Mervyn Sinclair, president of the Pennsylvania Council, Ann Connelly of Burlington, Vermont, and Sadie Jacobs of New Orleans. He warned Adelaide that Miss Jacobs was "a very small nervous person," and she was bringing her secretary with her, which might pose a problem. Adelaide was feeling optimistic: "Yesterday I put Debetaz through his first blindfold test with me. The dogs worked tic-tac, so three cheers!" She and Debetaz twice had dinner in restaurants in order to teach their dogs to lie quietly under the table. "Debetaz is doing very well. He will have two dogs to work every day in Harrisburg, and believe me, I am going to keep him busy. He is an awfully nice fellow and very willing."

On December 14, Adelaide and Debetaz drove to Harrisburg over ice-covered roads. There had been difficulty finding a lodging where Adelaide could be properly chaperoned. The YWCA was "too awful a place," but Mr. Sinclair helped to find her a room in the River View Manor. The following morning, she and Debetaz went to the railroad station to pick up the crates with the dogs. Harrisburg proved much larger than Adelaide had imagined and would present some problems. In the afternoon, the class assembled at the Hotel Colonial. In addition to the three workers for the blind, it included the Rev. C. E. Seymour from Baltimore and Clyde Hutley, a piano tuner from Jamestown, New York. Adelaide read aloud a letter from Morris and asked the students to sign a contract agreeing not to sell or breed their dogs. Mr. Hutley could not write and signed his name with an X. The distribution of the dogs went well, except for Miss Jacobs. "She is afraid of dogs, which makes it very difficult."

A few days later, Adelaide reported that the class had agreed to work on Saturday and Sunday, so as to have two days off for Christmas. "Miss Jacobs appears to have forgotten to be afraid of her dog, and the situation looks brighter, but she is so small compared to the dog. She doesn't seem strong enough to hold her. She is a little bit of a woman and only weighs 96 pounds. The dog is almost as big as she is. She has to run to keep up." Sinclair was doing remarkably well. "Everyone is very much in love with their dogs, and all the dogs are working well. Debetaz is having an English lesson with Rev. Seymour every night for a half hour. I am so busy with the blind that I find very little time to talk to him at all."

At the end of the first week, Fox Movietone News took films of Mervyn Sinclair with Kara. Things were going quite well, but Adelaide was beginning to wonder whether Willi Ebeling should come to Harrisburg to check the class. Morris reported that he had received most enthusiastic letters from Ann Connelly and Mervyn Sinclair and hoped the others were doing as well. He had bought a braille watch in Vevey the year before, and because these were not available in the United States he had ordered a shipment of them from the same jeweler. He would make them available at cost to any students who wanted them.

Two days later, Adelaide announced that "Sinclair is working beautifully with his dog, and I am more than pleased with him. He is really one of the nicest men I have ever worked with. His dog Kara has won him absolutely. Everybody else is doing very well except Miss Jacobs. Morris, she just can't seem to hold her dog as she is not strong enough. How to put enough strength in that left arm of hers is out of my line. I am doing my darndest to find a way out for her. She is certainly one terrible case."

Morris had a letter from Sadie Jacobs. She was "in love with her dog" and making a strenuous effort to succeed, "not only for herself, but for the host of friends who are all awaiting her return and she couldn't possibly disappoint them." Adelaide responded, "We have had a terrible time with her and still are. Up until today, she has worked like the devil. The big trouble now is that her dog is just about ruined and refuses to work for her. I am doing everything possible, but nothing seems to work."

In desperation Adelaide appealed to Willi Ebeling, who came to Harrisburg and observed for two days. Then he ruled that it was hopeless. "The case is such a pathetic one. A long trip for nothing. However, the fault lies absolutely with Miss Jacobs."

He composed a detailed analysis of the case. Her dog, a good worker with very strong nerves, "stood the gaffe as long as it could, then gave up and absolutely refused to do anything. Adelaide and Debetaz tried everything and nothing would go. When I got to Harrisburg, both were nervous wrecks over the case." Miss Jacobs might try again later, but "her secretary was a very bad influence, and it must be stated that she must come alone to the next class, absolutely alone, or her instructors will refuse to tackle the case. Her temperament is bordering on hysteria. Either she is giggling or sour as a lemon." She showers her dog with "a sort of hysterical affection that might possibly have fear hidden behind it. If so, no dog would ever take her over."

Willi Ebeling outlined a long list of conditions Miss Jacobs would have to fulfill before she could be allowed to try again. Broadened to apply to all students, they reflect the shaping of Seeing Eye policy in the screening and preparation of applicants for future classes. Students must come alone. They must take their own dogs out to empty. They must have no social engagements during the turnover. They must be able to walk with a light touch on a human guide, not hanging on their arm. They must be prepared to accept the mental and physical strain during the class. They must be genuinely fond of dogs and unafraid of them. They must be attentive to the instructor's words of explanation, must understand and remember them. Above all, they must be seeking a dog to gain their own independence, not for the effect the dog may have on other people.

The failure of Sadie Jacobs was a discordant note on

which to enter the new year, but 1929 had seen far more successes than failures. The school had conducted five classes, attempted seventeen turnovers, and graduated fourteen units working in nine states from coast to coast. It had been recognized by the Junior League, the Council of Jewish Women, the International Lions, and a number of workers for the blind. If it had alienated Herbert Immeln, it had won an important friend in Mervyn Sinclair. Best of all, it had learned from its mistakes. It would never again try to adapt trainers like Weber to its methods, but would train its own instructors. When cooperating with other organizations, it would insist on its own high standards of instruction and safety. Finally, it would be more selective in the acceptance of applicants to ensure that the case of Sadie Jacobs would not be repeated. With these lessons learned, The Seeing Eye was prepared to launch into 1930.

9

On the Road—Berkeley and Pittsburgh

At 4:30 in the afternoon of March 26, Adelaide Clifford kissed her mother good-bye in Grand Central Station and boarded a train for the West Coast with G. William Debetaz. In crates in the baggage car were seven dogs that the two had trained for an April 1 class in Berkeley. In May, they would begin training another string of dogs for a July class in San Francisco.

"Poor Mother must have been having fits," Adelaide recalled years later. "I would be gone for four months. I was only nineteen, and my chaperon was a young Swiss who spoke hardly any English. At 1:30 in the morning, the porter woke me up with a wire that I was to get off the train at the next stop. Of course, I couldn't, so I went back to sleep, and Mother got over it."

For four days and nights, their train rolled westward. At stops along the way, Debetaz and Adelaide let the dogs out to empty. In Cheyenne, one dog ran away, and the train had to be held until she was found. When they arrived in Berkeley at last, Dorothy Eustis and Gretchen Green were there to meet them. With Gretchen as booking agent, Dorothy was winding up nearly three months of lectures and personal interviews from coast to coast. Now they were headed east, so the reunion lasted only one evening.

The class began two days later. The students put up in a hotel with Debetaz, while Adelaide had a room in a chaperoned dormitory at the University of California. The

111

arrangements had been a year in the making. Mrs. Eddy had begun soliciting interest in a class the previous April. She had involved the local chapter of the Council of Jewish Women, and the American Foundation for the Blind had given Morris Frank a list of local workers for the blind to contact. Robert Irwin and the American Foundation had also helped Adelaide and Debetaz get railroad tickets for half fare.

The class of seven was the largest yet, and its makeup differed from those of the past. The 1929 graduates had included two doctors, two clergymen, two agency executives, and a law student. The Berkeley students worked at lower-level positions. They were Miss Marie Ward, a Dictaphone typist, Miss Mathilda Allison, a clinical stenographer, Miss Ethel Roikjer, a violin teacher, Miss Daisy O'Brien, a piano teacher, Mrs. Seeley, a housewife, Reginald White, retired on his veteran's pension, and Jack Stewart, a reed worker at Blindcraft, a sheltered workshop in San Francisco. Blindcraft was run by the Mrs. Quinan who had refused Helen Keller permission to visit, and at first she had insisted that there was no room for a dog in her shop. However, Dorothy Eustis had won over Mr. Roos, one of Blindcraft's most generous donors, and Mrs. Quinan had not only capitulated, but she had also permitted the enrollment of four more Blindcraft workers in the class scheduled for July.

The April class began and the students progressed well, with the exception of Mrs. Seeley, the housewife, who had too much residual vision to put complete confidence in her dog. Only one legally blind person in ten is totally blind, and the blurred and distorted lights and shadows that Mrs. Seeley saw confused her. Her failure to follow her dog confused the dog as well. She was still struggling with the problem when she fell ill and had to drop out of the class.

During the first week, they worked entirely in Berkeley, but the streets were very quiet, and to expose the students to real traffic, they had to go over to San Francisco. The Bay Bridge had yet to be built. They had to take a ferry across the bay to the foot of Market Street, cross the San Francisco version of "Death Street," and climb the hill beside the clanging cable cars. Looking back, Adelaide wondered how she and Debetaz had had the audacity to work new students through the noise and chaos. "I don't know whether we were young, stupid, crazy or all three." But everything went "tic-tac," the turnover was completed, and two weeks later, Adelaide reported on the graduates.

Debetaz had been up to Napa to check on Reginald White. "There is nowhere he won't go with his dog. Debetaz said he almost had heart failure watching him walk along the side of a cliff. Ethel Roikjer came to see me last night. She works tic-tac. She lives out of town and comes on the streetcar with her dog in one hand and her violin in the other. Miss Ward I see off and on, works okay. Miss O'Brien goes along the street like quicksilver."

Mathilda Allison belonged to a type that would cause recurrent problems—the active, flamboyant, and frequently accomplished blind person who is too involved in other affairs to make the working of a dog an integral part of daily routine. She was campaigning for Governor Young, "is all mixed up in politics and doesn't know whether she is coming or going. They tell me she never works her dog alone. If she doesn't work her pretty soon, it won't be much good to her."

When Jack Stewart went home, Adelaide sent the crate Mrs. Quinan had required to Blindcraft, but when Stewart and his dog showed up on Monday morning, "some woman stopped him and told him he was cruel to his dog and that the harness he was using was inhumane. She had a policeman with her. Later a policeman appeared at Blindcraft and told Stuart he could not keep his dog in such a small crate. Mrs. Quinan was in the East Bay when all this happened," but Adelaide was sure that "this was all nothing but a put-up job. On Wednesday," she said, "Roos and

I went to see Mrs. Quinan. We were there for two hours. Roos and Quinan did all the talking, and I never saw such sparks fly in my life. Of course, she denied that she had anything to do with the affair." The situation was still unresolved when Adelaide took time off.

She had planned to be away four days, "but I thought I'd better get back and see if the kennels were ready for the next load of dogs. Lucky I did. When I got there, nothing had been done."

The preparation of these kennels had been covered in detail in correspondence. Willi Ebeling had written Morris the specifications the previous August, but apparently personality clashes between Mrs. Eddy, the executive of the local Council of Jewish Women, and other area leaders had stalled progress. Adelaide "couldn't make out what all the trouble was, but it finally came to the point that Debetaz and I built a fence around a barn and cleaned the place out. We worked two days and got it finished an hour before the dogs arrived. The new blind leaders, having been in crates for six days, looked more like pigs than dogs. They were a sight." They also made sounds. They barked all night. "There was an apartment house behind us, and they were the first to complain." The chief of police gave Adelaide a week to find a new place. "Mrs. Eddy couldn't seem to find anybody to help me, because all of the club women for some reason were mad and were having some big club fight." Adelaide appealed to the mayor, the city manager, the Lions, and even the pound master to no avail.

"While all this was going on, Debetaz and I thought there must be a ring leader in the bunch that was doing all the barking. We decided on two dogs. Debetaz and I each took one. They didn't want to take the dog in the place I was living, but I finally got her in on condition that if she wet the rug, I would pay for it. At four o'clock in the morning, she woke me up having puppies!" Debetaz recalled being roused from sleep in the male sanctuary of the YMCA by a frantic Adelaide. "She was yelling bloody murder. She had the bitch downstairs in the taxi having puppies. The driver was mad as a hornet."

As Adelaide's tale continued, worse was yet to come. "Some kind persons got it into their heads to poison the dogs and poison the dogs they did. I had to get a vet, and one of the dogs almost passed out. Lucky I discovered what the matter was right away. The next day a policeman appeared at the kennel with a warrant for my arrest for violating the anti-noise ordinance."

There were some old houses on the Berkeley campus being demolished to make way for new construction. Adelaide changed her pants and boots for a dress and silk stockings to call on Mr. Nichols at the university. Using all the charm she could muster, she persuaded him to give her an old house through the month of July. "Debetaz and I built another fence out of nothing and cleaned the place out. It couldn't have been dirtier." It was Sunday, and they could find no one to help them move the dogs, but they could not risk another complaint. They borrowed a wagon, piled the crates of ten dogs into it, and, with Miss Adelaide Clifford, New York debutante, between the shafts and Debetaz pushing behind, they moved onto the university campus. And still their luck continued bad. Ina was hit by a car. "Debetaz had her out for a run, and she ran across the street just as a car was coming around the corner." She was only grazed, "but she is so car shy I can do nothing with her. Every time she sees a car coming down the street, she nearly goes crazy." Since they had ten dogs available for a class of eight, the loss of Ina was not critical. Having survived puppies and poison, arrest and an automobile accident, constructing kennels and carting crates, Adelaide and Debetaz were ready for their real work to begin.

The July turnover opened on July 5, so as to avoid the distraction of firecrackers. There were seven men and one woman. Ernest Blumenthal, A. Cunha, William Perkins, and Frank Klein worked at Blindcraft. Charles Brown and George Vahey were June graduates of the University of California and Stanford respectively. John Jacobs and Miss Ollie Gish were unemployed. All eight were successfully graduated on July 22. Ernest Blumenthal wrote:

> Yesterday was the last day of training for the class of which I was a member. It was a very delightful as well as an interesting and liberating experience. With the guidance of Flou I traveled home from the outlying districts of San Francisco on the streetcars, through the San Francisco Ferry Terminal, on the boat, and on the electric train to Oakland and a considerable walk burdened with a suitcase before I reached home. Through this entire trip I touched only one person in what might be called a collision when, as I was walking with the crowd going aboard the ferry boat, I bumped a person with my suitcase, and that was the other person's fault.
>
> An hour after I arrived home, I walked several blocks to a car line, taking the streetcar and going to the Berkeley Station to see Miss Clifford and Mr. Debetaz on their way east. From Berkeley Station I again took the streetcar and visited a friend in Berkeley from where I walked home, a distance of two miles across several busy boulevards with which I was unfamiliar. It is in reality a realization of independence to go about in this manner after having been so restricted for twelve years.

Late in July, the scattered personnel of The Seeing Eye began to gather at Openaka. Adelaide and Debetaz arrived from Berkeley. Willi Ebeling, recently returned from Europe where he had studied technique at the Oldenburg School and Vevey, drove to New York to meet a new Swiss apprentice, Robert Chapellet, and ten trained dogs from L'Oeil qui Voit. Adelaide took off for a vacation in Maine, but with Chapellet joining Debetaz in the help house and the arrival of Jack Humphrey on August 1, Openaka began to hum. Under Jack's supervision, Debetaz and Chapellet graduated a class of eight students in Morristown.

Chapellet's salary was set at $80 a month. Debetaz's was raised to $85. There was an elaborate system of bonuses and penalties based on each dog's score on the last blindfold test. A perfect score was 64. Both 64 and 63 were classified "excellent," while 61 and 62 were "very good," and so on down the line.

On September 1, Morris Frank arrived with Buddy. To test the practicality of a guide dog for the working blind and those in schools, they had spent a week in a sheltered workshop, making brooms, and another two weeks in a school for the blind. Buddy had passed both tests with flying colors. After a few days conferring with Willi and Jack, Morris left for Washington where he was received in the White House by Herbert Hoover. Morris exhibited Buddy's work and put her through obedience. She fetched President Hoover's handkerchief for him once, but when she was immediately asked to do it again, she realized it was simply "busy work." She fetched the presidential handkerchief and, pinning it to the floor with her paws, deliberately tore it in half to the amusement of the onlookers.

After this ceremonial occasion, Morris got down to business in a meeting with General Hines and Captain Miller of the Veterans Bureau. They were impressed by The Seeing Eye's nonprofit status and its turnover price of $300 per dog. Sinykin had been asking $1,000. There were no funds appropriated for the purchase of guide dogs, but Morris suggested they could be paid for from the same funds used to buy artificial limbs, glass eyes, or other prosthetic devices. Hines and Miller seemed favorably inclined and suggested circularizing the approximately 400 blind veterans with Seeing Eye literature.

The proposal reflected an ignorance of guide dog technique that would plague the school for years to come. To the average American, the guide dog was a miracle in an age of many miracles—the automobile, the airplane, the radio, the refrigerator, and talking pictures. But the guide dog was a biological, not a technological, miracle. The circularization of hundreds of blind veterans failed to take this into account. It implied that great numbers could be supplied simply by tooling up the assembly line to turn out guide dogs like Ford cars. The veterans could then be given a short course of instruction along with a manual to teach them how to drive these canine machines. Morris had to point out that establishing a harmonious relationship between a guide dog and a blind human was delicate and timeconsuming. If even 200 veterans wanted guide dogs, it would take from four to five years to supply them. Instead of mass circularization, he suggested that the government open its files to The Seeing Eye, so that the school could approach veterans selectively as dogs became available. Opening confidential files was a violation of government policy, but when Morris left Hines and Miller, he felt that they might ultimately agree.

In the fall of 1930, successes were offset by occasional failures. The Birmingham class had to be canceled again, but with the aid of Mervyn Sinclair, Morris was able to schedule a class in Pittsburgh. In September, two more students graduated in Morristown, and in October, Philadelphia followed Nashville and San Francisco in making public transportation available to guide dogs.

Chapellet began a class of five in Morristown and showed both courage and presence of mind on the night of October 13, when the Park Hotel, where he and the students were staying, caught fire. Under his supervision, the dogs guided their masters to safety. Two of these students proved special problems. Gilbert Newell of Greensboro, North Carolina, a reformed alcoholic, reverted to drink under the nervous strain and had to be hospitalized for several days. On his solemn promise never to use the dog while under the influence, he was permitted to complete the turnover and did so successfully. Gordon Lathrop, a writer from New York, had the twin problems of too much vision and too much intellect or, rather, too much intellectual pride. He insisted on knowing with certainty, something impossible for a blind master. He must leave the knowing to his dog and have the faith to trust its judgment.

Lathrop spoiled his first dog and returned to New York without her, but he hoped to try again later.

Following Jack Humphrey's departure in November, Willi began to notice careless work by the new apprentice. He wrote Dorothy Eustis, "Had a bust with Chapellet last night and almost sent him home. I am afraid he is a slacker, a man not to be trusted alone." On the other hand, Adelaide, returned from Maine, was working very well. "If she continues as she is doing now, our battles with her are over." Debetaz was "a man I can trust anywhere. He has just finished nine dogs for the Pittsburgh class, four excellent with 63 and 64 points, five, very good, 62 points, just one point below excellent. Beat that."

In Pittsburgh, Debetaz would face the acid test. He had been challenged in Harrisburg, Berkeley, and San Francisco, but there the main responsibility had been Adelaide's and she had been there to translate for him. As he was the first to admit, language was his most serious problem. For some students, his accent was impenetrable. Even after he had been in America many years, one woman wrote of him, "When I first came to Morristown, I thought it odd that The Seeing Eye should employ a man for such an important position who spoke no English. I could never understand how all the students managed to grasp what this man said. Then one day the light dawned, and I realized he *was* speaking English." His language was enlivened with quaint "Debe-isms." He telescoped "You would die laughing" and "You would laugh yourself sick" into "You would die yourself sick." A gala party or shindig became a "shinding-dong." But for all its color, Debetaz's speech was confusing, and the language barrier compounded the problems he faced in Pittsburgh.

He had seven students he had never met whom he must train on the streets of a city he had never seen in a language he was still learning. He had to match dogs unsettled by a long journey in an unheated boxcar to the appropriate students, making his decisions as fast as he opened the crates. A letter of November 30 gives vivid glimpses into both his problems and his English: "I arrive here yesterday morning with delay one hour, find two inches of snow, no dogs in station." At one in the afternoon he located the dogs, but was told they could not be delivered. He went to the station, "chanced to find the right fellow, who put my dogs on truck and sent to Y.M.C.A. At four o'clock, start to give the dogs."

There were two students surnamed Douglas. Paul was white; Herbert, black. "The white one does not be strong for Babe. Try to give Babe to Mr. Douglas black." The disorientation of the train trip was at once apparent. "Babe goes out from the crate and immediately jump on her new master and tries to bit him." Debetaz intervened immediately, but not before the black Douglas had a scare, and his attempts to smooth the snappish Babe failed. Since Douglas lived in Pittsburgh, Debetaz put Babe in his room in the Y and sent Douglas home for the night. He had his "other blinds" to think of.

He gave Night to the white Douglas, Billy to Mr. Altenhof, Fleury to Mr. Miller, Froelich to Mr. Burchfield, Peggy to Mr. Cravats, and Lisa to Mr. Wilson, "man forty-three years old, look fine, don't say word." The reason for his ominous silence surfaced when he failed to show up for dinner. Mr. Altenhof, his roommate, reported that Wilson was "mad and made his trunk to go home. I jump in his room, speak with that fellow for three quarters of an hour. He don't know himself for what he want leave, and after that he comes again perfectly all right."

Debetaz had dinner with Wilson and took him to his room. "He told me I will see you in the morning, good night. That was eight and a half. At ten and a half, I have the phone from the Y.M.C.A. office, saying he is gone and he leave his dog in his room." Debetaz lamented, "I can't put this man on chain for keep him. I am myself very sorry, because I see no reason why he can't have dog and make one nice piece of job. I will try today to give Lisa to the black Douglas and see what happens, because this man is now afraid about dogs." He shipped Babe and the empty crates back to Morristown. What had upset her remained a mystery, but she later recovered her good disposition and was turned over successfully.

Mr. Altenhof had physical problems. He was only forty-four but had been virtually chair-ridden since he went blind at six and "walk like if he is eighty years old, don't know nothing about walking alone, going down or up steps." He had to be carefully supervised on the stairs, and a few days of the lightest exercise made his feet and legs so painful that "in spite of all his willingness, he can't walk."

The weather did not cooperate. "Yesterday rain. Today snow. What is coming for tomorrow?" Later, "Sidewalks and streets covered by coat of ice that don't help." Debetaz was on twenty-four-hour call for all kinds of problems. If a dog emptied in her room, he cleaned up. He supervised trips up and downstairs between bedrooms and dining room, and out to the park for the dogs to empty. At meals he helped his "blinds" to eat. If they had mail, he read it aloud to them. If they had medical problems, he took them to the doctor. This was necessary for Altenhof at the end of the second week. The doctor prescribed liniment and foot-baths, which Debetaz administered, but the pain persisted. Altenhof walked too slowly to cross the street safely in traffic. At last, on Willi Ebeling's advice, Altenhof was dropped from the class, and Billy was matched with Mr. Miller, who had been having difficulty with his first dog.

The class, which was supposed to end before Christmas, lasted into the new year, but the black Douglas overcame his fear of Lisa, and Debetaz had the satisfaction of turning over five men and dogs on his own. Forty years later, Herbert, the black Douglas, wrote to him: "I am still able to walk about three miles every other day at the age of eighty-three years. I want to thank you for giving me the confidence to be independent and make a living and making it possible for my children to get a good education."

His classmate Paul, the white Douglas, who used Night to graduate from the University of Pittsburgh, wrote at the same time: "To you, Mr. Debetaz, I owe all my forty years of pure happiness and perfect independence." But that was in 1970. As The Seeing Eye entered 1931, the evidence that its work would succeed was less conclusive.

10
A Home at Last

In many ways 1930 had been a success. Dorothy Eustis's speaking tour with Gretchen Green had won contacts and converts across the country. Mervyn Sinclair was an enthusiastic supporter at the Pennsylvania Council for the Blind, and Robert Irwin at the American Foundation had been very cooperative. Morris and Buddy had been received by the president at the White House. Best of all, an instructor and two apprentices had graduated thirty-five blind students, more than double the 1929 output. But Willi Ebeling had misgivings.

Debetaz had proven his worth at Pittsburgh, but Willi had decided that Chapellet would not do. He was "too much the same type as Weber." Unless he was under direct supervision, he tended to take unsafe shortcuts and he would accept supervision only from Jack Humphrey. In December, Willi had sent him back to Switzerland. Adelaide, too, was becoming slack in her habits. She kept irregular hours and interrupted work on the streets of Morristown to gossip with friends. Her dogs were far behind schedule. In January, he redrew her contract. Two of her dogs were transferred to Debetaz, and the deadline for the rest was extended to April 1, allowing five months to complete what was ordinarily done in three.

Eighteen dogs were now scheduled to be ready for a class in Washington on April 1. It was essential to have eighteen blind students ready for them. Timing was crucial because dogs could not be brought up to pitch and then left in the kennels. They required the continuing challenge of work to keep from growing careless. Under the pressure of the upcoming deadline, Morris overcame the objections to mass mailing he had expressed to the Veterans Administration and sent a letter and literature to a list of 700 prospects whose names had been supplied by the Columbia Polytechnic Institute for the Blind. But by March 1, there was not a single response of any kind. At this stage in its history, The Seeing Eye was in need of the critical thinking Willi Ebeling was uniquely able to supply.

Like Jack Humphrey, Willi had a pragmatic and probing mind. But whereas Jack's restless imagination ranged over unexplored terrain, Willi's critical reason analyzed previously plowed ground to make sure he knew what lay beneath every stone. He reexamined policies and procedures across the entire range of Seeing Eye activities. Dorothy Eustis saw clearly in black and white. For this reason, on occasion she could be very wrong, as when she told Morris that the job of managing director would never take a man's full time. Morris was likely to jump to conclusions. For Willi, such conclusions became hypotheses to be tested, then tested again. He was forever weighing and measuring, probing and sifting.

The character of his mind was reflected in his conversational style. It was punctuated with question marks. As he talked, an eyebrow lifted quizzically and he queried his last remark with a "don't you know?" These "don't you knows" were like palpating antennae feeling out both the mind of his listener and the terrain they were exploring together.

He had serious doubts about the school's admission policy. Morris ought never to have accepted Altenhof in the Pittsburgh class. He was another Sadie Jacobs. All candidates should be required to take a brisk hour's walk each morning and afternoon to get in trim. Fifty or fifty-five was probably the upper age limit. It was foolish to place dogs in situations where they were not wanted, such as at San Francisco's Blindcraft.

Willi had come into possession of a disturbing letter that Kate Foley in Berkeley had written a third party. Initially a supporter of the school, Miss Foley had stated that although the dogs cost $300 each, their owners in the Bay Area used them primarily for recreation. For the same price, she could have bought seven typewriters or eight radios that would have done more good for their owners than dogs, without the expense of upkeep. Willi termed this "a vicious document, particularly coming from a professed admirer of the movement." More likely, it reflected a difference of perspective. Kate Foley taught braille. One of her students, John Jacobs, stopped taking lessons as soon as he was accepted for a Seeing Eye class. His decision was illogical and no fault of The Seeing Eye, but she may have concluded that the still unproven prospect of a guide dog was seducing her student from learning a basic skill.

Disquieting news from graduates in the field also worried Willi. In January, the Rev. Seymour returned Ellen because she had become gun-shy. When Morris had visited Seymour in the previous fall, he had concluded that Seymour must have corrected Ellen unjustly following a loud noise of some kind, so that she had come to associate loud noises with her master's displeasure. Seymour, Morris said, had accepted this explanation at the time, but now tried to place all the blame on Ellen. Willi pronounced him "another minister who should be shoveling coal instead of preaching the gospel." From Scranton came news that Alberta Edwards's Iris had died four months after graduation. The aunt in whose house she had lived had forced the dog to sleep in an unheated cellar during the Appalachian winter. Willi contrasted her callousness to the tenderness of an Italian piano tuner in Florence who left his dog at home when it rained and used his mother to guide him through the downpour.

Clyde Hutley wrote in great distress from upstate New York. During the winter, he had adopted the local practice of wearing "creepers," spiked metal frames clamped to his

shoes, for walking on ice. He had stepped on Sunny's paw
and was unaware of the wound until a companion had noticed her bleeding. He had rushed her to a veterinarian, but
she died the following day.

Edward Hoffman, who had graduated with Helga in
August, was having problems in downtown Philadelphia.
Although Helga had shown exceptionally strong nerves,
she was now reluctant to work in traffic. As Hoffman had
been taught, a guide dog requires its master's undivided
attention. Whenever walking with a friend, therefore, Hoffman should have put Helga at heel on short leash and used
his friend as a guide. Instead, he had been working her in
harness, while chatting with his sighted companion. Wit-
nesses had seen friends pulling Hoffman to the right in traffic while Helga was trying to lead him left. "No wonder
she had difficulty," Willi wrote. And of Hoffman's claim
of ignorance, he exploded, "I have no patience with smart
liars."

To have a dog spoiled for any reason was painful. What
gnawed at Willi Ebeling was a feeling that "we are getting
the greatest backlash from what we considered our best
students. The main blame for this, if it falls anywhere, goes
right into training headquarters, and I include myself." At
graduation, he and the others had been certain of students
who had developed problems later. "Are we all fools here?
They work all right when discharged, but the routine is not
deeply enough embedded in the minds of the pupils that
they will not vary from it. Perhaps one way we can protect
ourselves a little is to take the full four weeks of the turnover, even if they finish sooner, as that extra time should
make them firm in the routine. Perhaps we can draw up a
form letter asking them, 'are you still doing this, that or
the other thing,' enumerating the items they are apt to get
careless on."

His uncertainty regarding Dorothy Eustis's commitment to The Seeing Eye underlay his other misgivings. He
wrote to ask, "What part does America play in your pro-

gram? Is it a prime factor? Or is it going to become that?" In addition to her work with French, Italian, and Swiss blind, Dorothy was now beginning to excite interest in England. Making a new start in England when the American movement was still so precarious ran counter to Willi's conservative nature. "You have Italy, Switzerland, France, America and also England to cover. If help is needed, you have one man to send. If all the babies should cry at the same time, Jack has to be divided into fifths, and as science has not yet given us a practical solution for such a division, you will have neither five fifths nor one."

Despite all these doubts and misgivings, Willi Ebeling cherished an unshakable, almost a religious, faith in dogs. They were not only physical but also emotional guides. Gilbert Newell was an alcoholic, but he loved Hebe and he had vowed never to work her under the influence of liquor. If he loved her enough, that love would give him the strength to keep his promise. Gordon Lathrop had been a very difficult student. After failing once, he had returned to Morristown for a second try. It took twelve weeks and two spoiled dogs to achieve a successful working unit. Never mind. Willi would have invested more time, more of himself, even another dog, and still have considered it worth the cost. Willi sympathized with Clyde Hutley for the loss of Sunny and rejoiced in his turnover with Babe, who had recovered from her emotional upset in Pittsburgh. They performed "some of the finest traffic work I have ever seen." From irritation with Hoffman, he became all patience, carefully explaining his past errors and rejoicing in his new understanding.

Willi and Adelaide had been on a collision course for weeks, and late in February the clash came. A stormy scene ended with Adelaide's resignation. Later Willi blamed himself for losing his temper, and it was regrettable that they parted on bad terms. But hindsight made it clear that Adelaide's ultimate departure was inevitable. Even under Jack, of whom she was far fonder than Willi, she would have realized that she had neither the physical stamina nor the dedication to devote her whole life to guide dogs. Her work had been vital to The Seeing Eye during its first two years. Of the fifty dogs turned over, she was partially or wholly responsible for more than half, and she had been the only qualified instructor for a crucial fourteen months. Dorothy Eustis exaggerated only a little when she inscribed a Seeing Eye booklet "To Adelaide, without whom The Seeing Eye would not exist."

Her departure left the school shorthanded. By himself Debetaz was responsible for a Washington class that might have as many as fifteen students. Illness among his dogs had set their work back, and Adelaide's string was below par. The only recourse was for Willi to pitch in. At forty-nine he found it a strain. "Gosh, I'm sore," he wrote Jack. "I can hardly waddle."

What bothered him more than this physical challenge was his anxiety about Dorothy's commitment in England. The United Kingdom insisted on a six-month quarantine for any dog that entered, so it was impossible to train dogs in Vevey and ship them to England for immediate turnover. An instructor would have to stay in England long enough to train a string of English-bred dogs from the ground up. Except for Jack, no one in Vevey was qualified for the job. It was therefore assigned to G. William Debetaz, as he now called himself. Dorothy decreed that he would sail for Europe right after the Washington turnover and would not return until November. He would be lost to The Seeing Eye for nearly six months.

Willi took consolation where he could. "Hutley writes that he is just plain tickled pink with his new dog. He says, 'I am really stuck on this dog. She really has the goods.' Well, we had a devil of a time to convince him, but he is getting there now. Babe, you know, was just the opposite of Sunny. A year ago no other dog but Sunny would have done the trick. You should see the difference in Clyde today compared with when he came for his first dog. He impresses one as changed from poverty to prosperity. Delightful!"

There were other paeans from the field. Ann Connelly had used her new freedom to leave the Vermont Association for the Blind and start a gift shop, traveling to take orders for her wares. "Betty helps me to cover the ground rapidly. I can take her on any bus in the State of Vermont or the Central Vermont Railroad. I can take her to all hotels and to other public places. In my new work I find her a great help, not only as a guide, but as an attraction as well. People admit me and buy my wares many times to see Betty." Dr. Harris and Tartar were also traveling. "Tartar is working beautifully and I go about wherever and whenever I fancy. I have just returned from a trip through Northern Georgia with the finest four-legged guide in the whole wide world, even including Buddy. Tartar works in Athens, Atlanta, Augusta and Macon as accurately and safely as she works in Savannah. In hotels and on the streets I have no difficulty." These reports justified and fortified Willi Ebeling's faith in guide dogs, but they did not dissipate his awareness of serious weaknesses in The Seeing Eye, and he looked forward to Dorothy Eustis's arrival from Switzerland with a mixture of hope and dread.

The World Conference and the meeting of the American Association of Workers for the Blind followed each other in Washington in May. Dorothy reported to both on the use of the guide dog as a leader for the blind. Her presentation was clear, comprehensive, thorough, and persuasive. She began with a brief history of the guide dog, dating back to the writings of Father Johann Klein in Vienna in 1819. She sketched in the origins and development of the guide dog movement in Germany, noting that there were an estimated 4,000 units functioning there at present. She explained how her *Saturday Evening Post* article had brought Morris Frank to her attention and how this had led to the founding of both The Seeing Eye and L'Oeil qui Voit. Her commanding presence and clear, sensible exposition held her audience from the beginning, and she made some telling points. Instead of shrugging off difficulties, she emphasized them. Capable instructors were extremely rare. Guide dogs must be taught to disobey intelligently, and that was a difficult art. She explained the criteria for the selection of suitable dogs and stressed the crucial importance of the three- to four-week course for pairing dogs with masters. She cited percentages of dogs who failed their preliminary training (2 to 4%), who failed during the turnover (5%), and who failed after graduating with their masters (3%). In most cases, she said, the failures at home were owing to misuse by their masters.

She asked, "If we do actually know that some masters misuse their dogs, why do we not make a more careful selection of masters?" In answer, she admitted, "No school has yet evolved any method of examination by which they can tell which blind will make good with their guide dogs and which will fail. The records of every school are filled with cases of seemingly perfect students who failed and seemingly impossible students who have made good."

She stated her conviction that guide dogs should not be placed with all blind persons. Certain home or working conditions could render the use of a dog completely impractical. Since an instructor working full time could turn out only twenty to twenty-five dogs per year, only those who had prospects for real benefit from the use of the dog should be considered. She went on to state that the benefits for this limited number were improved earnings, improved health, and improved peace of mind, but she avoided exaggerated claims. She concluded with gracious thanks "to those organizations who have and are lending us their aid and experience."

Willi wrote Jack, "Dorothy went over big. Her speech won the greatest applause of the entire lot. Sinclair, Morris, and Mrs. Patchen with their dogs were a beautiful sight and certainly created a sensation." An incidental dividend was a report that Blindcraft in San Francisco was now wholly reconciled to workers having dogs. Willi exulted, "Smoke that one! Dandy! Just as soothing as your snuff."

The major reason for Willi's exuberance was Dorothy's renewed commitment to the American school. She was prepared for an aggressive new program that she would finance from her own pocket. She proposed closing the national office from August 1 to March 1. Instead of trying to line up classes by mail in various parts of the country, Morris should focus on Pennsylvania, New York, and New Jersey, working in person. With a car and driver, he would travel extensively through these states, studying local conditions, giving talks, and interviewing agency heads and blind candidates face to face. When Mrs. Eustis first unveiled this scheme to Morris, he was far from enchanted. "Suppose I'd rather stay in Nashville?" he asked.

"In that case, Morris," she replied, "there will be no Seeing Eye."

Morris surrendered, but that was only the beginning. Willi wrote Jack, "We are now out to find a house in Morristown for the blind and, if possible, something that will permit shifting of training headquarters under one roof." It was a good time to buy, because "everything is topnotch rotten." Dorothy's willingness to spend her money decisively was crucial, but The Seeing Eye was frugal. To save paper, Willi Ebeling made carbon copies of his correspondence on both sides of the page, and instructors made their own leashes, but Dorothy made sure that the school did not have to compromise its high standards for financial reasons.

The acquisition of a house in Morristown promised a sweeping reorganization of The Seeing Eye. Headquarters would be permanently moved from Nashville. The kennels would be shifted from Openaka. Students would be housed in the school's facilities, so that all operations would be in one location. Morris would be relieved of the administrative duties for which he had neither the training nor the talent. His major work would be in the field. Willi Ebeling would take over finance and administration, supervise training, and correspond with blind graduates on their problems.

In the interim there was much to be done. After completing the turnover of a class of seven students in Washington in May, Debetaz sailed for Europe to prepare the first string of guide dogs in England. Willi Ebeling followed a few days later for further study at both the German schools and L'Oeil qui Voit. He was hoping to hire an instructor from the school at Oldenburg, which was preparing to close. In New York City on her way to Switzerland, Dorothy hired as Morris's driver and secretary a young woman recommended by Gretchen Green, Marie MacKee. As Morris was winding up his insurance business in Nashville, he was awarded a commission as honorary colonel of the staff of the governor of Tennessee "in recognition of his signal contribution to the rehabilitation of the blind." On August 1, with a new car and a new secretary, Colonel Morris S. Frank and Buddy set off on a trip to explore and improve the opportunities for guide dogs in New York, New Jersey, and Pennsylvania.

At the end of August, Dorothy wrote, "I have arranged to buy the Schneider property on Whippany Road for The Seeing Eye. I shall try to hold it until such time as The Seeing Eye can afford to buy it from me for the price I paid for it plus interest." For fifty acres, a main house, gate house, and several outbuildings, she had agreed to pay $30,000. She planned to speed the time when the school could afford to buy it from her by negotiating with a young woman to organize a finance committee to raise funds when she returned to the States in 1932. It was high time for a program to buttress the personal philanthropy of Dorothy and a handful of her family and friends.

Morris and Mervyn Sinclair worked out a schedule for blanketing the Commonwealth of Pennsylvania with lectures and interviews. They estimated that the state had a potential of 600 guide dog users, but, lacking instructors, Morris confined recruitment to a class to be held in Morristown in November when Debetaz would return from England. On their travels in Pennsylvania, Morris was unhappy with Mrs. MacKee. Apparently she thought of herself as his impresario and manager rather than his secretary and chauffeur.

When Willi Ebeling returned from Europe in October, he took charge of many details of the purchase of the Schneider estate. He had the title searched and negotiated the tentative resale of twenty acres. He received shipments of furniture Dorothy sent from her house on the Main Line and New York apartment. On November 10 he wrote her, "The first load of furniture arrived today. How swell the home is going to be. Really too fine for the purpose." He took out fire and theft insurance, installed fire extinguishers, and sent his handyman to pick up furnishings contributed by the Alfred Kays, friends of Gretchen. He drove his Packard to the steamer to meet Debetaz along with ten dogs from Fortunate Fields for the next class. It opened on November 23 in the Washington Hotel in Morristown.

Dorothy was reassured by having Willi's hand on the tiller, but his last letter sounded an ominous note: "Now to something less pleasant. Frankness, I think, is in order." The depressed stock market had caught up with the Ebelings at last. They would have to cut back sharply on living expenses. "What I probably shall have to decide on is to go to Europe and remain with my mother until the financial sky shows a brighter face." The move, if it came, would not be until March or April, but it threatened a serious loss.

On November 30, Dorothy received a transatlantic phone call in Paris, where she was observing the turnover of five dogs to Frenchmen under Jack Humphrey and Missy Doudge. Willi Ebeling was on the other end of the wire with bad news. The local zoning board was about to ban the use of the Schneider estate for a guide dog school. There were only forty-eight hours left to act, and the school had a full class of students in progress. They decided on a bold stroke. Willi would move the class into the building and establish residence, so that the school could not be excluded after the fact.

It was a prodigious undertaking. The house was without heat, light, telephone, or water. Certain pipes were frozen and had to be fixed. Supplies must be bought, the kitchen equipped, and furniture arranged. Somehow they managed it. Willi wrote, "We moved heaven and earth and moved ourselves into the home and had our first supper there Tuesday night, fourteen at the table." Morris pronounced it "the realization of our dream to be at the head of the table with eight blind people and eight bright-eyed dogs under the table."

By the narrowest of margins, The Seeing Eye had been saved. The threat of exclusion had been nullified, but the class was presenting problems. The dogs from Vevey had little idea of traffic. Owing to the Depression and the decline of tourism in Switzerland, they had dealt with very few cars prior to their arrival in America. After two weeks, Willi gave a traffic test to Ann Connelly, back for a replacement, and reported, "She could have been killed three times." He and Debetaz would have to work the students singly rather than in pairs in order to give them the special attention they needed.

On December 6, Morris telephoned to report that the car in which Marie MacKee had been driving him to Pittsburgh had turned over twice and stopped six inches short of plunging down a two-thousand-foot precipice. Morris and Mrs. MacKee were only bruised but Buddy had suffered two cuts, and Morris was skeptical of Mrs. MacKee's alibi that a blowout had caused the accident. A couple of days later, when she neglected to inform him of a speaking date, he blew up, and there was a shouting match. "Uncle Willi," as Morris was now calling him, agreed to let Marie MacKee's contract terminate with the month of December.

The class ended before Christmas. Seven students graduated, and the two who did not owed the failure to their own defects, not to any fault of the dogs. The head of the Allentown workshop, which had sent three students, wrote Willi Ebeling on December 28: "The performance of these dogs has amazed our community. Thousands who have seen the dogs leading their blind masters through the crowded streets during these busy Christmas shopping days stand and watch in awe. They wonder, no doubt, who could have trained men and dogs to work together so perfectly."

Willi rejoiced that the class cost $360 less in the new home than it would have in the hotel, and he was feeling less pessimistic about remaining in the States. Florence Ebeling had always had servants, but she found she rather liked doing without them; living with her German mother-in-law was not an attractive alternative. Jack urged Willi, "You have made The Seeing Eye what it is in the States. For goodness sake, try to think of some way to stay." It was Dorothy Eustis who thought of a way for Willi Ebeling to stay. After she arrived in February, she brought him onto the school staff at a modest salary.

At the same time she reincorporated the school in New Jersey. The incorporators were Dorothy Eustis, her eighteen-year-old son, Harrison, Morris Frank, and the Ebelings. For trustees, she added her brother, Harry Harrison, and a local shepherd breeder, Charley Baiter. The officers were Dorothy Eustis, president; her brother, vice president; Jack Humphrey, vice president, Division of Training and Research; Morris Frank, vice president, Division for the Blind; and Willi Ebeling, secretary-treasurer. Three years before, she had urged Morris to form a board as representative as possible. Now that she had decided to take charge, she chose a board of only six, including three members of her family and two members of her staff with another staff member as third vice president. Dorothy liked to keep authority in her small hands. Be that as it may, through the purchase of a headquarters in Morristown and the new assignment of working roles, she had arrived at the basic formula that would guide the development of the school for the next decade.

III

MATURITY BY DESIGN

11
Philosophy at Openaka

On a June morning in 1933, Willi Ebeling herded four over-night guests at Openaka into his Packard to drive to the meeting of the American Association of Workers for the Blind in Richmond. They were C. L. Broun of the New York State Commission for the Blind, Mary Dranga Campbell of the Brooklyn Board of Charities, Mervyn Sinclair of the Pennsylvania Council for the Blind, with his dog, Kara, and his assistant, Elizabeth Hutchinson. They were good friends by now, but as he drove south, Willi Ebeling reflected that it had been their common interest in Morris Frank that had drawn them all together. Bringing these four to Openaka turned out to be a crucial service to the guide dog move-ment, because they played a vital role in shaping its philos-ophy.

Like Sinclair, C. L. Broun had been a successful busi-nessman before going blind. Director of Placement for the New York Commission for the Blind, he was a native Vir-ginian who retained the courtly manners of the Southern gentleman. He was too old to get a dog himself, but he was a believer in the guide dog movement.

Mary Dranga was one of the first workers for the blind with a graduate degree in social work, and she was widely respected in the field. When her sister died in 1911, she had moved in with her widowed brother-in-law, Charles Campbell, to look after his three children. The following year they were married, and professionally they made an effective team. She coedited *Outlook for the Blind* with Char-ley and served as assistant superintendent of the Ohio

School for the Blind. Temperamentally, however, they were hopelessly mismatched. Charley was a born extravert, all charm, wit, and diplomacy. Mary Dranga presented an impassive Viking facade. A no-nonsense professional, she could be devastatingly frank. Their marriage broke up, and after the war Mary spent three years working in child welfare in Serbia. She preceded Mervyn Sinclair as head of the Pennsylvania Council and went from there to the Missouri State Commission for the Blind and later to the Brooklyn Board of Charities. She had befriended Morris in Wawasee in 1929 and had recommended Mervyn Sinclair as an applicant for a dog.

Sinclair had become a "True Believer" ever since acquiring Kara in Harrisburg in December 1929, and the pair had enlisted the fourth member of the party, Elizabeth Hutchinson. A well-bred and extremely attractive Philadelphian in her twenties, Ibby had spent several years as an occupational therapist for the Visiting Nurse Service when a friend recommended she might like to work for Sinclair. Ibby recoiled. She wanted nothing to do with "The Blind" and would have refused even to meet Sinclair if a luncheon date had not already been arranged. She was waiting for him at the appointed restaurant "when the elevator door opened and out came this tall, handsome, very distinguished gentleman with a perfectly gorgeous dog." In that split second, Mervyn Sinclair and Kara shattered her stereotyped image of the blind man, and Ibby Hutchinson took a job with the council.

In her new job, she was assigned to drive Morris and Buddy on visits to various Pennsylvania agencies. "Morris could be perfectly awful," she recalled. At lunch in a restaurant she offered to pour cream into his coffee, "the way I would have for anyone. I wasn't even thinking about his being blind. He almost took my head off. 'I can pour my own cream!' That's the way he was." She laughed. "People either liked Morris or they didn't. I liked him."

The four were frequent weekend visitors to Openaka.

Morris was such a regular that he called Florence Ebeling "my northern mother." Dorothy Eustis and Jack Humphrey were a separate element of the Openaka mix. Like Willi Ebeling, they were primarily "dog people." C. L. Broun, Mary Campbell, Mervyn Sinclair, and Ibby Hutchinson had backgrounds in work for the blind. They were "blind people." The weekends at Openaka brought the "dog people" and the "blind people" together. In talks lasting far into the night, they blended their ideas. By degrees they shaped what was fundamentally a new philosophy of work with the blind. *With* the blind, not *for* the blind.

Morris always insisted that no one person deserved more credit than the others for this philosophy. Openaka provided the ambiance and the Ebelings' hospitality was a catalyst, but all of them made their individual contributions.

Certain fundamentals had already been established. Happily, The Seeing Eye did not include the condescending phrase "for the Blind" in its title. It had been consciously conceived, not as a charity, but as a service to provide guide dogs to deserving blind people at cost. The development of the school's financial policy involved trial and error. From the first, students of means were expected to pay for their dogs. Others were asked to contribute what they could to the revolving fund from the increased earnings their dogs made possible. In the early years the estimated cost of a dog fluctuated between $170 and $375. Since most blind people at that time would have found even the lower figure beyond their means, the school encouraged the granting of scholarships by individuals, clubs, or groups. The final selection of applicants was reserved to the school, but donors could nominate candidates of their choosing and were at first permitted to know who had received their scholarships. Unfortunately, one service club was so delighted with its generosity that it continually reminded both the recipient and the community at large who had paid for his Seeing Eye dog. He was expected to repay the club, not only with his gratitude, but also with the donation of his services as a pianist at the club's meetings. He found his situation humiliating, and to prevent any recurrence with future graduates, the school kept the identity of all scholarship recipients in strict confidence.

As the school's financial resources increased, the practical need for student payments diminished, but The Seeing Eye continued to ask its students to assume some financial obligation for their dogs. Morris did not want students "to look upon our work as something due them, accepted in the same spirit as favors received from other blind organizations." In 1933, a new contract requiring the students to pay $300 for a dog specified that the actual cost was "at least twice the price quoted." In 1934, the amount to be paid was reduced to $150. As Ibby Hutchinson put it, "No individual or organization can relieve the student of this obligation, for if he is unwilling to accept it, he is apt to be unsuccessful with a Seeing Eye dog." Willi Ebeling had an historical perspective: "Blind people have for centuries been prime objects of charity. They have many of them become used to the idea that people give things to them, and they have therefore relaxed their own efforts to do things for themselves. When a student undertakes to repay $150 for his dog, more often than not he is for the first time recognizing his capacity to do something for himself." This was a revolutionary concept among workers for the blind in that day, and it took time for the dog people and the blind people to agree that it was good for blind students to be challenged. It represented a sharp break with tradition.

In 1929, Edward Allen posed the following examination question for his Harvard students: "Comment on the statement 'What the public thinks the blind are, that they tend to become.'" Forty years later Robert Scott, a Princeton sociology professor, might have rephrased it as "What agencies for the blind think the blind are, that they will pressure them to become." Scott wrote a book, *The Making of Blind Men*, suggesting that agencies for the blind tended to make their clients blind, making them blinder than they really were by forcing them to conform to the stereotype of helplessness that justified the existence of the agencies. The message they conveyed to their clients was "Be helpless, so that we can help you." This is an oversimplification of Scott's thesis and an overstatement of the facts, but in the 1930s and much later, many agencies for the blind projected an unfortunate stereotype of blindness and tended to force it on their clients. As late as 1960, a highly reputable national agency mailed an appeal for funds that spelled the acronym BLINDNESS from the words Bewilderment, Loneliness, Insecurity, Neglect, Dependency, Nostalgia, Emptiness, and Sedentary Solitude. At about the same period, an equally well known agency rebuked a volunteer for having treated several of its blind clients to an evening that included cocktails, dinner, and a musical comedy at his own expense. He was accused, he said, of putting dangerous ideas into their heads. They might forget that they were Bewildered, Lonely, Insecure, Neglected, and Dependent.

Seeing Eye graduates were not expected to languish in sedentary solitude. They were challenged by more than an obligation to pay for their dogs. The ownership of a dog was itself a challenge beyond anything that blind Americans had experienced up to that time. Dorothy, Jack, and Willi, the dog people, looked at the human-dog equation from the canine point of view. They might have rephrased Edward Allen's statement to "What a guide dog needs its blind master to be, that he must become." There was no alternative. An educated guide dog was far too precious to waste on a human who was unable or unwilling to meet the challenge of ownership. Working a dog required strength, coordination, and orientation. The dogs walked fast, pulled hard, and must be worked two or three miles a day, if they were not to grow stale and unsafe. Generally, people over fifty-five could not meet the physical strain of a first dog. Those under sixteen tended to lack the sense of responsibility that ownership of a dog required. A master must have the courage to trust his dog's judgment and follow its lead, or it would stop working. There was need for moral courage, too. Newell had shown it in keeping his pledge not to touch alcohol, but Alberta Edwards had lacked the backbone to resist her aunt's demand that Iris sleep in a cold cellar. Hendrick had submitted weakly to his landlord's prohibition, "No dogs allowed."

It was the duty, nearly the mission, of all Seeing Eye graduates to get their dogs received in public places. They owed it to themselves and those who would come after them. If dogs were to be received, they must be made to behave. This imposed the far more difficult task of making the public behave. Having taught the dog to lie quietly under the table in a restaurant, the master must then teach the other guests not to tempt it to misbehave by patting it, talking to it, or, worst of all, offering food. Since the challenges of ownership were considerable, it was obvious that guide dogs were not for everyone, but, as Dorothy had told the World Conference and AAWB, it was very difficult to predict who would succeed and who would fail.

At Openaka, the "dog people" and the "blind people" gradually came to agree on screening procedures, but not until Sinclair had challenged one of the criteria for admission. Without testing the idea, The Seeing Eye had adopted the European belief that a dog should not be paired with anyone who had been blind for less than two years. The theory was that it took at least that long to "learn to be blind." Sinclair persuaded Willi Ebeling to accept three newly blind students in the same class with others of long standing. The newly blind learned faster than the others. They had a fresher recollection of their freedom, were more eager to regain it, and had had a shorter time to sink into habits of dependency and inertia. In other words, they had not yet learned to be blind. Thereafter, The Seeing Eye gave priority to the newly blind.

The "blind people" assisted in the admission process.

In a swing through Albany, Rochester, and Buffalo, Broun and Morris personally screened seventy-nine of the most promising candidates culled from the New York State Commission files. Both Mary Campbell and Ibby Hutchinson interviewed applicants. The complaints Ibby Hutchinson heard from graduates persuaded her that the school's teaching methods put too much emphasis on the dogs and made too little provision for individual differences in the students, but after spending a month as an observer in a class in May 1933, she changed her mind.

In the end, the "dog people" and the "blind people" arrived at a consensus that projected a new role for The Seeing Eye. Other agencies taught their clients to be blind. Seeing Eye students would be taught to be as normal as possible. The dogs would give their masters the freedom to move into the sighted world. For this reason, The Seeing Eye made the fewest possible concessions to its students' blindness. Headquarters had been a family dwelling and maintained a homelike atmosphere. The students slept not in dormitories, but in bedrooms on the second floor. Since the staircase had two landings and twenty steps in all, it offered plenty of practice in going up and down stairs. The living room was arranged with Dorothy's own furniture. In the dining room, students, staff, and visitors sat around a large family table. The men were asked to wear coats and ties and the women skirts or dresses at lunch and dinner. They were addressed as Mr., Mrs., or Miss, and they were expected to cut their own meat and butter their own bread. In short, they were treated like grownup ladies and gentlemen and were asked to behave like grownup ladies and gentlemen.

For those from families or institutions that had taught them to be blind, this was a challenge. Many had scant notions of table manners. One young woman of twenty-three, brought up in a foundling home, had never used a knife, fork, or spoon. She had eaten with her fingers. Others had never been to a hairdresser and had no idea of cosmetics.

Where blind people were seen only by their families or the staffs of segregated institutions, appearances did not matter. The Seeing Eye wanted its graduates out in the world. It could not attempt total rehabilitation, but it could provide some preparation for life in the sighted world. To assist in this process, in October 1934 Mary Campbell was hired as executive secretary of the Division of the Blind. Just a year later, Ibby Hutchinson became her assistant. If a student could not handle a knife and fork, he was given a private lesson. Ibby showed women students how to apply cosmetics; she also arranged appointments for them with a hairdresser.

There were many subtle ways in which students were helped to understand what it meant to be part of the sighted world. Perhaps I can best illustrate from my own experience. When I arrived at The Seeing Eye for the first time in 1941, I was twenty-one and had been blind for six months. My mother drove me to Morristown and we were met in the driveway by my instructor, Mr. Northrup. Following his directions, interspersed with many asides to my mother ("Let him do it himself, Mrs. Putnam"), I carried my bag up the stairs to my bedroom, was shown the position of my bed, bureau, and closet, the way to the lavatory, and was then left with my mother in the recreation room. After a parting conversation, I went downstairs with my mother to say good-bye on the front porch. Back inside, I crossed the hall and was groping for the banister of the staircase when Mr. Northrup called from the landing, "Keep your head up, Mr. Putnam, and stand straight."

This made me realize that my neck was sticking forward, apelike, in my uncertainty.

"I'm sorry," I said foolishly.

"It's a frequent mannerism of the new blind," Mr. Northrup explained, "but it's a good thing to catch early."

Within fifteen minutes of my arrival at The Seeing Eye, I'd had my first lesson in personal appearance in a sighted world. Two weeks later, Miss Hutchinson was reading me a letter from a college girl who invited me for a weekend in a ski resort. I laughed at the notion of myself on skis.

"Oh, I don't know," Miss Hutchinson said. "Maybe you ought to try it."

I had never been skiing before I went blind, but I did try it that winter and kept it up for the next thirty years or more. At least in part, I owe it to Elizabeth Hutchinson's having shaken my incredulity that morning.

Another student arriving at the school for the first time had very much the same experience as mine with Mr. Northrup. Having been blind much longer and sheltered by an overly protective family, he had become what Morris Frank called "blind-minded." He was flabbergasted when the greeting staff member told him to pick up his bag and follow him. The staff member talked him upstairs to his bedroom, showed him the position of his bed, bureau, and closet and advised him to unpack. This was too much for the newcomer.

"In case you haven't noticed," he said, "I am blind."

"So am I," Morris Frank answered, "but I never let it interfere with my appetite, and dinner is in twenty minutes. You better get unpacked."

Morris frequently used such shock tactics to stiffen the spines of the blind-minded. His message was clear, and it was startlingly different from that of most agencies for the blind in that day. Instead, of "Be helpless, so we can help you" it was "Help yourself, or we can't help you."

Figure 1. Architects rendering of Vincent A. Stabile Canine Health Center, which is scheduled to open in October 1997.

Figure 2. Jack Humphrey, Dorothy Harrison Eustis, and Morris Frank meet at The Seeing Eye soon after it was founded. At Morris Frank's feet is Buddy I, the first Seeing Eye dog.

Figure 3. A Seeing Eye graduate deboards a United Airlines plane after a flight accompanied by her Seeing Eye dog. Virtually all states and provinces have legislation that prohibits discrimination against a blind person accompanied by a dog guide. The 1992 Americans with Disabilities Act is designed to end discrimination for people with any disability, including visual impairment.

Figure 4. A newly renovated, single student room at The Seeing Eye. Notice the special sleeping mat for the dog.

Figure 5. Morris Frank traveling to work in Morristown with his Seeing Eye dog, Buddy.

Figure 6. Morris Frank navigates street obstacles with his faithful dog guide, Buddy.

Figure 7. As part of formal training, instructors put on a blindfold to test the dog's skills and progress before being placed with a blind student. Here, Dave Johnson under blindfold is followed by his supervisor Doug Roberts.

Figure 8. Dave Johnson and Doug Roberts use a decoy dog as a distraction for a Seeing Eye Dog in training.

Figure 9. A class of students in front of The Seeing Eye's Whippany Headquarters in 1949.

Figure 10. Trainer Drew Gibbon working a Seeing Eye dog on the streets of Morristown, New Jersey.

Figure 11. Paul Wilson departs a bus while an instructor observes. The Seeing Eye makes use of many forms of local transportation to accommodate its graduates many lifestyles.

Figure 12. Blanche Eddy of Berkeley, California, the first American woman to have a Seeing Eye dog, confidently walks across a busy intersection. She was a member of The Seeing Eye's second graduating class in 1929.

Figure 13. Portrait of Morris Frank and Buddy III.

Figure 14. A Seeing Eye dog safely leads its blind master down front porch steps.

Figure 15. A Seeing Eye dog safely leads its blind master through downtown stores.

Figure 16. A Seeing Eye dog safely leads its blind master through revolving store doors.

Figure 17. A Seeing Eye dog safely leads its blind master around construction obstacles.

Figure 18. A Seeing Eye dog patiently waits while its blind master tends to business.

Figure 19. Dorothy Eustis with her husband George at Fortunate Fields in Vevey, Switzerland.

Figure 20. The Five Founders: Dorothy Harrison Eustis, the lady who loved Shepherds; Elliott S. (Jack) Humphrey, geneticist and chief instructor; Morris Frank and Buddy, who proved that a dog and its blind master could live a normal life; and Willi Ebeling, the first expert breeder of Seeing Eye dogs.

Figure 21. Alexander Wollcott, famous writer, discussing the training of Seeing Eye dogs with Jack Humphrey, a self-taught geneticist and breeder who trained Morris Frank with the first Seeing Eye dog.

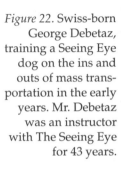

Figure 22. Swiss-born George Debetaz, training a Seeing Eye dog on the ins and outs of mass transportation in the early years. Mr. Debetaz was an instructor with The Seeing Eye for 43 years.

Figure 23. The Walker Dillard Kirby Kennel, dedicated in 1993, houses Seeing Eye dogs in various stages of formal training.

Figure 24. Steps are common obstacles with which master and dog soon become familiar. You see dog and master descend steps as confidently as if he or she had normal vision.

Figure 25. A Seeing Eye instructor is blindfolded twice during a dog's 12-week training period—once midway through the training to test the dog's progress and once at the end of the 12-week period as a final examination. Although not pictured, The Seeing Eye's director of instruction and training follows the blindfolded instructor to evaluate the dog's ability.

Figure 26. Guided by her Seeing Eye dog Patty, Norma Farrar of Winchester, Massachusetts comes down the gangplank of the Holland American Liner SS. Groote Beer after a visit to Germany.

Figure 27. Morris Frank follows Buddy as she leads him through the traffic of Vevey, Switzerland, during his indoctrination period in 1928.

Figure 28. Seeing Eye dog Heidi is permitted to accompany her master, David Chappell, into all places of accommodation. Heidi is exempt from the "No Pets Allowed" rule because by law she is a working dog, not a pet.

Figure 29. For 60 years, Seeing Eye dogs and their blind masters have shared a unique partnership unequaled in any other human—canine relationship.

Figure 30. Donald Roszmann and his Seeing Eye dog Ashley walked 2100 miles to raise funds for The Seeing Eye of Morristown, New Jersey.

Figure 31. A Seeing Eye dog safely leads its blind master across a street.

12

The Power of Light

Harking back to a spring morning in 1932, Margaret Kibbee recalled, "I was at the reception desk when Mrs. Eustis came into the office and announced, 'I have been told that Mr. Harold Strong is the finest fund raising man in New York, and I would like to see him.' She was a rather small woman, crisp and very direct in her manner and with a humorous gleam in her eye. The best word I can think of to describe her is perky. I remember we smiled at one another when I told her I would tell him she was there."

That marked the beginning of one of the most remarkable fund raising stories in history. With the deepening Depression, the increased expenses of the Whippany house, the expanding payroll and her other commitments, Dorothy was finding her resources strained. Charley Baiter, the new trustee, voiced his misgivings at the school's dependence on the personal philanthropy of Mrs. Eustis and a few friends. The death or disaffection of any one of them could cripple The Seeing Eye's program. It would be far sounder to build up a base of small contributions. A friend of Gretchen Green had recommended Harold Strong.

Dorothy Eustis liked the Strong company from the beginning. It was young, energetic, and highly organized. Although it would grow much larger, there were only four on the staff at the time: Strong, Dickson Hartwell, Margaret Kibbee, and a secretary. Dorothy worked with them on a personal basis.

"Their first task," said Margaret Kibbee, "was to set up a good solid sponsoring group made up of men and women who were dependable, highly respected, known for integrity, influential and with access to other people of the same type. I remember Mr. Strong and Mrs. Eustis spending days going over lists of people, the *Social Register*, club membership lists, etc., and discussing them before settling on Herbert Satterly as their first choice. They then discussed how to approach him, what program they would present to him and how to present it. Mrs. Eustis was enthusiastic, vitally interested and eager. She was full of ideas of her own and contributed a great deal to the plan."

Satterly was a well known New York lawyer, a brother-in-law of J. P. Morgan, and just the sort of person whose reputation for integrity would give the right tone to the committee. He was also hard to reach, but Dorothy was patient and persistent. It took her three separate meetings to persuade him to give a luncheon for a group of influential friends at the Downtown Association. Morris showed films and Dorothy spoke. No one was asked for money. The program was so well received that Satterly gave a second luncheon. A few members were added to the committee, but the recruiting process was highly selective, and it took time.

According to Margaret Kibbee, Gretchen Green was invaluable. "Her sense of humor was tremendous, and she knew how to use it to amuse and catch one's attention." Typical of Gretchen's attention-getting humor was her way of poking fun at her own appearance. She had a long neck and sloping shoulders. Somewhere she found a bed with posts carved to resemble the heads and necks of giraffes. She had herself photographed sitting bolt upright between the posts, looking uncommonly like a third giraffe. The result was an eye-catching Christmas card. With this unconventional turn of mind, Gretchen "had a remarkable ability to find ways for gaining access to someone we wanted or needed in the program."

Beginning in March of 1933 while Dorothy was in Switzerland, Gretchen played hostess at a series of teas in

Dorothy's New York apartment. Morris showed films and talked about The Seeing Eye, but there was not even a hint of an appeal for support. Gretchen's tea cakes were delectable, and, late in the afternoon, tea was followed by mulled wine. The guests were interesting people in their own right. As a result, invitations to Gretchen's select gatherings were envied and sought after.

Thanks to Gretchen's teas, the membership of the sponsoring committee was brought to full strength in May, but it was not unveiled for another six months. On November 14, 1933, the committee held a gala dinner at the Park Lane Hotel. The guest list of nearly two-hundred-and-fifty included such prominent New York names as Astor, Colgate, Cromwell, Davison, Harrison, Morgan, and Reid. Everyone was personally invited by a hostess and sat at her table. The dinner resembled a collection of private parties so well planned and executed that there was not an empty chair in the dining room. To represent its graduates, The Seeing Eye chose not Morris Frank, but Mervyn Sinclair. As a former business executive and Ivy League graduate, he was someone with whom this audience could readily identify. Alexander Woollcott, who had his first exposure to The Seeing Eye that night, described Sinclair following Kara through the eddying crowd "with the stately dignity of a tall ship surrounded by small harbor craft."

To the astonishment of the guests, there was no appeal for funds, but the arousal of Woollcott's interest were worth a fortune. With Dorothy Parker, he drove out to see the school at first hand. The more he learned, the more enthusiastic he became. He vented his enthusiasm in print and on his weekly radio broadcast, *The Town Crier*. An appeal for support on one of these broadcasts produced nearly $6,000, but the indirect benefits would prove far greater.

In the spring of 1934, The Seeing Eye staged its first benefit, the so-called "Hiss the Villain" party. It was a festive affair. New York's younger social set dressed in Gay Nineties costumes, arrived in horse-drawn carriages, buggies, and one hay wagon for a music hall performance of an old-fashioned melodrama, *The Drunkard*. It was featured in columns and photographs on the society pages of all the newspapers and netted The Seeing Eye more than $3,000, but it was never repeated. Critical analysis concluded that it had been a failure. Benefits are an expensive way of raising money. When they have no educational value, they produce money for the wrong reason. The frolicking masqueraders at the Hiss the Villain affair learned absolutely nothing about The Seeing Eye and would have enjoyed themselves equally at a benefit for widows and orphans of the Ku Klux Klan. The publicity on the society pages was equally irrelevant. From then on, The Seeing Eye gave up benefits.

The school's fund-raising philosophy evolved into the polar opposite of the Hiss the Villain party. Its whole emphasis was on education. If light stands for education and power for money, then light generates power, instead of the other way around. To some extent this is true of all fund-raising, but it was uniquely true of The Seeing Eye. Education was so thoroughly dominant that the term "fund-raising" was never used. The educational program was not distorted by propaganda or accompanied by sentimental strains of pity. There was not a hint of B is for Bewilderment, L is for Loneliness, and the rest. The Seeing Eye had a joyful story to tell. The best way to tell it was simply, clearly, and without embellishment.

The educational emphasis may have received its initial impetus from a tour of New England's private schools by Dorothy Eustis, Morris Frank, and Buddy in the fall of 1932. They visited eleven schools in all, including Phillips Exeter, St. Paul's, and Miss Porter's. Aided by the films, Morris and Buddy had an irresistible appeal for school audiences. The students raised contributions for Seeing Eye scholarships, and within a few years Morris and Buddy were covering some 175 private schools from Maine to the Carolinas at regular intervals. Many future business executives and society leaders had their first exposure to The Seeing Eye as members of a school audience. Meanwhile, the educational program for the adult generation was accelerating.

In 1935, the Park Lane dinner was transferred to the Plaza on a much larger scale. Alexander Woollcott was the main attraction. The following year Woollcott's profile of Jack Humphrey in *The New Yorker* conveyed a great deal of information about The Seeing Eye to an influential readership. Woollcott continued to tout the school on his weekly radio broadcasts, and there was an increasing number of human interest stories about Seeing Eye graduates in magazines and newspapers. The photogenic appeal of the dogs was immense. The Seeing Eye staged gala dinners in Boston and Philadelphia and, with the addition of Marian Jobson to the Strong organization, in Cleveland and Chicago. Jack Humphrey and Alexander Woollcott shared the podium before an audience of 2,600 in Boston's Symphony Hall and nearly 2,000 in Detroit's Orchestra Hall. Booth Tarkington, one of America's best-loved writers then recuperating from the temporary blindness of cataracts, addressed an audience in Evanston, Illinois, by long distance hookup from his home in Indianapolis. In 1935, the school began publication of *The Guide* to spread news to a growing constituency twice a year.

In the five years since Dorothy had first approached Harold Strong in 1932, his organization had grown enormously, and three of its members, Dickson Hartwell, Marian Jobson, and Margaret Kibbee, felt uncomfortable with its size and growing preoccupation with large impersonal affairs. Dorothy Eustis, too, was unhappy with the direction Harold Strong was taking, and in 1937, when Hartwell, Jobson and Kibbee formed their own firm, she directed Willi Ebeling to ask for a proposal. Of the five public relations firms submitting such proposals, Hartwell, Jobson and Kibbee was chosen. In consequence, The Seeing Eye's program for public support became even more personal. Its work was described, not as fund raising, but as "education and extension."

Extension meant enrollment of annual memberships. These might range anywhere from $5 to $500 or more. There was no pressure for large gifts. A golden egg was no good if it stopped the goose from laying. The school wanted memberships that it could depend on year after year, even if they were modest. Potential donors did not feel threatened.

Memberships were enrolled by volunteers. Initially a sponsoring or executive committee was chosen from among those who had attended one of the dinners in the various cities. Some were parents of students who had heard Morris Frank at their schools. Others were prominent members of the Junior League or Council of Jewish Women. With the painstaking organizational work of Marian Jobson, they met in groups of ten, preferably in someone's home. Dorothy Eustis reasoned that since the dogs loved their work, so should the volunteers. And they did. The emphasis was educational and personal. Morris and Buddy attended with Marian Jobson or another staff member, but he arranged to arrive and depart alone, thereby demonstrating the freedom of movement Buddy made possible. The groups were small enough, so that everyone felt they knew Morris and Buddy personally. When Morris had gone, the staff member organized the solicitation of memberships. Again the emphasis was educational. If a volunteer protested asking for money, she was told not to ask for money, but only to tell The Seeing Eye's story. The softness of the sell got on the nerves of one flamboyant young socialite from Grosse Pointe who insisted on whispering because, she said, "The Seeing Eye is so damned well bred." Requests were almost always to friends or acquaintances. Letters on personal stationery appealing for modest annual memberships were hard to resist. Marian Jobson kept painstakingly accurate lists of the names and addresses of volunteers and of those they solicited. There was no duplicate solicitation. Members were asked to give once a year only.

Within a very few years, the school had recruited roughly 1,000 volunteer workers for the committees of various cities. They in their turn enrolled some 15,000, then more than 20,000 memberships. Some were large, $100, $500 or more. The average was about $15, but the volume was more than sufficient to underwrite the school's operating budget. In 1933, The Seeing Eye's net cash assets were $43,000. Five years later, they were $400,000. In 1943, they surpassed $1,000,000. The school was beginning to benefit from a low key but carefully planned program to encourage testamentary giving that would ultimately increase its assets to many millions of dollars.

In strictly material terms, the program of Hartwell, Jobson and Kibbee was a fund-raiser's dream. It reaped a golden harvest. But its educational value was equally important. Annually, half of The Seeing Eye's 1,000 volunteers were new recruits who were thoroughly informed on the practice and philosophy of The Seeing Eye and who were stimulated to communicate what they had learned to thousands of others. Volunteers and members constituted an invaluable communications network to carry the school's message across the country. Many of them became powerful allies in other ways. They helped to open up mass transportation, restaurants, theaters, and other public facilities for guide dogs, to secure jobs for graduates, and to create a new awareness of and respect for the potentialities of the nation's blind population.

Morris was working on membership enrollment in Chicago one day when a volunteer informed him that the head of a cookware factory wanted to see him about a woman employee who was losing her sight. Morris toured the factory and found a job that could be performed by a blind worker. When he asked the president what had prompted him to turn to The Seeing Eye for advice, the man answered that they had been discussing the woman over the family dinner table at Thanksgiving, when his son, a student at Deerfield Academy, said he had heard Morris talk about blind factory workers.

In other words, The Seeing Eye's unique method of fund-raising produced light as well as power. It enlightened the American public as to the existence of a new type of blind people, ready, willing, and able to help themselves, if given an opportunity. And for this new type, it illuminated a path from the shadows of segregation into a bright new future in the American mainstream.

13

The Challenge of Freedom

"I was out of my cage the first day I walked down the street with my dog," a graduate exulted. "I was free and that was the way I was going to stay." An Allentown worker who picked up three graduates with their dogs to drive them home observed, "It is as if they had been released from prison, having been sentenced for life."

Prison is often used as a metaphor for blindness, and its psychological impact is often very similar. One type of convict becomes mutinous, bitterly resentful of everything and everybody, and there is a similar type among those who go blind. They are rebellious, resistant to any suggestion from outside, but they are a minority. In order to survive in an environment in which he is not free to make decisions, the average convict retreats into himself. Consciously or not, he cultivates the passivity and resignation that enable him to endure his loss of freedom. He becomes so accustomed to following prison routine that when he is released, he feels incapable of making the simplest decisions for himself. As a Trenton State Prison inmate put it, "When he goes through a door, he doesn't know whether to turn left or right. When he goes into a restaurant, he doesn't know how to choose a meal. When he goes to sleep, he doesn't know how to wake up."

Blindness can have the same paralyzing effect on the will and the decision-making faculty. Many blind people passively accept the estimate of their helplessness thrust on them by their families, friends, or agency. They become model workers, resigned to a future of making brooms or caning chairs. Students arrive at The Seeing Eye with attitudes that range from resignation to rebelliousness, but they leave them behind when they graduate. They have begun to change even before they arrive. The decision to get a dog reflects the decision to change their dependence on family and friends. The young sons of a Carolina farmer were so fearful that their blind father would hurt himself that they insisted on guiding him around the farm on his daily chores. To the question of why he wanted a dog, he answered simply, "So my sons can go to school and I can go where I like."

Booth Tarkington described a girl whose family "won't let her have a dog, because they think a guide dog will make them conspicuous, put them in the wrong, look as if they wouldn't take the trouble to lead the poor thing around themselves." This girl was the prisoner of her family's tyrannical charity. Her departure for The Seeing Eye would have been a declaration of independence. A young wife who wanted a dog, but whose "husband said no," touched on the most humiliating aspect of blindness. "My experience has been that people kill me with kindness. As long as I act feebleminded and partially paralyzed, I get along fine. I feel there is nothing wrong with my mind since losing my sight. I feel just as capable of making certain decisions as I ever did." During the blindness of his cataract operations, Booth Tarkington had a taste of the same humiliation when a friend read aloud from a book the words "He felt himself as unlike his fellow beings as if he had been blind or an idiot." Tarkington commented, "Among the nuisances of blindness to which I was imaginatively looking forward had not been that of relegation to the status of an idiot."

Many students arriving at The Seeing Eye were surprised that the staff addressed them all as Mr., Mrs., or Miss. They had been treated as children for so long that they expected to be called only by their first names. Each Mr., Mrs., or Miss reminded them that they were grown adults. The shock of this courtesy was followed fast by the shock of the daily schedule for the class. They were awakened at half past five in the morning to dress and take their dogs out to empty in "the park," a large rectangle of gravel behind the house.

The trip to the park was a challenge in itself. It began at the top of the steps on the second floor and proceeded as follows: Descend five steps, turn right on landing, find top step, descend five steps, turn right on landing, find top step, descend ten steps to hall, cross hall, find knob of inner door, drop harness, open door, enter, and close door, pick up harness, find knob to outer door, drop harness, open door, exit, close outer door, pick up harness, cross porch, find top step, descend porch steps, turn right on sidewalk for about twenty paces past corner of building, turn right to edge of driveway, pause, cross driveway to sidewalk, pause, walk forward about fifteen paces to next driveway, pause, cross first driveway, pause, forward into park.

In the course of this trip, there were no fewer than eighteen commands to be given in the proper order with the proper inflection and accompanying body movements. Each command properly obeyed must be rewarded by a cheerful "Atta *good* girl!" Students must avoid crowding each other. Each student must open and close the inner and outer door unaided. The dogs must be corrected for sniffing or being distracted by other dogs. To the right of the porch steps there was a stone balustrade that inflicted many a charley horse in the thighs of the unwary. There were no curbs on the driveway, so it was easy for dogs to run the edges and difficult for novices to tell that they had. Instructors posted along the route pointed out errors.

Once in the park, the students removed the harnesses and followed their dogs around the large gravel rectangle on long leash, being careful not to get dogs and leashes tangled. Emptying on leash was something the dogs had not been taught previously, and it took time to learn. With two classes in session, there were sixteen human minds focused on canine bowels and bladders. This was faintly amusing at first, but the amusement wore thin as a quarter of an hour in the chill dawn stretched to twenty or thirty minutes. When the dogs had emptied at last, the route had to be worked back to the second floor to wait for breakfast at seven o'clock.

The first trip was at eight. One at a time, four humans and their dogs climbed into a station wagon, and their instructor drove them to Morristown. There were six or seven routes, varying from a few blocks on Maple Street to the four-mile "Boy Scout route." After 1931, a rigid U-shaped harness handle replaced the flexible strap Morris had used with Buddy; it gave a more precise definition of the dog's direction. The dogs were bigger, stronger, and harder[1] than those the school now uses. They walked at three and a half miles per hour. It was not unusual for a student to drop out from inability to stand the strain, but many returned later after conditioning themselves with exercise.

Mrs. Rita Duren described the impact of her turnover with a dog with the appropriate name of Urge. "My experience of The Seeing Eye was explosive. It dynamited me out of the protective shroud I had built around myself. I was bewildered and cogs of my brain didn't work, but there was no going back. Urge was always pulling forward, and the staff was there to say in effect, 'What is making you hesitate? The world is yours.' " Mrs. Duren had been blind and relatively immobile for many years. "I was tense with the abrupt transition from slow motion to speed and danger. I was dying from being jerked around by the dog, not having enough hands for dog, comb and brush and feed pan, from trying to remember routes, from managing the stairs and trying to keep my body intact."

There were many individual problems. Mr. Finch had

---

[1] The terms "hard" and "soft" as applied to guide dogs refer to emotional sensitivity to correction. Hard dogs tend to ignore corrections that soft dogs take seriously.

trained his own dogs for eleven years. They had guided him on leash, and the changeover to a rigid harness handle was not easy. "I had eleven years of acquired bad habits to unlearn in three weeks." Emil Buchko was only four feet tall, crippled, and unable to ascend a curb without the helping pull of a dog that had to be trained specially for him. Many students had only the most rudimentary notions of orientation. Others had difficulty giving commands with authority. Mr. Whitman, who was partially deaf, remained stalled so long at one corner giving quavering "forwards" to Betts that he finally lost his temper and shouted, "Betts, forward! Right! Left! Take your pick, damn it, but do something!"

Incidents of this sort could seem hilariously funny to a class, and if there were anxiety, confusion, and physical discomfort to overcome, they were frequently dissolved in laughter. I myself went to my first class at The Seeing Eye with the same dread I might have felt at the prospect of a Women's Christian Temperance Union prayer breakfast. To my surprise I laughed more than I had on the Princeton Triangle Club's Christmas tour. What was so funny? Nothing except that I had come with a heavy heart, and suddenly my heart was high. I have witnessed the same metamorphosis in dozens of others.

It begins with the exhilaration of that first walk. Stepping out with the breathtaking new freedom of a tugging harness handle, students feel their backs and shoulders straighten, their lungs fill, their hearts beat. They feel suddenly taller, like real men and women again. They praise their dogs with laughing voices and become laughing men and women. "The habit of bestowing praise is a very beneficial one for human beings to acquire," wrote Booth Tarkington. "It is likely to enlarge their hearts." At The Seeing Eye, students who must bestow praise on their dogs literally hundreds of times a day feel their hearts enlarging.

Dogs offer students a kind of freedom they have rarely received from human guides. As one woman put it, "A dog would not be guilty of imposing her wishes on me because she felt that I was blind and incapable of thinking. She would not enrage me to tears by insisting that she spread my biscuit or butter my toast. She would not insist on taking my arm and half carrying me down steps with the result that I never quite know just where my foot is going to land. She would not do that because she would 'feel safer' regardless of how safe or unsafe I feel." Guide dogs do not impose their wills on their masters, and they do not condescend. They look up to them, and the sense of being looked up to is one some students may not have had for a long time.

The affection between dog and master is transforming. One young man who came to the school in a state of active rebellion against practically everything gradually mellowed. He had arrived unkempt and carelessly dressed, but he began to take pains with his appearance, combing his hair before every meal, shaving daily instead of every two or three days, and borrowing his roommate's brush and polish to shine his shoes. When asked what had come over him, he answered, "Well, you know, my dog is such a lady." The head of a local welfare board gave his impression of a young father who had just returned from The Seeing Eye: "I have never known anyone changed so much in four weeks as Mr. C. He now holds his head up, throws his shoulders back, is in better physical condition, and for the first time since the loss of sight, is anxious to work and support his family."

Changes of this sort were not due solely to dogs. The school was teaching more than guide dog technique. Ibby Hutchinson read students their mail in private, and the readings led easily into conversation. Once they had their dogs, she said, they would be spending far more time in the sighted world, getting out into public places, doing things they had not done for years, if ever. They might like some suggestions other students had found helpful. She offered tips on grooming and taking care of their nails. One of the most sensitive subjects to broach was the appearance of their eyes. I remember my own experience. I had been blind about four months when I had a visit from a former college roommate.

"Putnam," he told me, "you ought to wear dark glasses."

Inwardly I winced. The bullet that had severed my optic nerves had not touched my eyes, and, after some initial swelling had subsided, I had assumed that except for my closed eyelids I looked quite normal. None of my extended family had hinted anything to the contrary. It took the candor of a peer to inform me that my lids were red and one eye was distractingly half open. I have blessed him many times since.

Some blind people are hard to convince. Those who have been born blind cannot picture how important the appearance of eyes can be. Often their attitude is "If I can put up with my blindness, so can you." Frequently, their families protect them against what they regard as unfeeling attacks. Other blind people feel that wearing dark glasses will draw undue attention to their blindness. They are unaware that unsightly eyes are far more distracting than glasses. A few seem to feel their blindness entitles them to ignore social conventions. The Seeing Eye's position is that if you want to be treated as an equal in the sighted world, you should conform to the standards of the sighted world, including its visual standards. Ibby Hutchinson was so completely and obviously a lady that almost no one could take offense at her suggestions, and she set students of both sexes straight on many details of dress, manners, and appearance. Graduates back for second dogs were often able to reinforce her message.

The total impact of the school amazed observers. Writing of a new graduate, a social worker struck a common theme: "I have never seen such a change in anybody in four weeks. He has developed character, initiative and independence. He is neat and clean and so polite now, and so much more particular about his person. I do not see how you do it in such a short period of training."

Years later, Albert Gazagian recalled the importance of some advice Willi Ebeling gave him on his eighteenth birthday. "I had come to your office to discuss my leaving for home. When I rose to leave, I failed to start in the right direction. I was not going straight for the door. You advised me always to pay careful attention how I entered an office, so that I could make a good exit and not give the person I had been talking to the impression that I was not capable of getting about." This little tip, he said, had been important in his success at the John Hancock Insurance Company.

Victor Parez Collazo wrote, "I will always remember that when I reached the school, my whole personality was disturbed, that I was afraid to face my new life and that you all contributed to help me in my moral and psychological reconstruction. I do not doubt that, if I am writing from this desk [as a district judge in Puerto Rico], it is greatly due to the hearty push you gave me."

The moral and psychological reconstruction of a big Pennsylvania Dutchman named Pfeiffer surprised even The Seeing Eye. His wife was opposed to his getting a dog. He could get around the block with a cane, she said, but Pfeiffer replied, "Yes, and the block is my prison." He enrolled in the school, and Debetaz decided he would make a likely partner for Lisa.

Lisa was an excellent guide in every respect but one. In training, she and Debetaz had been near the corner of Park Place and South Street when a freight elevator had clattered up through the sidewalk. It made such an indelible impression on Lisa that Debetaz was never again able to work her past that corner. Nothing could persuade her, and because guide dogs must be educated, not trained, she had to be persuaded, not forced. However, since Pfeiffer's sleepy little village had no freight elevators, Debe decided Lisa would do nicely for him.

The turnover was successful, but some three months

later Debetaz saw Pfeiffer and Lisa get off the bus in front of the school and walk up the driveway. Sure that something had gone wrong, he hurried to meet them. Pfeiffer was all smiles. He had been off on an excursion to Harrisburg, Philadelphia, and New York. He was just stopping by to say hello. In response to Debe's questions, he said that Lisa had guided him through all the noise and confusion that New York could offer. Half disbelieving, Debe asked if Pfeiffer would mind going down to Morristown, so he could watch them work. Pfeiffer agreed, and, following them around the streets, Debe directed them to the fateful corner of Park Place and South. Unhesitatingly, Lisa walked her master past the very spot where the elevator had popped up, then looked over her shoulder at him. Her look, he said, spoke clearly: "I'll do it for this guy, not for you."

The block had been Pfeiffer's prison. When Debe turned him over with Lisa, he had thought she would give him the freedom of his village. The love and gratitude he had lavished on Lisa had unlocked the door to a much wider world. There were no prisons now.

14

"Never a Dull Moment!"

"Never a dull moment at The Seeing Eye!" was the laughing comment Ibby Hutchinson repeated so often that it was finally embroidered on a sampler and hung above her desk. It might have been mounted over the door the day the first class moved in, because it was true from the beginning. Lila Rich, who became Willi Ebeling's secretary in that first December, recalled arriving for work to find that the heating system had broken. "There was ice in the goldfish bowl, and Mr. Ebeling was sitting at his desk in his raccoon coat."

Morris Frank and Debe Debetaz shared bachelor's quarters on the third floor and became fast friends. As soon as Debe had completed a class, he would confide the care of the kennel dogs to Sita and Adolf, the German couple who served as cook and gardener. Then he and Morris would head for New York City. At Mandelbaum's, their favorite speakeasy, Buddy sat on a chair between them and was served a saucer of milk with each round of drinks. Once, when Mandelbaum's was closed, they were referred to another speakeasy and told to ask for Tony. The name worked like magic. Every time they asked for Tony, they were brought drinks on the house, but Tony himself never appeared. They later learned that the presence of Buddy had convinced Tony they were federal agents.

As part of the school's education program, visitors were frequently invited for meals, and Gretchen Green decided the dining room needed brightening. From Schumacher's in New York she cadged a sample roll of wallpaper, a green ivy-leaf pattern against a cream background. Then she bought scissors, brushes, paste, and rolls of plain green and cream wallpaper to match the Schumacher sample. After supper one night, she and Debe papered the entire dining room in cream, then painstakingly cut out ivy leaves from the green paper and pasted them on the cream background. They did not finish until three in the morning.

Dorothy decided that Morris, too, should be spruced up for visitors. She took him to Brooks Brothers and had him outfitted in a sports jacket, grey flannels, and a tattersall vest. Morris was delighted until he learned he was paying the bill. "It cost me damned near a month's salary, but you didn't argue with the Boss."

In his new finery, Morris was showing a lady visitor through the building when she asked to see "some of the poor dear blind people."

"You're seeing one now," Morris told her.

"But your eyes look perfectly normal."

"They should. They cost $25 each."

During the summer of 1933, the Gate House was remodeled into apartments, one for Dorothy Eustis on the second floor and another for the Humphreys on the first. Nettie Humphrey moved in that fall in time for young George to start school, but Jack and Dorothy were still in Vevey. During the last half of 1933, Debe was there, too, studying guide dog theory and psychology. In exchange, L'Oeil qui Voit sent over another young Swiss apprentice named Dardel.

Dardel had a weakness for practical jokes. When a student was taking a shower, he would turn on all the hot water taps in the sinks, so that the shower would run cold. When he tried this on a student named Messler, it worked the first time, but Messler was large and powerfully built. The next time, he held Dardel under the water, fully clothed, until he was soaked to the skin. Dardel proved to have other problems and returned to L'Oeil qui Voit in 1934.

In August of that year, a car drove up to the school with a young blind lawyer from Chicago. His named was Herbert Geisler, and he had come "for the purpose of examining the guide dogs on hand and selecting one which I could take home to Chicago." Amused by young Geisler's presumption, Willi Ebeling explained that one does not choose a guide dog like an animal in a pet shop and drove Geisler into Morristown to observe a pair of students in a class under Debetaz. Undaunted, Geisler announced that he was ready to begin training at once and would postpone his return to Chicago as long as necessary. After a hurried conference, Debe agreed to take on an extra student. In September, Herb Geisler went home with Nubia as his guide.

Chicago had not yet had its first membership enrollment, and nothing had been done to educate the city to the virtues of guide dogs. Banned from public transportation, Geisler and Nubia had to walk miles to and from work, and Nubia was not allowed in Geisler's office building. Geisler rented a room for her in a neighboring hotel and made his way to his office alone. At lunch time, he came back to feed Nubia and take her out to empty. Then he returned her to the hotel room for the afternoon. Later the volunteers of the Chicago committee became his allies, but at the outset he was alone and had to devise his own strategies for breaking down the barriers.

Debe witnessed one of these strategies when he stopped to see Geisler on his way home from a class in Berkeley. They met for lunch at the Sherman Hotel, but had hardly been seated in the dining room when the headwaiter objected to Nubia. He refused to acknowledge Geisler's argument that he needed the dog because he was blind. Suddenly the lawyer handed Nubia's leash to Debe and told him to take her out. When they were halfway to the door, Geisler stood up and turned over his table. The headwaiter protested. Geisler said he was blind and did not know how to get out of the room without his dog. Then he turned over a second table. He was groping toward a third when the headwaiter surrendered.

Thanks to the fighting tactics of graduates like Morris Frank and Herb Geisler and the diplomatic and educational efforts of volunteers, the school gradually won acceptance of its dogs in public facilities, but there were some wry by-products of victory. The Delaware & Lackawanna Railroad Station in Morristown bore a sign proclaiming "The Chicago Express will stop to discharge Seeing Eye passengers and corpses only."

Before Morristown had begun to take pride in being the home of The Seeing Eye, there had been problems with the local residents. The school was using public space as its classroom for both dogs and students. Inevitably this caused some inconvenience for the sighted public. When a dog came too close to a moving car in the street, the instructor slapped the fender with a *pfui!* The sound of a thud on the rear fender could be a chilling experience for nervous drivers. Small children were likely to carry ice cream cones at a level with a dog's mouth, and occasionally one disappeared as a German shepherd shot past. One elderly woman stepped back suddenly into the path of an oncoming student and broke her hip in the fall. Others were bumped or had their feet stepped on by students not yet experienced in following their dogs.

The bank had the only revolving door in town, and the school received permission to expose its dogs to this type of problem. One day an instructor was just halfway through the door when his dog suffered an attack of diarrhea. His desperate attempts to clean up were complicated by a continuous flow of customers entering the bank.

Some dog lovers complained of cruelty, but even kindly intervention could be disconcerting. In the early years students were trained with white canes. When Debe found that one of his students was confused by the cane, he relieved him of it and sent him off on a solo. As he stood watching his student, an old lady offered to lead him across the street. Taking the line of least resistance, he accepted, thanked her, and had resumed watching his student on the other side when another woman offered to take him back across.

In February 1934, Dorothy closed L'Oeil qui Voit, and in December, Jack undertook to train a class of eight American apprentices. This greatly increased the activity on the streets of Morristown, and one of Jack's training techniques was alarming to onlookers. Periodically he would drive down a street where students or apprentices were working their dogs and wheel suddenly into driveways to give traffic checks. This was questionable as a training technique, because the dogs soon learned to identify the sound of Jack's engine and were ready for him, but Jack seemed to enjoy it for its own sake. Fortunately Messler, the student who had drenched Dardel in the shower, was a local resident with relatives on the police force, and Jack cultivated the friendship of the chief. But on one occasion it did not avail. Right after he had executed two or three spectacular cuts on Maple Street, a state motor vehicle inspector who happened to be passing through confiscated Jack's license on the spot for reckless endangerment. To the secret delight of the apprentices, Jack had to walk to the police station to square accounts with the chief.

Visitors to the school could be a problem. If they followed too closely on the streets, they distracted the dogs. When they made ill-advised remarks at the school, they upset the students. One numbingly tactless woman spent lunch comparing dogs in a voice of brass: "Your dog isn't half as handsome as Mrs. Jones's." Or, "The dog with the man from Pittsburgh looks kind of sickly." Eventually visitors were strictly limited, but occasionally they arrived uninvited. Ibby Hutchinson recalled a Hindu woman, complete with sari and caste mark, who appeared without warning late one afternoon to announce that she was an official representative of work for the blind in New Delhi. She insisted on being put up at a Morristown hotel at

Seeing Eye expense and spent the following morning at the school, insulting one member of the staff after another. After lunch, she cached all the cold cuts and rolls she could gather into a basket she carried and boarded a New York bus, threatening to report The Seeing Eye's inhospitality to her government. Subsequent inquiry revealed that she had no official status whatever. She was an impostor pure and simple.

The school did not need visitors to provide variety. Students came from widely divergent backgrounds, regions, educational levels, and walks of life. At various times, they included a woman watercolorist who was still painting, a black pugilist who had fought champion Tony Zale, a former minor league baseball player, an Eskimo, and a Russian nobleman who claimed God had blinded him as punishment for having killed so many men. I once shared a class with a former professional gambler, an army veteran who had lost his left hand along with his sight, a black cabinetmaker, a hypnotist, and the first pregnant blind student to attend the Sorbonne on a Fulbright scholarship. Hector Chevigny, the author of *My Eyes Have a Cold Nose* and *Lord of Alaska*, a definitive, scholarly history on Russian settlements in North America, also wrote a popular radio serial, "The Second Mrs. Burton." Bernice Clifton was much in demand on the lecture circuit. Roy de Groot, gourmet author of *A Feast for All Seasons*, appeared regularly on NBC's "Today Show." Catherine Smith was a columnist for the *Buffalo Express*.

Subjecting this varied human assortment to an experience not unlike boot camp produced tensions. There were occasional flare-ups. Under the strain of the course, students came to words and, at least twice, to blows. Jack Humphrey got into a running battle with an impertinent male student who insisted on smoking a pipe while working his dog. One evening when the class was on its way to give the dogs an airing, Jack spied the offending pipe through his living room window. Throwing it open, he shouted at the student, who removed his pipe, turned it upside down to prove it was empty, and insolently replaced it in his mouth. The tale of the smart aleck smoker had an Aesopian ending. As a news vendor in the Bronx, he ignored Seeing Eye rules by leaving his dog to guard the newsstand while he went to lunch in a nearby diner. He was not using his dog when he fell into an open manhole and was killed.

There are many stories about the early years: about the time Arthur Meeker, the burly groundskeeper, collared a suspicious stranger skulking in the bushes who turned out to be Henry Colgate, chairman of the board, inspecting the lilacs he had donated to the school; the time the cooks had quit without notice and Aunt Mary Campbell and Ibby Hutchinson were pressed into service to cook the salmon caught personally by Mr. Colgate; or the time during the war when Agnes Fowler, a board member, had donned blue jeans to help muck out the kennels and was pressured for a date by the Polish kennel man. But not all the stories were about the early days.

In the 1960s, after Dorothy, Jack, Willi, and Morris were out of the picture, George Werntz, Willi Ebeling's successor, had an idea for a public relations photograph. One of the kennel men went without shaving for three days. He was then outfitted in disreputable clothes, dark glasses, a tin cup, and a sign reading "BLIND." He was paired with a scrawny mongrel at the end of a heavy, rusty chain. The photograph was intended to lampoon the obsolete stereotype of the blind beggar, but while George Werntz and the photographer were still in the act of posing their subjects on a street corner in Morristown, a gentleman in a Homburg paused, reached into the pocket of his tailor-made suit, and dropped fifty cents into the tin cup. Old stereotypes die hard.

15

The Achilles Heel

With her customary insight, Dorothy Eustis labeled the difficulty of finding suitable instructors as "the Achilles heel of The Seeing Eye." The problem had arisen first in the summer of 1928, when she and Jack had searched for an instructor for Morris Frank. Since Germany had been turning out guide dogs for a dozen years, they had assumed there would be a plentiful supply of competent German instructors available. They discovered that, although there were many apprentices capable of teaching particular aspects of guide work under supervision, there were only a handful sufficiently familiar with all phases to provide that supervision.

The experience at L'Oeil qui Voit confirmed the difficulty. Of more than fifty apprentices who enrolled, only three qualified as full instructors. Liakhoff, a Russian, went to England to carry on the work begun there by Humphrey and Debetaz. Gabriel became chief instructor in Italy. Only Debetaz was left for the American Seeing Eye.

In February 1934, Dorothy closed down L'Oeil qui Voit, and in June, Jack Humphrey set forth the plan of an American school for instructors. It was an Americanization of L'Oeil qui Voit. The Swiss school had been educating instructors, and the instructors had been educating guide dogs supplied by Fortunate Fields. Many of these were sold to The Seeing Eye and sent to the United States. The new American school would work in the same way. Jack Humphrey, his salary still paid by Fortunate Fields, would be its head. Since most of its expenses would be underwritten by

175

a fund donated by Helen Hubbard, the woman who had financed Jack's scholarly publications, it would be called the Hubbard School for Instructors. The dogs that its apprentices educated would be sold to The Seeing Eye. Everything was located on the Whippany property, and the Hubbard apprentices taught Seeing Eye students under the supervision of Humphrey and Debetaz.

Only male apprentices were accepted. Adelaide Clifford and Missy Doudge had done excellent work, but Adelaide had tired of the mental and physical strain, and Missy had fallen into that most dangerous of traps for professional women: marriage. Certainly there was an element of male chauvinism in the decision, but women, it was decided, were a poor risk. Jack planned a comprehensive curriculum for the Hubbard apprentices. The course would last four years and be "the equivalent of a college education." In addition to the theory and practice of guide dog education, they would study and hear lectures on such topics as animal psychology, animal physiology, animal husbandry, principles of breeding, genetics, and the anatomy of the eye. When Jack had typed them up, the Hubbard lectures filled 3,000 pages.

The school opened in December 1934. Eight apprentices were selected from nearly a hundred applicants. They lived on the grounds of The Seeing Eye in a remodeled barn and began by going through the entire routine of a class under blindfolds from the time they woke up until they went to bed at night. The hours were long, the work was hard, and the pay was low, but the country was in the depths of the Great Depression, and a job of any sort was prized. Dorothy's attitude toward instructors' salaries was revealed in an interview with Debetaz at the close of his first year in America. Noting that he had been paid $75 a month above his room and board, she asked him how much he had put aside. He admitted he had saved nothing. She feared that he was squandering his pay on beer and frivolous amusements and advised him to open a savings account at once. Meanwhile, she had a gift for him. If he expected a cash bonus to start his savings account, he was disappointed. It was a signed photograph of herself.

Apprentices were regarded as subordinates who were expected to keep their place. When two apprentices approached Dorothy Eustis for a raise on the morning a class was to begin, she sensed blackmail and did not hesitate. Tapping on the glass of her office for the bookkeeper, she had her draw checks for two weeks' salary and told the young men to have their personal effects off the premises by nightfall. "She would have fired the whole staff the same way," Morris commented. "Nobody threatened the Boss and got away with it." Willi Ebeling was reasonable and courteous, but instructors who entered his office to complain soon found themselves backed up against the mantelpiece.

Jack Humphrey was just, but he expected hard work and he minced no words. Ned Myrose recalled applying for a job as apprentice in the fall of 1937. Jack told him he would have to spend the first six months working in the kennels and offered him $50 a month plus board and lodging. Myrose took it and remembered Jack as a harder worker than any subordinate. "Many a morning, he was in his office two hours before daylight, typing up the Hubbard lectures, and he was all over the school and the streets of Morristown the rest of the day. I used to love to hear him talk, but he could be a terror."

Once, when an apprentice was having difficulty teaching a stubborn animal in obedience, Jack stepped in to demonstrate, but the dog continued mulish. For once, Jack lost his temper with an animal and fetched it a clout on the ear. Immediately he spun on the apprentice, pointed his finger and snapped, "If I ever catch you doing that, I'll fire you on the spot."

Another time, he gave one of Myrose's female students a traffic check and ran the car over her foot. She habitually took another step after her dog stopped, and Jack decided that was the only way to teach her. He coddled apprentices less than students. When Curtiss Weeman was taking a blindfold test, Jack allowed his dog to walk him into a steel post at full speed. Weeman split his forehead, but Jack's position was that since instructors were asking blind students to trust their dogs, they should learn from experience what could happen with an untrustworthy dog. Debe recalled an experience with Jack in Liverpool, England. He had worked one dog before breakfast when Jack showed up unexpectedly over coffee and suggested a blindfold test. Debe figured to have an easy time of it, walking the same dog over the same route. In the middle of the fourth block, the dog stopped in an area where Debe knew there was no obstruction. When she refused to budge after repeated "forwards," Debe committed the unpardonable sin. He stepped in front of the dog and into a scaffold that had been erected during his breakfast. "Jack was across the street, laughing, and I was pulling splinters out of my forehead the rest of the morning."

Of the first eight Hubbard apprentices, only Weeman and Hauptmann became instructors. In the fall of 1938, Jack started a new class recruited from college graduates. Of 150 applicants, the school chose six. Only three, Dickerman, Lee, and Northrup, became instructors. Their life had certain compensations. For the right sort of man, exercise in the open air is preferable to sitting in an office. Working ten to twelve hard-pulling dogs ten to fifteen miles a day kept them lean and muscular, but some broke under the strain.

Dog fights were a hazard. At first, the school had used only bitches, but as the demand for dogs grew, males were added. Until 1939, the bitches were not spayed, and their coming into season stimulated aggression among the males. There were some bloody battles in the kennels. Once, Northrup was struck in the chest by a big boxer and went down amid a snarling pack. Dickerman later claimed that his intervention may have saved Northrup's life. Myrose had one class that included four males who hated each other and two bitches in season. "Maybe you think it wasn't a scramble keeping them apart in the recreation room."

The safety of eight pairs of students and dogs was a heavy responsibility. After a couple of days, student-dog pairs worked two at a time, one in front of the other. The lead pair waited at down curbs for the other to come up, so that they would not get too far separated. To keep both pairs in view, the instructor positioned himself in the rear and had to move fast if the lead student got into trouble. He first had to command the rear student to put his dog at sit, so that he could give the lead pair his undivided attention. Once, having failed to take this precaution, Myrose found himself racing forward after one student while looking over his shoulder at the other. A moment later, he was doing a somersault over a fire hydrant.

The nervous strain was considerable. As experienced graduates returned for second dogs, the problem eased. Graduates required less strict supervision than first-timers, but even veterans could make stupid mistakes. During a class with my second dog, Wick, I commanded him forward at a busy intersection. I was unaware of a large puddle in the gutter in front of us. To avoid it, Wick gave a bound that pulled the leash and harness out of my hand. It was an inexcusable lapse on my part, and Dickerman's heart was in his mouth as he leaped into the traffic to retrieve Wick. At any moment, instructors must be prepared to rescue students from unexpected cars, ditches, obstructions, or their own mistakes. Hauptmann broke under the nervous strain and retired a little more than a year after his graduation.

Instructors developed strong bonds of affection for their dogs during the three months before class. The dogs loved their work, and when the door of the truck in which they were driven to Morristown was opened, they greeted their heroes with furiously wagging tails and clamored to be first. This was heartwarming, but after instructors had

paired their dogs with their new masters, they had to ignore those pleading eyes and wagging tails, so that the
dogs would transfer their affections to the blind students.
It was thrilling to watch a novice taking his first walk, but
it hurt to see the bafflement of a dog whose master had
given the wrong command or failed to follow a clear signal
and stepped on its paw. Puzzled by its new master's inepti-
tude, a dog would look to its instructor to ask, "Why are
you doing this to me?" Students could be exasperating.
Told to go left, they turned right. They got lost on their trip
to the dining room, showed up late for the drive into town,
and discovered halfway there that they had forgotten their
gloves or their dog's muzzle. It was difficult to be patient
with a slow-witted student who was ruining a favorite dog.

During the three months' preparation, apprentices
worked twelve hours a day, six days a week. During class,
they slept in the main house within earshot of their students and were on call twenty-four hours a day. The last
student in a class generally left on a Friday. This gave the
lucky man a whole weekend free before starting to train a
new string of dogs on Monday. It is not surprising that so
few of the apprentices lasted the full four years. One recruit
got cold feet the first night and left the following morning.

Despite the difficulty of finding instructors, The Seeing
Eye had been graduating a larger number of students each
year. From a low of eleven in 1931, the number had risen to
forty in 1934 and exceeded one hundred in 1938. There
were not enough rooms in the main house to accommodate
all the students. A temporary solution was to start a class
in the main house; then after two weeks move the male
students into the former apprentice quarters to make room
for a new class. In January 1940, the construction of a wing
that included a new kitchen and dining room downstairs
and six bedrooms and a recreation room upstairs permitted
two classes to run at the same time. The Seeing Eye graduated a record 144 students that year.

Finding suitable dogs for so many students was a serious problem. To avoid even the semblance of conflict of interest, Willi Ebeling had given up his breeding program in 1932. Fortunate Fields continued to supply dogs until Dorothy Eustis closed it down in 1938. The school sought out breeders known to Dorothy, Willi, or Jack. Shepherds were in the majority, but Jack believed that the qualities that made for a good guide were more a function of the individual than of the breed. The school was soon training boxers, Labradors, Dobermans, Briards, golden retrievers, and mixed breeds. Ultimately, more than thirty breeds were represented, but good dogs of any breed were hard to come by. A number of dogs were donated by owners who could not keep them for some reason, but these sometimes changed their minds. Two elderly sisters in nearby Bernardsville offered a beautiful male shepherd because one of them was allergic to dog hair. Three days later they telephoned in tears to get him back. When the allergy was aggravated, they donated him again. In all the dog went back and forth from Bernardsville to Morristown eight times before the ninth donation proved final.

Dogs of this sort, accustomed to a home environment, did not adapt well to kennel life. Clean and friendly in a family setting, they became dirty and snappish in confinement. Often they rolled in their own excrement. It seemed impossible that these foul-smelling and ill-tempered animals could ever become proper companions for blind graduates, but as soon as they were taken into the main house during class they became their old selves, housebroken and amiable.

Another source of supply was a certain Mr. Krause, who came by two or three times a month with a truckload of dogs he had picked up around the county. "Probably stole some of them," Myrose conjectured. It is amusing to think of the aristocratic Dorothy Eustis as president of an organization trafficking in stolen goods, but the need was great and the dogs Jack picked from Krause's assortment were sound, healthy, and intelligent.

In 1940, The Seeing Eye began breeding shepherds for the first time. Unhappily, none of the Fortunate Fields breeding stock had been preserved, and the war in Europe put dogs from Germany out of reach. Jack Humphrey collected seed stock from various sources, and they were housed in a new kennel built on the Whippany property. When nine of the twenty-one bitches proved unsuitable as breeders, they were spayed and trained as guides.

The breeding program had barely started when the United States entered the war. Partly to relieve the problem of care during the manpower shortage and partly to isolate the puppies from the danger of contagion in the kennels, Jack proposed an ingenious idea. At Fortunate Fields, puppies had been farmed out to peasant families to gain the social experience so valuable for working dogs. Jack persuaded the 4H Club of Morris County to make the rearing of Seeing Eye puppies one of their regular programs. The Seeing Eye agreed to pay food costs of about $5 a month for each dog, and thirty-five puppies were farmed out in 1942. From this modest beginning would grow one of The Seeing Eye's major programs and one later adopted by other guide dog schools.

World War II affected The Seeing Eye in several ways. Debetaz, Weeman, Dickerman, Lee, and Northrup were granted draft deferments, but the kennel men, who also taught obedience, were swept into the armed forces. The kennel maids who replaced them were inadequate to teach obedience, and that had to be added to the workload of the instructors. The war made it impossible to recruit new instructors, and, worst of all, it took Jack Humphrey. In June of 1942, he entered the Coast Guard with the rank of lieutenant commander to organize and run a school for dog trainers in the armed forces.

Jack had worked hard and brilliantly for The Seeing Eye, but it had never occupied his entire horizon. Until 1938, he was on the payroll of Fortunate Fields, which he still visited regularly, and was technically only on loan to

The Seeing Eye. His contributions to the science of genetics were well known, and as distinguished a scientist as Alexis Carrel regarded The Seeing Eye as an unfortunate interruption of Jack's real work. At Fortunate Fields, his scientific methods had raised the percentage of dogs put into service relative to the number bred from 16 to 94 percent, but there were still vast areas of genetic research with dogs to be explored. When Dorothy closed down Fortunate Fields, Jack was shattered. Willi Ebeling recalled, "I never saw a sadder man. Tears rolled out of Jack's eyes. He felt he had only begun."

Confined to The Seeing Eye, he had occupied his restless mind by constantly experimenting with new methods. He was never content. In the year the school graduated more than a hundred dogs for the first time, he devised and put down on paper a scheme of instruction intended to turn out four times that number. His decision to go into the service may well have reflected his craving for a new challenge. By the time he left the service, his principal link with The Seeing Eye, his old friend and former employer, Dorothy Eustis, was in seriously failing health. As Willi Ebeling put it, "After the war, Jack went back to his first love, the west." He settled in Arizona.

Meanwhile, The Seeing Eye had done its part in the war effort. The day after the United States declared war, the board of trustees resolved to provide dogs for all qualified blind veterans, free of charge to either themselves or the federal government, and to offer them preferment on the waiting list. At Seeing Eye expense, Morris Frank went on the road for months at a time visiting army, navy, and veteran's hospitals. He showed films and lectured to doctors, nurses, and staff on the treatment and rehabilitation of blind people. He distributed copies of a booklet Mary Campbell had prepared for The Seeing Eye, *The Newly Blind*. It embodied the school's philosophy of rehabilitation and may have been the most influential piece The Seeing Eye ever produced. Accompanied by his wife, Lois, Morris and Buddy visited a total of ninety-six hospitals, where he conducted extensive interviews with blind veterans. Many of them later came to the school, and by 1950 The Seeing Eye had provided dogs for 163 veterans.

War industry also increased the demand for guide dogs. Starved for manpower, employers were willing to hire handicapped workers as never before. Blind men and women needed dogs to get to their jobs, and by the end of the war some 15 percent of the school's approximately one thousand graduates were working in war-related industries.

The war also stimulated a boom in guide dog schools. In the thirties, Synikin, Weber, another German named Kreimer, and one or two more had trained guide dogs for sale to the blind, but their number was insignificant. In 1939, Leader Dogs for the Blind was founded in Michigan, but it began modestly. A law promising federal funds to underwrite guide dogs for blind veterans produced a rash of new "schools." By 1952, there were twenty-seven of these, nineteen in California alone. Most of them were one- or two-man operations. When the California legislature required the licensing of schools based on blindfold tests in traffic for all trainers, fifteen of the schools evaporated almost overnight. Others were hand-to-mouth operations. But Leader Dogs grew, and so did the newly established Guide Dogs for the Blind, first in Los Gatos and, later, in San Raphael, California.

Willi Ebeling did not think much of the competition. In his view, the small schools were far more interested in raising money than educating dogs. None approached Seeing Eye standards of safety, and none required a financial obligation on the part of the student. Donaldson, who headed Guide Dogs for the Blind, had failed as a Hubbard apprentice in Jack's first class, as had his successor, William Johns. Willi Ebeling did not take them seriously. His main fear was that the slipshod work of one of these schools might result in an accident that would reflect discredit on the guide dog movement as a whole. It never occurred to him that rival schools might one day pose a threat to his own staff.

A more immediate threat was the booming postwar economy. Job security was no longer the adequate recompense for long hours and low wages it had been during the Depression. In 1945, Northrup left the school to go into business. Several promising new apprentices were enrolled, but discontent was brewing under the surface. Agnes Fowler, the trustee who had voluntarily worked in the kennels all through the war, sympathized with the instructors. She urged Willi Ebeling to raise their salaries substantially, but he was adamant. He was duty-bound, he said, to be thrifty with philanthropic dollars, and he pointed out that Debetaz had worked much harder for less pay under more difficult conditions.

Any comparison of the new instructors with either Humphrey or Debetaz was bound to be unfavorable. Jack was a genius. At L'Oeil qui Voit, he once finished a dog in only twelve days and scored 62, just 2 points short of perfect, on the blindfold test. Debe had trained dogs in cities around the country under conditions no instructor had to put up with in Morristown. In Kansas City, he had been attacked on the street by an hysterical woman with two policemen who claimed that the dog he was training was her Fritz. Happily, the dog was a bitch, and he could prove by lifting her forepaws that she was no Fritz. In the White Curtain Hotel in Berkeley, a dog he had medicated for worms failed to respond for thirty-six hours, then emptied in the hotel dining room at lunch hour with 160 guests at table. Debe hustled his blind students into their rooms and fled for the afternoon to let the management cool off before making his apologies. No apologies would have been necessary in the Whippany dining room.

Debe's capacity for work bordered on the superhuman. After completing a class in Denver before Christmas, he received a wire to report to Los Angeles on the morning of January 1 to begin a new class of eight with a string of strange dogs being crated from Morristown. He did so, and in the process managed to meet and fall in love with Lou Dahl, the sister of one of the students. On their honeymoon the following year, he turned over two dogs with students in Gallup, New Mexico. He did countless odd jobs as well. He not only wallpapered the dining room with Gretchen Green, but also constructed beautifully scaled wooden relief maps of Morristown with the streets marked in braille, so that students could trace and learn the routes. There were no challenges in the lives of the new instructors that were not dwarfed into insignificance by comparison with Debetaz's past.

Willi Ebeling's view of The Seeing Eye posed another problem. To him, it was not simply a philanthropy, but a way of life, a religion. He wrote, "The dogs are the soul of our organization. They need to be taught, but at the same time they teach. They drive home the lesson that to be understood is to understand, and because they are the symbol of truth, they demand truth. One must believe this, and one must live it to render the service to which our students are entitled." Willi Ebeling himself believed it, and he expected the instructors to do the same. He worked long hours at a quarter of the salary he could have earned in the business world. So should they. The primary satisfactions of working for The Seeing Eye were not material, but spiritual. His was the philosophy that justified underpaying ministers because they are otherworldly beings who do not seek earthly rewards.

In the end, Agnes Fowler's misgivings were justified. In 1950, Robert Lee, who had a bad back and an academic background in science, left The Seeing Eye for a job in jet engineering. He had been with the school for twelve years. In 1951, Curt Weeman, a veteran of seventeen years, went to work as a draftsman. A few months later, a fourteen-year veteran, Harold Dickerman, and a four-year man, David Evans, also left. In less than two years, The Seeing Eye had lost four instructors with a combined total of forty-seven years of experience. After more than twenty years of recruiting and training apprentices, the lack of an adequate staff of instructors was still The Seeing Eye's Achilles heel.

16

Love in the Lead

Alfreda Galt, who worked on public relations with Marian Jobson, recalled showing Willi Ebeling some copy she had written for the annual report. As he read, he squirmed restlessly in his desk chair. She could see he was uncomfortable. Finally he looked up with a pained expression.

"It seems so proud, don't you know. So proud." He hesitated for a moment, then waved at the walls of his office. "We here are not The Seeing Eye, don't you know? The Seeing Eye is not the staff or this building. The Seeing Eye is the graduates and their dogs out in the field."

Through his extensive correspondence with the graduates, Willi Ebeling was acutely aware of the challenges they faced. Those first walks at home could be a test. John Gates of Artesia, New Mexico, wrote Willi Ebeling of an experience typical of the novice first trying his wings:

> I was approaching the railroad track here about the third week home, when I heard an oncoming train I had not realized was so near. Terror seized my exploding brain as the train bore down upon us, and while my impulse was to break and run, mentally I could hear my instructor shouting, Follow your dog! so follow I did, expecting to be hamburger at any moment. Then I realized the engine had passed in front of us. Dodie and I were still walking briskly and no one was dead. I stopped and planted a big kiss on Dodie's cold nose.

The jealousy of a spouse could wreck the partnership of dog and master. Two weeks after leaving L'Oeil qui Voit, the dog of a French veteran was returned to the Vevey railway station without explanation. It developed that the dog had enabled the old soldier to resume an independent social life. Leaving his wife at home, he had gone to a café to hobnob with his old cronies. Resenting his freedom, the wife had sent the dog back. A similar scenario has been repeated several times at the American Seeing Eye. On one occasion, the wife of a classmate told my wife she liked having a blind husband she could "keep around the house." Three weeks after he graduated, his dog was sent back on the pretext that it was unclean.

The mother of a teenage boy, Miner Clites, was more generous toward his dog, Joy. "One evening he didn't appear for dinner. I finally located him by telephoning around to his friends. When he came home, I sputtered and scolded and said the dog would go back if I had to hunt him for his meals. But sputtering was all, because he got a kick out of it. Joy couldn't go out of his life now. Honestly, I got a lump in my throat, and I got a real thrill out of the fact that he could go out and be late for dinner like other mothers' sons." When Miner Clites returned for his second dog, the gangling 120-pound adolescent had filled out into a young man of 170 pounds who laid it to "being able to get out and exercise after I got Joy."

Family, friends, and the public at large had to be taught to keep hands off a graduate working his dog. Edward Hoffman's friends nearly ruined Helga by pulling him one way while she was trying to lead him another. A dog who is wearing a harness is on duty, working or not, and should never be patted or spoken to. A graduate who had ignored this rule returned to The Seeing Eye during my first class. He had allowed strangers to pat his dog so indiscriminately that she continually whined for attention and was a nuisance in public places. At the school he stubbornly disclaimed any responsibility for having spoiled his dog and was sent home without her.

It is hard to convince Americans that they ought not

pat other people's dogs, but Jack Humphrey made his point with a woman on the Whippany bus. After she leaned down to pat a dog he was training, he reached over and patted her knee. Stiffening, she gasped, "How dare you! You don't know me."

"No," Jack shot back, "and you don't know my dog."

Occasionally graduates try to work under conditions that are too much even for a well-adjusted dog. A young woman who lived in Brooklyn took a job in Trenton that required her to commute nearly three hours each way. Her dog became extremely nervous, and the school advised her to find work closer to home. Agnes Stone, a diminutive teacher of braille, was paired with a shepherd who was too strong for her. It pulled right out of her grasp to chase squirrels. Miss Stone was retrained with a Weimaraner better suited to her size and strength. Rosa Buchko reported a problem with her dog that defied analysis by long distance, and Debetaz was sent to watch her work. Half a block from her apartment, her dog had to pass an organ grinder with a monkey. In the wink of an eye, the monkey was on the dog's back, to the distress of the dog, the mystification of Rosa, and the amusement of the passing yahoos. Subsequently Rosa was retrained with a more spirited dog, one who knew how to get a monkey off its back.

Several times the school had reports of graduates begging with their dogs. Nearly all of these were false. The beggars were not Seeing Eye graduates. Some were not even blind. But a Seeing Eye dog had to be taken from a graduate caught begging in Philadelphia, and on another occasion Morris Frank reclaimed the dog of a young woman graduate attending a school for beggars in Chicago. Twice the threat of recalling dogs spurred their owners to find gainful employment.

Willi Ebeling regularly received letters and phone calls from students having difficulties. Harold Rosenthal phoned one day in a panic because his Prancer refused to walk down a certain street. Willi concluded that he must have corrected her unjustly on that street and now she was avoiding it in the fear it might happen again. Rosenthal wrote him later, "Your suggestion was that I walk down that street and, if necessary, get down on my knees and try to talk her out of it, and do you know, Mr. Ebeling, I literally did just that—with success."

With his passionate faith in dogs, it was emotionally impossible for Willi Ebeling to admit that they were ever in the wrong. The master must always be at fault somehow. Today, the school admits that dogs are not infallible, and sometimes the problem may lie in the particular personal chemistry of dog and master, for which neither is at fault. Dogs have been known to suffer psychosomatic illness from mismatching. When recalled to the school and paired with different masters, their health problems disappear, while their former masters have no difficulty adjusting to new dogs.

What can be difficult for masters to understand is that every dog is a distinct individual. All of my dogs have been shepherds, and all were taught to do the same job by the same methods, yet all have been endowed with their distinctive personalities and idiosyncrasies. Because the relationship between dog and master is so intimate, these individual differences can be troublesome. Debetaz used to warn students that comparing a second dog to the first was as dangerous as comparing a second spouse to the first, but it can be hard to avoid. Minnie, my first dog, was a hard puller and so fast that we were never passed on the Princeton campus except by someone running. My second dog, Wick, ambled along at a slower pace with less pull. It took time, patience, and concentration to get used to the change. Some graduates seem unable to make the emotional investment required to achieve full partnership with their dogs. Yet this investment, the ability to give fully of yourself to your dog, to confide your whole trust and to show your concern and affection, is even more important than physical coordination and orientation. Emil Buchko,

Rosa's husband, dwarfed in stature and so lame when he came to the school that he depended on his dog's strength to pull him up a curb, proved to be an excellent worker and wrote the following letter:

> During the war I was commuting to New York City and working in a defense plant. I was coming up the subway stairs from the Long Island subway to Grand Central Station proper when a man offered me assistance. I said no thank you. I had just a few minutes to walk through the station to make my train. Going down the first ramp, another man approached me and said, "May I assist you, sir?"
>
> Not pausing to reply because of time, I said, "No, thank you. I know where I'm going."
>
> This did not seem to satisfy the two men following me. I could hear one say to the other, "I wonder how he knows where he's going."
>
> I turned my head slightly, while still walking with Gulpin and said, "Don't worry. My dog reads the signs."
>
> Little did I realize these men would take me so seriously. When I reached the main concourse of the lower level, Gulpin turned into a gate marked Track 116. Behind me I heard one man mutter, "Well I'll be g— d_____!"

There seems no limit to what a well-adjusted dog can do for its master. On a second trip to San Francisco, Debe was mystified to find that the dogs of his first class never made a mistake in boarding the correct trolley cars to take their masters to and from work. He concluded that they identified them by smells peculiar to the quarters of the city through which they ran. When my wife and I were unsure where we had left the car in a huge parking lot, I would simply follow Sarja, who went straight to the car with no hesitation.

On the occasion of his retirement from The Seeing Eye after twenty-five years, Willi Ebeling received literally hundreds of letters from graduates. Passages from them will give an idea of the extraordinary variety in the lives of

Seeing Eye graduates and their dogs. Maxine Hansen, whose job took her all over the state of Wisconsin, wrote, "In our life of almost continual travel, Pansy never forgets which is our hotel room nor where the hotel is when we have left it. Wherever we have left our things is home, and she knows where home is. The lapse of time means nothing. Having been there once, she can recognize the place any length of time later. I wish someone could tell me how a dog can remember that way."

Munroe Fox's dog allowed him to enjoy nature in the country around Albuquerque. "Missy has made it possible for me to spend long quiet hours alone fishing in some lake, secure in the knowledge that I have a faithful pair of eyes to guide me back to camp and that I need ask the aid of no man to enjoy the quiet and solitude of our lovely mountains." Thousands of miles away in New York City, Harman Gainer lived in anything but solitude. "Sarge knows every subway entrance and exit that I use in my daily work as a salesman. He finds a seat for me in the subway and the buses that I use each day. He knows at my command when to go to the change booth and when to go through the turnstiles of the subway station. He knows every building and office that I go into."

Fran was a great help to Jennings Lattimer in his work as a piano tuner. "We have been visiting all the 130 Pittsburgh Public Schools periodically, keeping their pianos in good repair. Fran soon learned to know her pianos, too. When I walk into a school room and she gets her eyes on a piano, she takes me straight to it. This is a big help, for we often go early in the morning before the teachers arrive, as that is when we can work without being disturbed. As soon as I begin putting my tools together, she is up and ready to go. In the school wash room, she takes me straight to the wash bowl. I can leave my coat in one room, go to several other rooms to work, and then when I tell her, 'Get my coat,' she will almost invariably go straight to it."

Ralph Stewart from Salt Lake City felt some uncertainty about Rollo in the beginning. "I was worried about having Rollo guide me and my wife, who is also blind, uptown for the first time, but he did a super job of taking us, and he is working out beautifully. The only trouble I have with the big lug, he loves stealing kiddies' ice cream cones. He is so big that he sticks his head over their shoulders and slurp, it is gone, all unknown to me until I hear a scream, and I have to pay for his fun. But he wags his tail and is so pleased with himself that I haven't the heart to scold him."

Henry and Mary Driskell, a blind couple from Chicago, each had a dog. She wrote Willi Ebeling, "If you could be here in Chicago when the four of us start out from home, you would see Mr. Driskell and Muffer speeding on a way ahead, and Una and me coming along as fast as we can. We're still slower than they are. Of course, Muffer always stops at the end of each block and looks back to see if Una is coming all right. Folks tell us it looks as if she were looking out for her little sister. In our home, Una and Muffer would put on one of their boxing matches for you. They get out in the middle of the room and tumble and box each other and expect much praise and rooting from their audience. I might add that they do stop the show instantly when we give the command."

When Mrs. John Stern had her baby, Val became more than a guide. "For instance, when the baby was still quite tiny and lying in her bassinet, she would throw her rattle to the floor. Without a word from me, Val would walk over to the rattle, pick it up, place it in my hand, curl up and go back to sleep until she again heard the rattle hit the floor. The baby is now a little over a year old. Val picks up toys that are out of her reach and takes them to her."

Dogs have adapted themselves to a variety of professions. C. L. Finch's Trooper made himself at home in the courtroom:

After graduating from The Seeing Eye, Trooper and I opened a law office in Antigo, Wisconsin. One day when I was presenting a case, the judge interrupted me. "Mr. Finch, all during this trial, your dog has been sitting beside you holding a glove, a dollar bill and a document in his mouth. Do these things have any bearing on the case?" I explained that Trooper was only doing his job, picking up after his untidy master.

Trooper almost had his own day in court. I had a call from the sheriff one morning. "Mr. Finch, is Trooper in your office?" I thought he was. After looking under my desk, I replied, "His leash is here, but he isn't."

"Well," came the dry voice of the sheriff, "he's up here at the county jail. I just booked him on a count of lewd and lascivious behavior on the courthouse lawn. He wants you to spring him and his girl friend."

Dr. Jack Wilcox got his Ph.D. in clinical psychiatry at Michigan. He comments:

King's calmness and imperturbability are his outstanding traits. This has turned out to be a very fortunate circumstance in my work. I have worked with him in mental hospitals where I might at any time run into disturbed patients who make all sorts of approaches to him. Even when their behavior is what might be considered threatening by most dogs, King pays absolutely no attention and calmly concentrates on taking me where I want to go. He also makes himself inconspicuous when a patient comes to the office, and only once in all my experience have I had a patient sufficiently frightened by him to make it necessary to put him in another room. Very often his presence is a definite contribution to a patient who finds it difficult to talk. Almost all of them have a dog story that comes to mind and furnishes a beginning topic for conversation.

In the IBM laboratory in upstate New York, Dr. Glaser's Pal found his preoccupation with computers boring. "I am sure she sometimes thinks human beings are demented creatures. One particular activity that is necessary from time to time is the plugging of wires into the control panel of the IBM machine. The first time I occupied myself with this ridiculous conduct, Pal became perturbed. It seemed futile to her to spend so much time placing the ends of wires in small holes in a useless piece of plastic. However, her training and good manners came through, and now if I drop a wire, she will pick it up for me and put it in my lap."

The key to all these adaptations is the praise that makes it clear to the dog that their masters appreciate what they are doing. Work then becomes a pleasure. Don Faith reported Otis's reaction to construction work in Chicago:

> They now have the Midway torn up, and they are installing lights at the intersection. This makes it necessary for Otis to make a detour which the average person would consider a bother. Otis, however, looks forward to this detour work and regards it as a challenge which he truly enjoys meeting. Whenever he comes to the barricade, he pulls with that sure steady eagerness of one who enjoys his work, yet knows its every intricate detail. He then has to pause to peer around a tar truck to see if anything is coming. After we listen to the traffic, I give the command of forward and we proceed across the street.
>
> Because of the difficulty of the barricade plus a blocking truck, I give a strong reward. Sometimes this is taken by Otis as a matter of course, but every once in a while he has to stop and lift his big shaggy head up to my right hand and lick it, as if to say, "Aren't I the smartest person you ever saw!"

We graduates have all felt the contagion of our dogs' pleasure in a challenge. On her first trip through Philadelphia's Thirtieth Street Station, my Hessa seemed to swell with pride. I had the distinct impression she was walking down the exact center of the great room, looking from side to side with regal interest at the peasantry. An earlier dog, Sally, spent five years with me in the solitary occupation of a writer before I took a job that required me to fly 50,000 miles a year. One two-week trip took us to Pittsburgh, Cincinnati, Chicago, Omaha, San Francisco, Portland, Seattle, Los Angeles, Minneapolis, St. Paul, and New York. I was in a different hotel almost every night. That meant that Sally's "parks" were constantly changing, but she ate, emptied, found her way in and out of hotels, elevators, restaurants, and offices, followed passenger service representatives through airports as though she had a radar fix on them, and was always ready to wag her tail at a word of praise.

Genevieve Wiley described her Rene's response to a different sort of challenge:

> Four years ago the city was making extensive repairs for a number of blocks along our main thoroughfare here in Pasadena, putting in a complete new set of pipes. After two weeks the day came when I was to have my hair done. I heard machinery in the distance, but decided to go on.
>
> I soon found myself right in the midst of the work, which was plenty noisy. Rene was on the outside, the side of the machinery, but aside from slowing up a little, she kept steadily on her way. One of the workmen shouted that the dog was doing fine, but I noticed that she kept pushing me very close to the buildings, almost against them. When I reached the shop and mentioned the way we had come, everyone was simply horrified. All along the block where Rene had kept me so close to the buildings was just a narrow strip of sidewalk. The rest was a great hole where pipes were being laid.

Several graduates have reported narrow escapes. Albert Korp lived five miles outside Grand Junction, Colorado. "I decided one day to go into town and while walking along a country road, Queenie turned sharp, took me across the ditch and never stopped until we were against the fence. By that time I heard something coming down the road. It was about fifty head of rodeo horses that were being driven by some men I knew. They told me they saw what happened. Without the training of Queenie, I would have been trampled by the horses, because they could not stop them or get to me in any way."

Ray Coffey of Lenore, South Carolina, had two close calls with Pram:

> One day I went up to Collettsville in Caldwell County to visit an uncle. Pram and I got off the bus on the main highway and took a road leading to my uncle's home. When we got to a bridge over a stream of water on this road, Pram stopped. I talked to him, but he would not go a step further. I knew something was wrong.
>
> We turned back and went to a store nearby where I had a cousin working. The cousin took us in his truck back to the bridge. He found that two planks were missing, making a space wide enough for me to fall into the water below.
>
> In 1952, Pram showed an unusual alertness for my safety. We were riding home in a bus. Without any warning, Pram jumped from the seat and started with me for the door. When we reached the door, the driver announced the bus was on fire and ordered all passengers off. Pram and I were the first passengers off the burning bus because he was the first to know the danger.

City life could be dangerous, too. George Cohen and Bambi were caught at a busy intersection in Montreal at a time when some bank robbers were trying to make a getaway:

> We were crossing a street at a traffic light when some shots rang out. At first I thought it was some leftover fireworks, but I felt Bambi freeze against my legs, blocking my path. I realized something serious was wrong when she took the lead firmly and jaywalked as fast as she could through the cars across to the other corner and into a doorway. I knew it must be serious if she would break one of the strictest rules of her training by cutting through traffic. Her quick thinking and pulling me into that doorway almost assuredly saved me from what might have been serious injury. At almost the

exact spot where we had been standing, a Royal Canadian Mounted Police pursuing the robbers was shot and killed.

With her Heidi, Ethel Stevens operated a candy stand in a New Haven hospital. On her way home one evening, she was stopped and told of a shooting in a theater and that one of the bandits was hiding in a building not far down the street.

> My first thought was to return to the hospital, but I learned that all streets in that direction were blocked while the police looked for the second bandit around that way. I had no alternative but to command, "Heidi, forward!" Heidi appeared to be thinking for a minute or two. Then she turned, retraced her steps to Broad Street, turned left and waited for a policeman to allow us to cross. We then proceeded for a full block to High Street. Here, amid police whistles, automobiles, and pedestrians, she turned a sharp left and worked her way two blocks and then right in the direction of home. When we passed the city's leading hotel, a shot was fired. One of the bandits had killed himself. People and police were everywhere, but Heidi walked steadily forward to the bus stop. By the time we reached the bus stop she was sniffling hard and rubbing her face against my coat. My eyes were watering and burning, too, for we had walked two blocks through where tear bombs were used. Until now, Heidi was most calm, but now that we were safe from danger, she began to tremble a great deal. All evening she was very nervous, but the next morning she was as usual.

Edward LeMoine wrote a letter printed in the September 1964 issue of *The Guide:*

> Lina and I had just boarded the bus when the rain started. Thirty minutes later, we stepped off the bus into several inches of water. By the time we had gone three blocks, it was up to my ankles on the sidewalk and nearly up to my knees crossing the street, as the water poured down from higher ground.

Crossing the third street, the water came almost to my hips. Lina, it seemed to me, must actually be swimming, but she slowed down perceptibly at the point where she calculated the curb should be and, so help me, it was. We went another block in water up to Lina's chest, and she again found the curb down, but only after she showed me a low-hanging tree branch. I lifted it, and we passed under unscathed. We crossed the street in somewhat unorthodox fashion, angling to the left away from the intersection and almost directly to the house of my friend, where I was expected for dinner. When we reached the porch, I leaned down to hug and praise her, and she was all over me, licking my face and emitting little squeals of joy. All through our ordeal I had talked to her in a calm voice and encouraged her frequently with "Hopp, hopp. That's a good girl!" We knew we needed each other to get through safely. With this kind of understanding and love, we could go any place.

The point of all these stories is not their melodrama, but the love and understanding between dog and master, the sense of needing each other. Lisa and Heidi and Bambi were heartened by knowing that their humans trusted them, spoke to them calmly and encouragingly, and followed the signals they gave through their harness handles. People do not go to The Seeing Eye expecting to be rescued from rodeo horses, burning buses, bank robbers, or flash floods, but for freedom of movement. Jeanne Pechtel remarked:

People are so often disappointed when they expectantly ask if Nellie has ever saved my life and I answer no. Oh, of course, she has got me out of the way of backing trucks, but it is for the freedom to be in such situations that I am grateful for Nellie. A guide dog's business, after all, is not rescue, but safety maintenance. It is the certainty that she will keep me out of situations from which I would need rescuing that makes it possible for me to cross un-stoplighted busy streets, to catch an el in a rained-on rush-hour mob, or for that matter to run in fluffy new snow.

There is an emotional support in the partnership with a dog that is unquantifiable. In January of 1942, when I sought readmission to Princeton University with my first dog, Minnie, we met unexpected opposition. I'd thought the matter had been settled before I went to The Seeing Eye, but now the college authorities were telling me that I ought to spend six months to two years in a school for the blind first. They wanted me to learn to be blind. I pled my case passionately, but I am not sure I would have prevailed if I had been pleading only for myself. I was pleading for Minnie, too, or, rather, for our partnership. We needed the meaningful challenge of my return to college. My deep-seated conviction of this was my strongest argument.

Other graduates have experienced the same positive reinforcement. Gabe Fuqua was discontentedly running a candy stand in Jackson, Mississippi, when he heard a radio interview of Hamilton Jenkins in Chicago. Jenkins, a former middleweight boxer, was returning to Denver from The Seeing Eye with his second dog. This inspired Fuqua to go to Morristown for his own dog, Xon, and that led him still further. He wrote Willi Ebeling:

> Xon and I went to school this summer at the College of Swedish Masseurs in Chicago. I had never been to a place as large as Chicago in my life before. A friend wanted to know if I'd be afraid, and I said, 'Afraid of what? Xon and I can go anywhere anyone else can go.' So off we go to Chicago. We didn't know anyone there, but before three nights were up, Xon and I had many a new friend. Now I have a good job at the Jackson Y.M.C.A. Health Club as a masseur, but I know in my heart that, if it had not been for Xon, I would never have had the courage to make the grade.

Xon would not let Gabe Fuqua stop there. As he recalled later, "Xon lit a fire in me and opened new doors I only dreamed about before. I went back to school and completed college and law school. Now I am a member of the Mississippi Bar Association and a justice of the peace."

The courage and confidence that Xon's love inspired led Fuqua from behind a candy stand to membership in the Mississippi Bar as surely as her harness handle guided him through the streets of Jackson. The love of a Seeing Eye dog is a pearl beyond price, and so is the love for a Seeing Eye dog. It has suffused the hearts and minds of thousands of men and women and given them the courage to do what would have been impossible without it. Their mutual love leads them both. That love is the heart of The Seeing Eye.

IV

SECOND GROWTH

17
A New Approach

"I knew I could never replace Uncle Willi," George Werntz recalled years later. "Gosh, no one could. He was one of a kind. But Henry Colgate thought we needed a new approach."

Henry Colgate became president of The Seeing Eye on the death of Dorothy Eustis in the fall of 1946. It was he who had brought in George Werntz to replace Willi Ebeling. A few years earlier, fate seemed to be preparing a different successor.

Dorothy's younger son, Harrison, had taken an active interest in The Seeing Eye at a young age. When the school was reincorporated in New Jersey in 1932, he was both an incorporator and a trustee at eighteen. Before that, he had worked with dogs at L'Oeil qui Voit. Later, he learned to work dogs under blindfold. After he graduated from Harvard in 1936, he took a job working on membership enrollments with Marian Jobson of Hartwell, Jobson, and Kibbee. Both she and Debe believed Harrison was being groomed for a position at The Seeing Eye, ultimately as Willi Ebeling's successor. He was highly intelligent, personable, and sensitive. He would have been the logical choice, but in the spring of 1938, while working for Hartwell, Jobson, and Kibbee, he contracted a fatal illness. Because of Dorothy's Christian Science, it was never precisely diagnosed. Instead, Dorothy accompanied him on his last trip to Europe that summer. He died in Switzerland in September.

It was a terrible blow for Dorothy. When she came back to America, instead of returning to the Gate House in

Whippany she retreated to her New York apartment. She had probably intended to withdraw from The Seeing Eye in any case. The board of trustees had been expanded, and since 1936 Henry Colgate had been serving as chairman. Her active leadership was no longer crucial, but if Harrison had lived he would have provided a strong emotional tie. As it was, her withdrawal to New York removed a vital presence from the grounds at Whippany.

It was the first of a series of changes. The newly married Debetazes moved into Dorothy's Gate House apartment. When Jack Humphrey went into the Coast Guard, the Myroses took over the ground floor. Dickson Hartwell, who had just completed *Dogs against Darkness*, the first history of The Seeing Eye, was off to the war, and Marian Jobson, who carried on the firm, was elected vice president.

Following the war, there were further changes. Aunt Mary Campbell retired in 1945. The death of Dorothy Eustis in 1946 virtually coincided with the elevation of Ibby Hutchinson to vice president of the Division for the Blind and Debe Debetaz to vice president of the Training Division.

The income from memberships was so much in excess of expenditures that Marian Jobson was instructed to slacken the pace of enrollment, but legacies continued to swell the school's net worth. It surpassed $2,500,000 in 1948 and continued to grow in spite of several capital expenses. New training kennels had been constructed on the Whippany property in 1945. In 1948, the breeding stock was moved into new kennels on a hundred-acre tract purchased in nearby Mendham. The segregation of the breeding stock was designed to free it from the contagious diseases that handicapped the program at Whippany. John Weagley, who had been specially educated on Seeing Eye scholarships at Rutgers, took charge of the breeding farm.

In 1950, the school opened a women's wing. There had been a relative scarcity of women in the thirties. Now they were a growing minority, and "the harem" gave the school the capacity to house 240 students a year. A record 187 students graduated in 1950, but the most important event of the year was the appointment of Willi Ebeling's assistant and eventual successor.

After graduating from Colgate in 1933, George Werntz taught for four years at Irving, a private boys' school in Tarrytown, New York. When Henry Colgate inquired at the university for a likely undergraduate to act as companion and athletic coach for his sons during the summer, young George had taken the job and spent several summers with the Colgates at Lake Placid. In 1937, when the Irving School closed down, he got a job in the admissions office at Colgate. He became its director just a month before being called into the navy in 1942, where he spent three and a half years as personnel officer on the staff of the commander of the Air Force Pacific Fleet. Returning to Colgate after the war as a lieutenant in the Naval Reserve, he became assistant dean.

In physique, background, mind-set, and style, George Werntz was very unlike the man he was to succeed. Willi was short, slight, and wiry. George was tall, broad, and muscular. Both were conservative, but whereas Willi's mind was intuitive and mercurial, George's was rational and pedestrian in the sense that it moved logically, a step at a time. Willi had come from the business world. George's background was largely academic. It was natural for him to call Debetaz "dean of the faculty," and Ibby Hutchinson "director of admissions and dean of students." Willi Ebeling ruled The Seeing Eye with the religious zeal of the abbot of a medieval monastery. George Werntz had the air of the congenial headmaster of a boys' boarding school.

He began work on August 1, 1950, and spent nearly three and a half years as Willi's assistant. Under Debetaz, he learned the technique of guide dog instruction and personally trained two dogs and adjusted them to a pair of students. In Marian Jobson's New York office, he worked on every phase of education, extension, and membership enrollment. By the time he took over on January 1, 1954, he had a thorough grounding in all the school's programs as they had been in the past, but Henry Colgate was calling for a new approach.

George described it this way: "Willi used to say that if we built a better mouse trap, the world would beat a path to our door. Mr. Colgate thought we should be improving the path ourselves." This was basically a matter of public relations, and The Seeing Eye had three problem areas.

The first was the attitude of workers for the blind toward guide dogs. Willi Ebeling had long ago made peace with Herbert Immeln at the Lighthouse, and as Seeing Eye graduates rose to positions of importance in various agencies, the school had won friends. But there were still many workers who were hostile for one reason or another. Blind people who went to The Seeing Eye came back changed. They left sheltered workshops to take better-paying jobs in industry or business. With their newfound freedom, they had less need of the agencies, and workers did not like feeling unneeded. Many counselors secretly feared, disliked, or distrusted dogs and advised their clients against them. Others envied The Seeing Eye's spectacular financial success and minimized its achievements.

A second problem was the continuing proliferation of guide dog schools. Leader Dogs for the Blind in Rochester, Michigan, and Guide Dogs for the Blind in San Raphael, California, were becoming well established, but there were a number of others, frequently one-man operations, hand-to-mouth affairs that confused the public and produced substandard dogs. Returning graduates reported that, after the deaths of their old dogs appeared in the papers, representatives of other schools wrote or telephoned to offer them replacements free of charge and even promised to pay full transportation.

More pressing than either the hostility of agency workers or inferior guide dog schools was what George Werntz labeled "The Seeing Eye's No. 1 public relations problem."

In a memorandum to the board on August 1, 1954, he drew attention to the increasingly embarrassing public awareness of the school's net worth. It had surpassed $4,500,000 in the previous fiscal year and was growing annually because annual income exceeded expenditures by a wide margin. Under the circumstances, it was difficult to justify asking for membership contributions. The National Information Bureau, a private nonprofit corporation that monitored philanthropic fund-raising for interested contributors was becoming critical.

One way of decreasing the surplus was to increase expenditures. The school hired a resident nurse to monitor the health of the growing number of diabetics attending classes. George also arranged to have a doctor come to the school to examine diabetic students on the first or second day of class. But expenses of this kind were a mere drop in the bucket, and Werntz proposed to the board several options involving sizable outlays of money. One was the establishing of a program to make grants to related philanthropies. The second was the opening of a branch school in another part of the country. But it would be foolish to open a branch for which there was no need. There were many different estimates of the number of potential users of guide dogs, but there was no reliable information on the subject.

In true academic fashion, Werntz proposed that The Seeing Eye use a substantial part of its surplus to finance a scientific survey of the potential demand for guide dogs, to be conducted by a competent outside organization. The board of trustees approved, and in due course the Columbia School of Social Work was chosen to do the research. It planned to assign a team of social workers to conduct personal interviews with a sample population of 500 blind men and women. It would cost some $250,000 and would take seven years to complete. Pending the outcome, the board would make no decision regarding a branch school.

In the interim, George devoted himself to improving

relations with other agencies. Unlike Uncle Willi, who had loathed meetings, George was a good mixer. He took an active part in meetings of the American Association of Workers for the Blind, where he enjoyed the old-school-tie spirit of the annual reunion breakfast with Seeing Eye graduates and their dogs. With Ibby Hutchinson he attended other conferences, where he made a good impression on several agency executives. With some justification they had felt that Uncle Willi looked down on them.

In 1956, George's efforts bore fruit. On the recommendation of the Texas Commission for the Blind, a committee studying the advisability of founding a guide dog school in Texas came to The Seeing Eye. George described the Columbia study in progress, expressed his doubts as to the need for another school, and pointed out that, since The Seeing Eye now paid all travel costs in excess of $50 per student, Morristown was within the reach of blind Texans. The committee was dissuaded from founding another school.

At about the same time, a New York legislative investigation of charity rackets exposed the fact that a professional fund-raiser had collected $57,000 for an organization called Guiding Eyes for the Blind; it had never supplied a guide for a blind person, never trained a dog for guide work, and never employed a guide dog instructor. Scandals of this sort hurt The Seeing Eye by association. More serious harm was to come. Behind George Werntz's back Guiding Eyes succeeded in hiring away Edward Fouser, an instructor with eleven years' experience at The Seeing Eye and junior only to Debetaz and Myrose. Of nearly seventy-five men apprenticed over the years, only six now remained at The Seeing Eye. Six others were working for rival organizations.

On April 25, 1956, the school experienced a major personality change. Precisely on the twenty-eighth anniversary of his arrival at Vevey in 1928, Morris Frank retired from The Seeing Eye which he had helped to found and of which he was a living symbol. From the outset he had served as its roving ambassador, traveling literally hundreds of thousands of miles across the United States and Canada. Since his marriage in 1942, his wife, Lois, had generally accompanied him. In 1954, they had completed a three-year program of travel, interviewing 300 ophthalmologists and a majority of Seeing Eye graduates in all forty-eight states and Canada. They had been on the road for eighteen of thirty-six months. Enough was enough. Morris felt he had done all he could for the school. It was time to move on. As he had once demonstrated that a guide dog was a safe and effective travel aid, he now planned to prove that a blind man could be a success in business. At forty-eight, he launched his own insurance agency in an office at 10 Park Place North in the center of Morristown.

To succeed Morris, George chose a very different sort of person. The thirties had required a brash young rebel like Morris to break down the barriers, but times had changed. The need now was for diplomacy. Robert Whitstock was a graduate of Hamilton College and Harvard Law who had received his first dog, Nesta, in 1952. Bob was soft-spoken and articulate, clear-thinking and deliberate. He inspired such respect in his fellow workers that they ultimately elected him president of the American Association of Workers for the Blind.

A valuable supplement to Bob Whitstock's fieldwork was underwritten by another financial windfall. A legacy provided a sizable fund for Seeing Eye publications, and in 1957 it underwrote a revised and handsomely illustrated version of *The Newly Blind* under the title, *If Blindness Occurs*. It was widely circulated to hospital staffs, social and rehabilitation counselors, and other groups whom Bob addressed in the course of his travels.

In the fall of 1957, George supervised an innovation in alumni relations. Members of the staff made a long-playing Christmas record mailed to all graduates. Familiar voices sent season's greetings and reported recent developments with an immediacy of impact far beyond that of any written message.

The Christmas record was a triumphant success, the first of many, but in October, while it was still in its planning stage, George had word of the death of Henry Colgate. It terminated twenty years of productive service and leadership. George was saddened by the loss of his longtime friend and patron, but he was fortunate in the election of his successor. James Carey, a vice president of the Bank of New York, had been The Seeing Eye's treasurer for many years. He assumed the presidency at a critical stage in its public relations problem.

The National Information Bureau had become strident in its objections to an organization with assets now in excess of $10,000,000 that persisted in raising funds for its annual operating budget. Jim Carey and George Werntz proposed to appease the N.I.B. and court public favor with a two-pronged solution. The Seeing Eye would establish a program of grants to philanthropies in related fields and extend all memberships for one year without asking for contributions. To several conservative financiers on the board, this seemed fiscal madness, and it took all of Jim Carey's persuasiveness to win their approval. The grants program was inaugurated with a gift of $30,000 to the Retina Foundation, working to prevent blindness, and The Seeing Eye membership was informed that, as of October 1, 1959, no contributions would be needed for the year ahead.

The response to this unprecedented action bordered on the ecstatic. Letters poured in, congratulating The Seeing Eye on its enlightened policy and promising renewed support whenever it was needed. This public approbation and the legacies that continued to increase the school's net worth thoroughly convinced the board. On June 1, 1959, it voted to extend memberships without contributions indefinitely.

The abandonment of membership enrollments cost The Seeing Eye more than dollars. There had been an exhilarating ésprit de corps among the network of volunteer fund-raisers across the country. They had loved working for The Seeing Eye, and they missed it. The Jobson office sought to keep their interest and enthusiasm alive by mailing copies of the school's quarterly newsletter, *The Guide,* to the entire membership of 15,000. On the positive side, the cessation of fund-raising mollified agencies for the blind that had envied The Seeing Eye, and the grants program transformed the school from a rival to a potential source of support.

To improve relations with other guide dog schools, George Werntz had taken a step that would have been unthinkable for Willi Ebeling. Uncle Willi had encountered so many unscrupulous opportunists and downright frauds in the guide dog movement that he was highly suspicious. For him, former Seeing Eye instructors came under two headings. Either they had failed to meet Seeing Eye standards and were incompetent, or they had gone over to the enemy and were traitors. George had a different perspective. "Having been in the educational field, where we had things like the Headmasters' Association and meetings where we could let down our hair and exchange ideas, it always seemed very strange to me that there was no framework for cooperation among the various guide dog schools."

The preliminary findings of the survey on the demand for dog guides had given him food for thought. It indicated that the primary reservoir for guide dog users was only about 1% of the legally blind population. There were an estimated 3,270 persons who combined sufficient motivation with the physical capacity to learn to use guide dogs successfully. Of this number, only about one in eight, or 425 persons, could be expected to apply for dogs within the next year. The Seeing Eye, Leader Dogs for the Blind, and Guide Dogs for the Blind, the three major schools, had adequate facilities to supply this population. From George's point of view, therefore, these three schools should cooperate in every way to improve standards, expand their programs, and discourage the creation of new schools or the continuation of those that were substandard.

In 1958, at the initiative and expense of The Seeing Eye, the leadership of Guide Dogs for the Blind and The Seeing Eye met for a two-day seminar in Denver. Later, George arranged for a similar conference with Leader Dogs in Michigan. In neither case did the schools come to anything like a complete meeting of the minds, but an avenue of communication had been opened.

The Demand for Dog Guides by Samuel Finestone, Irving Lukoff, and Martin Whiteman was published in 1960, but The Seeing Eye was familiar with its contents long before then. In addition to the primary reservoir of dog users, there was a secondary reservoir of some thirty-four hundred people who possessed the mental and physical qualifications, but lacked the necessary motivation to use a guide dog. The study revealed that there was a good deal of misinformation about guide dogs among nonusers. As a result, George Werntz decided to put more emphasis on the education of potential dog users and their counselors. In August 1959 he hired a second field representative to supplement the work of Bob Whitstock. Norma Farrar was an extremely attractive, bright, and capable young graduate of the University of New Hampshire who had received her first dog in 1953.

To provide television and radio exposure, Marian Jobson Associates arranged for the taping and filming of a number of public service announcements emphasizing the practical value, public acceptance, and availability of Seeing Eye dogs. Their effectiveness was proved by a marked increase in requests for information about The Seeing Eye from potential applicants. The Jobson office prepared a digest of *The Demand for Dog Guides* and distributed thousands of copies to better business bureaus, chambers of commerce, and rehabilitation agencies. It emphasized that no new guide dog schools were needed and made clear what the school had been stressing ever since Dorothy Eustis reported to the World Congress and AAWB in 1931: that guide dogs were not for every blind person and that The Seeing Eye had no desire to monopolize the field.

George Werntz's new approach was clearly illustrated in The Seeing Eye's relationship to mobility instructors. The first systematic study of cane travel had occurred during World War II. Dr. Richard E. Hoover had designed a light aluminum cane long enough to enable the user to swing it from side to side, making certain of safe clearance for each foot as it came forward. Hoover developed methods for teaching the use of his cane, but for some years there was no uniform system of instruction. In 1961, Boston College established the first program for mobility instructors to teach the Hoover cane and other travel techniques to the blind. Western Michigan University followed suit the next year. Soon courses in mobility instruction, or peripatology, would be available in ten colleges or universities, but George Werntz did not wait. He realized at once that graduates from Boston College would go out to teach mobility training at rehabilitation centers and schools in various parts of the country. Now was the time to acquaint them with The Seeing Eye. In 1962, The Seeing Eye paid all expenses to have three Boston College groups, a total of sixteen students with their instructors, spend two nights and a day in Morristown observing a class in action. Seven students from Western Michigan visited The Seeing Eye on the same basis in the same year. From that time forward, The Seeing Eye annually organized and underwrote workshops for mobility instructors from each of the growing number of college programs.

At these workshops, The Seeing Eye did not proselytize or vaunt the superiority of the dog to the cane. *The Demand for Dog Guides* had made it clear that only a small percentage of the blind population could become dog users. The guide dog posed no threat to the cane. As a result, there was no tension. The workshops stimulated a new appreciation of guide dogs, and in time mobility instructors were referring qualified students to The Seeing Eye.

In developing a new approach, George Werntz made a significant contribution to The Seeing Eye. He lacked Willi Ebeling's intensity and his incandescent faith in "The Truth" the dogs represented. Under George, there was no longer the sense of being engaged on a religious crusade, but it was impossible to maintain crusading zeal indefinitely. George's style was more relaxed, less despotic than Willi's, Jack's, or Dorothy's. Their methods had worked in the thirties, but they were no longer appropriate in the fifties. As The Seeing Eye entered the sixties, George was making plans for the most ambitious undertaking of his tenure, but it would once again expose the school's Achilles heel.

18
A Better Mousetrap

The thirty-third annual report of The Seeing Eye held two special features that contrasted sharply. One was a moving tribute to Willi Ebeling, who had died on December 12, 1961, just thirty years and ten days from the frantic move into The Seeing Eye's first home of its own on Whippany Road. The other was an exuberant column that looked forward to leaving that home.

A new building was much to be desired. What with renovations and additions, the old plant incorporated seven different furnaces in its antiquated heating system. The Victorian structure was not fireproof, and the thought of dogs and students trapped on the second floor was a nightmare. The training kennels had been outgrown. The office staff was cramped for space.

In 1960, Jim Carey had appointed a long-range planning committee of three trustees. The following year, the committee engaged Francis Comstock, a Princeton architect, as a consultant. Later, Comstock was chosen as architect for the new building. At first, the committee thought of building on the old grounds, but the offer of $250,000 for the school property by the neighboring Bell Laboratories was an incentive to move. The committee explored a number of sites before settling on the Kemie Estate, a tract of 120 acres on the Washington Valley Road between Morristown and Mendham. In August 1963, the school agreed to pay $250,000 for the property. Since this was the amount Bell Laboratories was offering for 25 acres in Whippany and the school later sold 60 of the Washington Valley acres

219

for a reservoir, the net result was a financial surplus. The plans were drawn. A contractor was hired. Construction began. The cornerstone was laid on June 5, 1965. The first class of students entered headquarters in October.

The new building was a handsome red brick Georgian structure overlooking the Washington Valley. A spacious entrance hall was bisected by a corridor running down the long axis, flanked by offices on either side. At one end was the student wing; at the other, the dining room, kitchen, and a large living room known as the Eustis Lounge. The women were housed on the ground floor, the men upstairs. Each bedroom had its own bathroom, a decided improvement over the community washrooms in the old school. The construction was fireproof, and the whole building was air-conditioned, a boon for dogs, students, and staff alike. The recreation rooms were spacious. Other features were a separate lounge for instructors, an outdoor patio, and a basement laundry room with washing machines and dryers for the students. There were also an elevator and revolving door for teaching purposes.

The new place looked like a million dollars, its approximate cost, but returning students found drawbacks. One thing they missed was Elizabeth Hutchinson. After more than thirty years, she had retired just before the move. Her replacement, Paula Pursley, a Smith graduate and trained social worker, was thoroughly competent, but veterans missed their old friend. At Washington Valley the park was right next to the building, and returning graduates preferred the longer walk they had known at Whippany. Another objection was more serious. The new bedrooms were too small to contain a desk for a typewriter, and it was difficult to write letters amid the noise of the recreation room. The Eustis Lounge was situated at the furthest possible point from the students' quarters, and they renamed it the Useless Lounge.

Despite these objections, the new building functioned well. Within a year of the move, however, The Seeing Eye lost three members of its instructing staff to Guiding Eyes for the Blind. The two events were not unrelated.

Geoffrey Lauck left in December 1965 to become Guiding Eyes' chief instructor. William McCracken followed in February 1966. Theodore Zubrycki joined them in September. Guiding Eyes was guilty of raiding the staff of a rival school, but The Seeing Eye had rendered itself vulnerable to the raid. While it had spent a million dollars on its fine new building, it had continued tightfisted in the matter of instructors' salaries. The school's Achilles heel was of its own making.

In 1954, George Werntz had pronounced the school's increasing wealth its major public relations problem. Five years later, that wealth had become so embarrassing that the school stopped raising money and began to give it away instead. Yet in that same period, the average annual salary of an instructor rose from $4,164 to $4,716. The average annual increase was only $110.40, a fraction more than 2 percent.

In fairness to George Werntz it should be stressed that the school's policy on salaries had been set under Willi Ebeling. For Willi, working for The Seeing Eye required material sacrifice, rather like taking a vow of poverty upon joining a religious order. Low salaries were the rule at every level, including that of chief executive. George Werntz did a good deal to improve working conditions and fringe benefits. Instructors were given medical insurance, a pension plan, and a modest life insurance policy with premiums paid by the school. Hours were much shorter than in the thirties. Instructors worked only a five-day week. After the first week of class, they rotated night duty, so that one instructor could go home. George arranged a lecture series for the instructors to raise their level of cultural awareness, but lectures put no meat on the table.

On October 1, 1965, The Seeing Eye's assets had reached a new high of $17,000,000. In the previous fiscal year, the Grants Program had given away $93,000, more

than enough to double the salaries of the entire staff of instructors. Charity, they felt, should begin at home. Geoffrey
Lauck had taught in England and San Raphael before coming to The Seeing Eye, yet he was making only $6,400 a
year, including a housing allowance.

The annual report that recorded the defection to Guiding Eyes seemed to waver. On the one hand, it declared,
"We have vast resources with which to pay salaries that
would soon become so high as to be inconsistent with the
type of organization we conceive this to be. To attempt to
meet salary offers of pirating organizations is to surrender
to a kind of extortion that could result in administrative
chaos." Nevertheless, in effect, the school surrendered. It
adopted a new salary schedule for the instructing staff that
provided increases of between 16 and 25 percent. "The me-
dian salary being paid mobility instructors, most with a
master's degree, is $7,740. The median Seeing Eye instruc-
tor will receive $7,950 for the new fiscal year."

With a better-paid faculty and a new plant, guide dog
production began to climb. In 1952, when the school had
graduated 187 students for the second year in a row, the
long-sought goal of 200 dogs a year had seemed within
reach. Instead, production fell off sharply and sank to 148
in 1956. Generally the demand for replacements held
steady or increased, but The Seeing Eye was not attracting
its share of new students. For thirteen years in a row, replacements outnumbered first-timers, frequently by a large
margin. A number of new students were lost to rival
schools. Others were discouraged by unfriendly counselors
who used *The Demand for Dog Guides* to argue that guide
dogs were only a passing fad. The pattern changed in 1967.
The new building had received favorable publicity, but far
more important was a three-part Walt Disney television series, "Atta Girl, Kelly." George Werntz had managed to interest the Disney studios through Jules Stein. The
celebrated songwriter, a friend of Disney's, had approached the school for a grant for research to prevent blin-

dness. Following "Atta Girl, Kelly," there was an avalanche of inquiries from potential applicants. In 1967, new students outnumbered replacements for the first time in fourteen years. In 1968, the school enrolled 200 applicants for the first time in history.

Thanks to Disney, applicants were beating a path to The Seeing Eye's door. Thanks to the breeding program, they found an improved quality of dog waiting for them, but quantity was a problem. The program had started slowly and suffered various setbacks. In 1950, it was discovered that an imported brood bitch with an excellent temperament was thought to have transmitted a tendency toward car sickness to all her puppies. A few years later, an outbreak of distemper and hepatitis carried off nineteen puppies. Only about 70 percent of the dogs bred qualified for training, and a physical weakness began to reduce this number.

For some time an unrecognized defect had been plaguing dogs of the larger breeds across the country. Hip dysplasia was a progressive degenerative bone disease to which large dogs were especially vulnerable. A cumulative process of growth and change in the bone caused a poor fit between hip socket and the hip bone, and this led to arthritis. A weakness in their hips was especially undesirable for guide dogs, whose forward thrust is generated by their hind legs. What made hip dysplasia insidious was that it frequently failed to appear until the dogs were two or three years of age or more. When X-ray proved to be a diagnostic tool, The Seeing Eye X-rayed all its puppies, and for a three-year period, one in every four puppies was disqualified for unsound hips. Diagnosis was valuable, but the only cure lay in breeding, and the genetic complexity of hip dysplasia would take years to understand.

While the breeding program sought to improve the puppies genetically, the 4H program worked to improve their social environment. By 1949, it had so expanded that Robert Curtiss was hired to supervise it, and his became a full-time job. By 1950, there were 150 dogs boarding in 4H homes in ten counties. Many of these dogs came not from the breeding farm, but by purchase or as gifts from friends of the school. Without the 4H, the school could not have raised these puppies and would have lost many desirable dogs. Bob Curtis visited each home four times a year to examine the puppies and discuss their progress with their families. When a dog was mature enough to go into training, he tried to replace it immediately with a new pup to ease the pain of parting with the old. Families with several children could handle more than one puppy at a time. Over time they might raise as many as ten or fifteen dogs. Miss Evelyn Henderson, who raised her first pup in 1951, later devoted herself to bringing up fifteen foster children. With this brood to look after puppies, she could handle as many as a dozen pups at one time. In 1978, she received The Seeing Eye's Buddy Award for the incredible feat of having raised more than two hundred puppies.

Families were encouraged to expose their dogs to a variety of experiences, to take them for rides in a car or, if possible, on a bus or train, to walk them on crowded streets, past noisy construction, inside shops and supermarkets—anywhere they might be likely to accompany their future master or mistress. The one thing forbidden was to make them walk at heel. They were meant to become guides, pulling ahead, not following behind. They must be allowed to tug to their heart's content. A straining adolescent dog of ten or twelve months could be hard to hold, but the trouble 4H boys and girls took with their dogs was well worth it. When they went into training, they proved far superior to kennel-raised dogs.

The student population was aging. It included more women and diabetics. Graduates coming back for a third or fourth dog might not be able to handle one as strong or as sharp as their first. Women, especially first-timers, needed dogs who did not pull too hard, and the same was true for diabetics. Patience and friendliness became increasingly desirable as urbanization exposed dogs to ever more crowding, confusion, and confinement in cramped space. The breeding program sought to produce smaller, gentler, and softer shepherds, but often Labradors and golden retrievers that had been purchased were preferable. The school's inability to procure enough of this type of dog might keep a first-time woman applicant on the waiting list for more than a year.

After the school moved into the new building, production of both dogs and students picked up. In 1964, when hip dysplasia was widespread, only 26 dogs from the breeding farm were sent into training. In 1966, the first year at Washington Valley, nearly three times that many were graduated with students. From 1967 to 1972, the average number of graduates was 188. The average number of Seeing Eye bred dogs paired with them was 94, precisely half the total. New students outnumbered replacements every year, and the proportion of women graduates climbed. In 1972, 88, or 44 percent, of the 198 graduates were women. But just at this point there was renewed discontent in the instructing staff and a serious setback in the breeding program.

Inflation had been eroding the value of salaries. The area around Morristown attracted many high-income families, and the demand for housing sent real estate prices soaring. It was impossible to live nearby on an instructor's salary, and driving many miles to work made the instructors feel like second-class citizens commuting from low-income ghettoes. Their awareness of the expanding grants program was an additional irritant. In the decade from 1958, The Seeing Eye had given away more than $2 million. In January 1967, when a full-time executive was put in charge, the grants program accelerated. In the next five years, average annual grants exceeded $900,000. Yet even with this largesse, the value of Seeing Eye securities had risen above $29 million. The trustees could hardly cry poverty.

The instructors petitioned the board to conduct a comprehensive review of their salary structure. This time, George Werntz and the board took their request seriously. Personnel officers from Merck and the Bank of New York were engaged. They recommended a salary schedule providing for increases of from 14 to 22.5 percent, which the board formally adopted in May 1973. The new annual salaries ranged from $8,400 for a beginning apprentice to $25,000 for the director. George Werntz declared that instructors' salaries were at last competitive with those of other educational institutions in the area.

It was time to deal with the breeding program. The record high of 120 Mendham-bred dogs graduated in 1970 had fallen in the following years to 100, to 81, and finally to only 74. Because the size of the average litter had decreased, even lower production could be expected in the future. In this emergency, Debe Debetaz was called out of retirement and put in charge of the Mendham farm. His analysis revealed a whole range of defects. The breeding stock was too limited and too closely related. Of the twenty-four bitches and four studs, only two bitches came from outside blood lines. Bitches and studs were over-age, and the bitches had been bred too frequently. The strain of producing the bumper crops of 1969 and 1970 had exhausted the stock, which ought to have been renewed. The school had been investing too much in grants and too little in dogs.

Even with money to spend, good breeding stock was hard to find. Some of the most desirable dogs were not for sale. Many of those with good temperament were dysplastic. On a trip to Switzerland and France, Debe found that all the dogs with sound hips were either too large or too sharp. While new dogs were being sought, over-age animals were retired. A new breeding schedule permitted brood bitches to rest for one season in every three. Plans for enlarged and up-to-date breeding kennels were drawn.

The breeding program had been thoroughly overhauled when George Werntz retired on August 1, 1975. It was the twenty-fifth anniversary of his arrival at the school. For more than twenty-one of those years, he had been its chief executive officer. The most immediately apparent achievement of his tenure was the Washington Valley campus. The new building had some disadvantages, but it was a well-built, up-to-date facility in a fine location with ample room for future expansion, a place that promised to serve as the school's home for an indefinite future.

Equally important, George had overseen the transition from the era when Willi Ebeling acted as patriarch of a quasi-religious movement staffed by votaries to a secular school employing a decently salaried faculty. In this connection he had initiated a change that would have been impossible before the retirement of Debe Debetaz. After a lapse of more than forty years since the days of Adelaide Clifford and Missy Doudge, he had added women apprentices to the instructors. He broke with The Seeing Eye's former aloofness from other guide dog schools and agencies for the blind and established friendly relations with both guide dog schools and the students of cane travel at a dozen universities across the country. Finally, in 1974, as a consequence of all these policies, George Werntz had the satisfaction of achieving The Seeing Eye's long-sought goal, graduating 200 students (201 to be exact) in a single year. He could retire with the sense of a job well done and the school's future firmly secured. It would be some years before the leadership recognized that it was lulling itself into a false sense of security.

19

The Monastic Mind-set

The successor to George Werntz was Stuart Grout. He had earned his Ph.D. in university administration from Chicago in 1956 and for nearly twenty years had worked in administration at both Arkansas and Boston University. He reported for work on May 1, 1975, and, like George Werntz, prepared two dogs for a class of students. In sharp contrast to George, whose apprenticeship under Willi Ebeling had lasted more than three years, Stuart took over as chief executive in August 1975 after only three months.

His executive staff was well seasoned. Marian Jobson, vice president for Public Relations, dated back to the 1930s. Bob Whitstock, vice president of Programs, had joined the staff in 1956. Paula Pursley, vice president of Student Services, had succeeded Elizabeth Hutchinson in 1966. Dick Krokus, director of Instruction and Training, had begun as an instructor thirty years earlier.

With such veteran personnel, many programs launched under George Werntz were continued. Enlarged, modern breeding kennels were constructed. In 1979, for the first time, the school began to breed Labradors as well as shepherds. Labradors are husky, strong dogs, but they have a shorter and choppier gait than shepherds. With a side-to-side motion, a Labrador's forward pull is not as hard as that of a shepherd with its longer forward stride. This made Labs easier to handle for older, diabetic, or frail students.

The 4H program continued to expand, and by 1979 it was nearing the target of 300 puppies boarding with families. An 1,100-square-foot veterinary clinic was constructed on the Washington Valley campus. It included a holding pen, operating room, recovery room, and an X-ray room for diagnosing hip dysplasia. Local veterinarians held regular office hours in the clinic, eliminating the necessity of driving dogs to and from the vets' offices for routine examinations and treatment. Another physical addition was the construction of an outside walk and gazebo on the grounds of the campus, allowing students and dogs to stretch their legs between trips to Morristown. Women instructors remained an integral part of the teaching staff, and with four teams of three instructors each, the school continued to graduate more than 200 students annually.

With Bob Whitstock's elevation to executive status, David Loux, another graduate, had taken over his role as ambassador at large, traveling the country, visiting graduates, interviewing candidates, and representing The Seeing Eye to workers for the blind. Dave also played host to the teams of student mobility instructors when they came to the Washington Valley campus on their annual visits.

One major change under Stuart Grout was a radical departure. The grants program was sharply reduced, renamed the Support Program, and the position of director was abolished. The new program limited funding almost exclusively to various veterinary research projects such as the development of an effective vaccine against the parvovirus.

Although there had not been an active fund-raising program since 1959, a series of bequests had continued to swell the endowment. The income from the endowment had also grown, but it was no longer adequate to meet increasing costs and the impact of inflation. In 1976, the board of trustees authorized a second significant change from the Werntz era. It endorsed the resumption of a low-key program of membership enrollment addressed to former supporters and friends.

In January 1979 the school observed its fiftieth anniversary, but it reserved the main celebration until June, when, to mark the occasion, the U.S. Postal Service issued a special commemorative stamp picturing a Seeing Eye dog. A gala audience was assembled for the celebration. It included the postmaster general and a galaxy of those who had made the school what it was, including Morris Frank, Adelaide Clifford, Debe Debetaz, Elizabeth Hutchinson, and George Werntz. At ninety, Jack Humphrey was unable to leave his nursing home in Phoenix, but he was represented by his son, George. There were a number of speeches, and when Morris took the podium, it was the first time he had officially represented The Seeing Eye in more than twenty years. Now over seventy, he seemed as vibrant, as energetic, as fully charged with youthful optimism as he had been in his thirties.

He recalled interviewing a potential male applicant in his home in the South. The yard was unkempt, the house dilapidated and in need of paint. The applicant, a man of about forty, was unshaven and dispirited, but Morris had persuaded him to go to The Seeing Eye. A few years later, Morris called on the same man again. This time, the garden was neatly trimmed. The house had been freshly painted. The graduate welcomed Morris and Buddy heartily. Later, his wife showed Morris in to the kitchen. She explained that, before her husband had gone to The Seeing Eye for his dog, she had been forced to pawn one family treasure after another. The one thing she had been able to save was a beautiful silver punch bowl they had received as a wedding present. Now that her husband was earning a salary again, that bowl, carefully polished, stood on the kitchen floor filled with water for the dog that had made it all possible.

I cannot reproduce Morris's words, or his delivery, but his charisma at that moment dramatized what The Seeing Eye had been missing for more than twenty years. Unhappily, this proved to be Morris's swan song. He died in November of the next year; Jack Humphrey expired the following summer, and Adelaide Clifford in the year after that. Time was marching on.

In 1980 The Seeing Eye graduated 231 dogs and students, a new high. With the confidence their dogs had given them, graduates were pioneering new careers and areas of independence. In July of 1979, Maureen Young had sung the role of Mimi in *La Boheme* for an audience of 12,000 in New York's Central Park. She wrote, "I feel that it was a kind of break-through for blind people, showing that it could be done, that there are roles we can handle." There were other roles graduates could handle. With an M.A. in French and Ph.D. in Spanish, Denise Decker with her Lila was working in the State Department as a researcher for the Agency for International Development. Following sixteen years in the Texas legislature, the Honorable Criss Cole, blinded in combat in World War II, was serving as a judge.[1] Albert Gonzales with Ebony was practicing law in New Mexico. Jo Taliaferro with her Hattie was a Presbyterian minister in Niles, Michigan. Rosemary Goodrich with Arden was a medical transcriber at the Mt. Sinai Medical Center in Milwaukee. Together these six graduates were making their way in opera, the foreign service, the judiciary, law, the ministry, and the health profession.

The story of two other graduates illustrates a serendipitous by-product of The Seeing Eye experience. When Tom Dekker came to the school for the first time, he met Ted Glaser, a Dartmouth graduate who had worked as a computer scientist at IBM and MIT. Glaser's success in computer science helped to encourage Dekker's ambition, and with Glaser's recommendation, he later landed a job with the Mitel firm in Ottawa. There were many similar examples of successful Seeing Eye veterans heartening younger students with their "can-do" spirit. Nor was this spirit confined to students. In the spring of 1983, a pregnant instruc-

---

[1] The Criss Cole Rehabilitation Center in Austin, also the site of the Texas Commission for the Blind and Visually Impaired, was named in honor of Criss. His statue—with his Seeing Eye dog—stands in front of the center.

tor, Joan Markey, completed a class just two weeks before she delivered her baby.

The trustees and staff could take great satisfaction in success stories like these. There was measurable progress in the health care of the dogs and in the breeding program. With Betsy Keuffel as the newly appointed director of Development, the annual fund-raising goal rose from $300,000 in 1983 to $400,000 in 1984. The endowment was up to $40 million. Substantial raises for the training staff had improved morale. The school was graduating over two hundred students annually.

Everything seemed satisfactory, but looking back, a later member of the executive staff compared The Seeing Eye at this period to a medieval monastery. The comparison had some validity. Although the "monks" were no longer expected to take vows of poverty, as in Willi Ebeling's time, they were zealous, hardworking, and dedicated to improving the product. Instead of wine or liqueur, the product was guide dogs, and that product was being improved. Pioneering work in genetics was in progress and would ultimately result in remarkable success at the breeding station. The puppy-raising program was expanding. But the vision of The Seeing Eye leadership was focused primarily inward. In anticipation of the fiftieth birthday, Stuart Grout had invited me to write the first edition of this book, but a history looked to the past. The Seeing Eye's leadership did not yet recognize the challenge in its future.

Like a monastery, the school was isolated from the outside world. Symbolic of this isolation was the sign at the entrance to the Washington Valley Campus. To discourage uninvited guests who would interrupt the training, the sign was so small and unobtrusive as to be nearly invisible. Inmates of the monastery must not be disturbed. To the casual observer, the handsome Georgian structure on the crown of the hill could have been almost anything. Thousands of cars drove past daily on Route 24, but not one motorist in ten was aware of passing The Seeing Eye.

The quarter-century hiatus in fund-raising had allowed the vital connection with thousands of enthusiastic donors to wither. The Friends of The Seeing Eye, groups that Morris and Marian Jobson had galvanized in major cities across the country, had gone out of existence. In 1980 Stuart Grout let Marian Jobson go. He was economizing, but in so doing, he had moved the conduct of fund-raising and public affairs from a vital communications center on Rockefeller Plaza to an isolated and understaffed basement office in Morristown.

There was a more serious problem than public awareness. In 1960, the Columbia School of Social Work's study, *The Demand for Dog Guides*, had proposed 5,000 as the maximum number of blind people who could be motivated to use guide dogs. This had convinced George Werntz that the four largest schools, Guide Dogs for the Blind, Guiding Eyes for the Blind, Leader Dogs, and The Seeing Eye, were adequate to meet the future need for dogs with relatively little expansion. Twenty years later, the situation had changed. The breeding of Labradors and of smaller and softer dogs had brought guide work within the physical capability of many who could not have handled the dogs available before 1960. If The Seeing Eye was no longer well known to the public at large, the school's efforts to educate mobility instructors and rehabilitation counselors had made guide dogs well known to the blind and their advisers; a growing number of blind people wanted access to the sighted world. As a result, there was a demand for dogs far larger than the school could supply.

The Seeing Eye could replace the dogs for old-timers fairly promptly, but the waiting time for new applicants was growing so long that many chose to attend schools with shorter waiting lists. Returning graduates were taking up so much room in the classes that the shrinking supply of new applicants was inadequate to replenish the alumni body. If this pattern of admissions were not reversed, the school would find itself serving a constantly aging and diminishing number of old grads. This was a recipe for extinction, and the dawning realization of this fact shook the monastic mind-set.

In 1981, thanks to the urging of Stuart Grout, a Long Range Planning Committee was established, and it began very tentatively to explore the problem. The school could not favor new applicants over "retreads" without betraying its alumni. Gradually the committee recognized that the only solution was to expand enrollment to include substantially more new applicants. In 1983, an architectural firm was hired to do a survey of future building needs. The tentative goal was a plant capable of graduating 300 dog-student teams a year. It would require the construction of new student quarters, expanded dining and kitchen facilities, new training kennels, and an enlarged staff of instructors and support personnel. Both the breeding and puppy-raising programs would have to be substantially increased.

By the spring of 1984, it was becoming clear that the school's annual fund-raising campaigns were inadequate to underwrite the investment in a plant of such dimensions, and The Seeing Eye's vision was distracted by certain peripheral concerns. The heating and air-conditioning systems in the main building had to be replaced at a cost of $350,000. A new office building in Morristown threatened to limit essential parking at the Schuyler Place lounge. A new location had to be found, purchased, and renovated at an ultimate cost of more than $500,000. Such preoccupations made it easy to overlook the necessity for a major capital campaign, but Stuart persuaded the trustees to take what would prove a decisive step. The Seeing Eye engaged the firm of Staley/Robeson/Ryan/St. Lawrence to conduct a feasibility study, and the report was completed in May 1985.

Its summation began reassuringly:

It is our conclusion that the program of The Seeing Eye is an excellent one and has the warm endorsement of both the

board of trustees and the school's many friends. It is also
our opinion that there is general approval for most of the
projected needs, particularly for those items relating to the
expansion of enrollment. However, there is some concern
about the cost and question as to whether such high expenditures are necessary. This concern is shared by a number of
both trustees and friends. At the trustee level, there are also
reservations about the need for raising additional endowment and a feeling on the part of some that it might be possible to fund several of the needs out of bequest income. The
needs require much more board examination and discussion
before they are approved. Few people are thinking in leadership terms. It is likely that most gifts would be at the four or
low five-figure level, rather than at the needed six and seven-
figure levels.

In view of the need to identify and cultivate many
large donors, the report concluded, "It would be unwise to
launch a major campaign at this time. Three to five years
would be needed to place the school in an appropriate position to raise a major sum."

The Staley Robeson report was a shock to the trustees.
They had not been with The Seeing Eye in the days when
fund-raising was vital to its existence and a major board
responsibility. Talk of a multimillion-dollar campaign, of
"six-figure or seven-figure gifts," and the prospect of the
contributions they themselves would be expected to make
took their breath away. It was like announcing to the assembled brethren of a monastery that they must leave their
comfortable cloister to conduct a major missionary crusade
in an alien country. They swallowed hard. Their ambiva-
lence is clearly revealed in the minutes of the meeting in
June 1985. These summed up board reactions to the Staley
Robeson report under two headings. The first stated "that
The Seeing Eye defer plans for a major capital fund-raising
effort and instead look ahead at this time." But instead of
looking ahead, the next comments looked backward:

That the first step should be a review of projected needs to reduce cost of enrollment expansion to a level where they might be funded out of existing resources. A number of Trustees were rather appalled at figures presented to them, including $5 million for the kennels. It was thought it would be better to go back to the drawing board and see if we can't achieve increased enrollment at some figure we could handle.

On the one hand, it was "back to the drawing board." But on the other hand, at this same meeting, the trustees and staff, despite their hesitancy, began to explore a number of fund-raising strategies: the use of direct mail appeals managed by a commercial house, the establishment of friends' groups in various cities, the recruitment of a graduate to act as a roving ambassador in the Morris Frank tradition, the expansion of fund-raising staff under a vice president for Development and Public Affairs, and the inauguration of a deferred-giving program.

It would take time to digest the implications of the Staley Robeson feasibility study, but ultimately it turned The Seeing Eye's vision from the inner to the outer world. The metamorphosis was slow, but this was the beginning of the end of the monastic mind-set.

20
From Drift to Drive

The monastic mind-set was only a partial explanation for The Seeing Eye's drift in the 1980s. As a member of the board from 1981 to 1990, I had some insight. We met in a private dining room of the Downtown Association in New York City. I was acquainted with several of the other trustees, including fellow Princetonians Jim Carey and Landon Peters, and a remarkable woman, Walker Kirby, who had joined the board in 1971. But from my perspective on the periphery, the principal roles seemed to belong to three others, Wallace Jones, Dorrance Sexton, and Stuart Grout. They appeared to me to create a balance not of power, but of inertia. As a result, The Seeing Eye was adrift.

Wallace Jones was chairman of the board. A member of the law firm of Davis, Polk & Wardwell and the stereotype of the perfect gentleman, he conducted our meetings with courtesy, patience, and firmness but with absolutely no sense of urgency. Dorrance Sexton was chairman of the executive committee. The retired president and CEO of Johnson & Higgins, he was Wally's temperamental opposite. He was impatience personified. Before an hour was up, Dorrance was restlessly shifting in his chair and looking at his watch as if afraid he was going to miss the last train back to Connecticut. By seniority and force of personality he seemed to command the most authority, but he apparently lacked the patience, the time, or the desire to assume the leadership. As chief executive officer, Stuart Grout might have taken command, but both he and Wally Jones seemed more interested in stewardship than leadership. To lead meant to go somewhere. They were happy where they were. After all, The Seeing Eye was the Harvard of guide dog schools—the first, the best, the wealthiest. Why should it change?

Something or someone else would doubtless have brought an end to this drift, but fate seemed to assign that role to W. Sydnor Settle. Syd was a resident of nearby New Vernon, a lawyer with the firm of Simpson, Thacher & Bartlett in New York City, and chairman of the board of Hampden-Sydney College, from which he had graduated before attending the University of Virginia Law School. He joined The Seeing Eye board in May 1984, and it was not long before he made his presence felt.

For many years the management of The Seeing Eye's endowment had been left to the sole discretion of the Bank of New York. Syd Settle's experience in the business world and as chairman of Hampden-Sydney convinced him that banks were far less effective as investment advisers than were money managers. At a meeting of the executive committee, Syd proposed that the endowment be confided instead to three different professional money-management firms who would have to account for their performance month by month. Landon Peters, chair of the Finance Committee, agreed. To Syd's surprise, the proposal was immediately and enthusiastically seconded by Dorrance Sexton, then unanimously approved by the rest of the members. They may have been questioning the investment policy, but had been reluctant to rock the boat.

Gradually, drift was transformed into drive. In the fall of 1985, the open houses held on the campus once a year were replaced by weekly guided tours arranged in advance by appointment and conducted by trained lay guides under the leadership of Walker Kirby. It was she who had recruited "Walker's walkers," several dozen volunteers who exercised the breeding stock at Mendham. Now she assembled a corps of docents for the Washington Valley Campus. The annual open houses had attracted crowds of thousands, but for this very reason they had provided no opportunity to establish the personal touch that would lead to a financial commitment. The intimate weekly tours, led by attractive and knowledgeable volunteer guides who imparted their contagious enthusiasm, stimulated the affection and commitment that had animated the school's benefactors in the old days.

A filmed version of Morris Frank's life, *Love Leads the Way*, provided another sort of showcase for The Seeing Eye. A benefit preview performance was arranged in New York in September 1984. The film included some glaring inaccuracies. For example, Morris Frank's mother had gone blind when he was three, while Morris's movie mother had her vision throughout. Some in the audience were aware of such errors, but when the film ended there was not a dry eye in the house including my own. The details might be wrong, but the central message and the magic were there. In May of 1986, *Love Leads the Way* was shown by the Disney Channel on Sunday television. It had an estimated audience of sixteen million, and one California viewer mailed in an unsolicited contribution in five figures.

Legacies and improved money management were continuing to swell the endowment year by year. By 1987 the income from annual giving had risen to $865,000, but two fund-raising ventures introduced in the fall of that year were ill-conceived. The first of these was a dinner benefit at the Pierre Hotel in New York. It was inspired by the benefit showing of *Love Leads the Way* but it lacked both its relevance and its impact. As a transparently artificial pretext for the occasion, the Dorothy Wood Eustis Humanitarian Award was manufactured and presented to Judith Peabody. Mrs. Peabody was justly celebrated for her work on behalf of AIDS patients and was deserving of a humanitarian award, but her efforts had no connection with The Seeing Eye. The award was as irrelevant to its purpose as the Hiss the Villain benefit had been more than a half-century before.

A less fortunate effort was largely Stuart Grout's pet project. As a trustee of the Morris Animal Foundation, he had been impressed by a commercial fund-raising firm that had conducted a phone-mail campaign for the foundation. He prevailed, over the objections of several board members, and the firm began its campaign in the fall of 1987. It managed to increase the gross revenue collected from the selected donors, but at an inordinate cost both in dollars and good will. All of the prospects had already been longtime loyal contributors, and many of them protested so indignantly against phone solicitation that the experiment was not repeated.

Meanwhile, a problem that had its roots in 1983 was finally resolved. In that year, the plan to construct a new office building next door to the Schuyler Place Lounge had threatened to eliminate essential parking for The Seeing Eye's training vans. Even after a new site was found, the negotiations to buy the building, to get approval from the zoning board, and to complete the renovations were so protracted that the Mt. Kemble Lounge was not opened until the fall of 1987.

That summer saw a far more important change. Wally Jones retired from his law practice and, in June of 1987, Syd Settle replaced him. Stuart Grout still had some time to serve before his scheduled retirement, but a severe illness that struck his wife had seriously complicated his domestic life. In 1988 he was pleased to accept a proposal for early retirement. There was some irony in the timing of his departure. Over the course of thirteen years, the breeding and puppy-raising programs had been improved and expanded, production had been maintained, and annual fund-raising had been revived and revitalized. Gradually, painstakingly, Stuart had cleared the obstacles and prepared the way for a major campaign that would now be left for a successor to lead. In June, a search firm was hired to look for that successor. The following month, Dick Krokus, a veteran of forty-two years, retired as director of Instruction and Training. A major changing of the guard was in process.

The board's choice to succeed Stuart Grout was a man with long experience as a professional fund-raiser. Dennis Murphy, a graduate of Michigan State with an M.B.A. from the University of Miami, had spent twenty-five years with the United Way. He had held key positions across the country and at the national headquarters in Alexandria, Virginia. Dennis joined the staff on January 1, 1989. Before assuming the presidency, he trained two dogs and turned them over to students. In April, he was ready to begin.

A whole series of personnel changes followed. To summarize and oversimplify, in 1989 Joseph Funke became director of Administration and Finance; Peter Guimes took over Buildings and Grounds. The following year, Rosemary Carroll became director of Development and Public Affairs. In 1991, Dr. Dolores Holle was appointed to the newly created position of director of Canine Health Management. With the retirement of vice presidents Paula Pursley and Bob Whitstock in the winter of 1991–1992, Judy Deuschle became director of Student Services, and Douglas Roberts director of Programs.

With the exception of Doug, who had begun as an apprentice instructor in 1968, all of these people were, like Dennis himself, "outsiders," but as the progress of the next few years would show, they were outsiders of extraordinary talent and energy. They worked well together as a team, but on occasion, Dennis said, innovations encountered resistance from the "insiders." His strategy for dealing with those fighting to preserve an old practice was to ask whether it was a custom or a tradition? If he could show that it was simply a custom or habit, the ground was cleared for change. Change was imminent.

In the fall of 1989, the board voted to go ahead with Phase One of a major expansion. It involved enlarging the kitchen, the conversion of the old Eustis Lounge into the Morris Frank Dining Room, the addition of a new Eustis

Lounge, and the appropriate electrical and site work. The estimated cost of Phase One was slightly more than $2,100,000. The overall cost of the whole project was estimated at just over $9 million.

The Seeing Eye's financial position was much improved. The year had seen a record high of nearly $6 million in legacies. The endowment totaled $83 million, and income from investments, annual giving, and other sources came to $5.6 million. The financial situation might have emboldened the board to proceed with Phase Two, the expansion of the student quarters and the construction of a new training kennel, if it had not been for a troublesome defect in the original design of the Washington Valley Campus.

The engineers of the kennels had designed septic systems for waste disposal, but they had overlooked two crucial problems in disposing of waste from kennels. Septic systems depend on bacteriological action to consume waste, but the antiseptics used to maintain kennel hygiene neutralize bacterial action, and the dog hair washed down during cleaning clogged the lateral drains. As a result, the septic tanks had filled up with the accumulated waste of more than twenty years and had to be pumped out regularly. The Seeing Eye purchased its own pump truck, and by the spring of 1989, it was pumping out 35,000 gallons of waste per week. To expand, it was essential that The Seeing Eye hook up to the Morristown sewer system, but the town issued a ban on further expansion. The construction of Phase One did not increase the burden on the drainage system, but the enlargement of student quarters and a new training kennel would. The school tried to obtain approval for a sewer hookup for more than three years. Phase Two was stymied until The Seeing Eye could come to some arrangement with the Morristown sewer authorities.

While these negotiations dragged on, Rosemary Carroll helped to stimulate progress on the fund-raising front. She revived a practice that Dorothy Eustis had used to great advantage. Groups of Friends of The Seeing Eye held meetings in Morristown, Washington, D.C., and Dallas. New "Friends" groups in other cities such as Boston, Greenwich, Philadelphia, Chicago, and Toronto were in the process of formation. A Heritage Society was formed for those who had provided for The Seeing Eye in their wills. Mark Smith, a racing driver at the Meadowlands, announced that he would give half of his winnings annually to The Seeing Eye.

In the fall of 1990, the new kitchen and dining facilities in the west wing were opened for use. With Phase One complete, The Seeing Eye formally announced the opening of the campaign for Phase Two. It was combined with graduation ceremonies for the school's ten thousandth dog. She was Zabrina, a German shepherd, the fourth dog for Bonnie Lanzet, who had paired with her first dog twenty years earlier while attending graduate school. Bonnie was a rehabilitation counselor with the Delaware Department of Health and Social Services. Other graduates attending the ceremonies at the school were Jamie Hilton, chief executive officer of the New Jersey State Commission for the Blind and Visually Impaired, John Turner, a trustee from Dallas, and Bill Irwin, who with his dog, Orient, had accomplished the incredible feat of hiking the entire length of the Appalachian Trail, a total of 1,200 miles, between March and October. Bonnie and Zabrina were later welcomed at the White House by President Bush, who had previously proclaimed The Seeing Eye one of his "Thousand Points of Light."

In April of 1991, with the endowment fund valued at $91 million, the board voted to float a bond issue for $10 million, of which $9 million was to be used to complete Phase Two of the expansion. While it remained in the endowment fund, this money was earning in excess of 12.5 percent in total return. Since the debt service on the borrowed money was only 7.3 percent, The Seeing Eye was actually making money on the arrangement, having its cake and eating it, too.

Better still, the school at last arranged to hook up with the sewer system, and although the agreement required

The Seeing Eye to construct several miles of sewer line, a pumping station, and a public toilet on some neighboring green space, delay was at an end. The sewer contract was awarded in April, and construction was ready to begin.

In the following March, an unseasonable blizzard turned groundbreaking to "snow-breaking" ceremonies for the new training kennel and student wing. At about the same time, the F. M. Kirby Foundation pledged $600,000 to general operations over three years, "one of the largest single gifts ever received." Soon afterward, thanks to James Storer, a graduate and board member, the George P. Storer Foundation made a grant of $50,000 to equip the student wing with an Information Center including personal computers, scanners, printers, and the software for synthetic speech, enlarged print, and refreshable braille. Construction proceeded on schedule, and on May 21, 1993, both the student wing and the Walker Dillard Kirby Canine Center were opened for inspection at a reception dedicating the latter.

The new facilities were splendid. The school could now serve 24 students at a time, providing an annual capacity of 300 graduates. The number of student bedrooms was doubled from twelve to twenty-four, each with its own bathroom, telephone, tape player, and radio. Students had the option of rooming alone or with another student. There were new laundry facilities and an enlarged area for grooming dogs inside. But the comfort and convenience of the student quarters were eclipsed by those of the new training kennel.

The Walker Kirby Canine Center enclosed 40,000 square feet of floor space on three stories. It was capable of housing 120 dogs, forty to a floor. Dr. Holle, the school's first full-time veterinarian, had pressed for a modern ventilating system capable of twenty-two air exchanges per hour to prevent the spread of infectious diseases, and climate-controlled humidity to decrease skin and ear problems. Each of the three floors was divided into quadrants, and each quadrant housed an instructor's string of ten dogs. Each dog had its own sleeping box, drinking spout, and exercise run. Each quadrant also had a communal exercise yard sheltered from rain and snow for the dogs' play time.

Each floor provided a support room for bathing, dipping, medication, and treatment of the dogs. The building also contained a lounge for the staff. The floors were linked, not by stairs, but by ramps coated with high-traction material that made for safe footing for instructors tethered to dogs. The impermeable epoxy flooring was free of crevices that could harbor the growth of parasites.

In short, the Walker Kirby Canine Center had been carefully planned and constructed to provide the safest and most healthful, comfortable, and convenient environment possible for the education of guide dogs. Nothing could have provided more convincing proof that The Seeing Eye's erstwhile drift had been transformed to drive.

21

A Breed within a Breed

The new student wing and the Walker Kirby Canine Center were obvious outward signs of progress, but there had been extraordinary strides at the breeding station in Mendham, and closely related, a new and very comprehensive canine health program at both Mendham and the Washington Valley Campus. In 1975, only 23% of the dogs going into training had been bred in Mendham. Ten years later, the number had risen to 90%. This development took place under three different directors, but the main credit for The Seeing Eye's breeding success was a team of outside expert consultants.

Dr. Eldin Leighton was a geneticist at the University of Maryland and a friend of Seeing Eye board member and veterinary doctor Donald Patterson of the University of Pennsylvania, himself a genetic expert of international stature. Leighton had taken his doctorate in quantitative genetics at Iowa State, where he developed extraordinary proficiency in computer technology. The blending of genetics with computer science was the key to success. As a consultant for The Seeing Eye, he spent two and a half years developing computer software for the breeding program. It stored data on a wide variety of genetic traits for at first 3,000, and then more than 5,000, dogs. Dr. Patterson pronounced it "the most advanced and practical system ever devised for the scientific breeding of dog guides."

Dr. Leighton made this computer software available to Marian Jerszyk, a Ph.D. in genetics who became manager of the breeding station in 1985. In a sense, history was repeating itself. The Seeing Eye was using the same breeding strategy of opening up blood lines that Jack Humphrey had introduced at Fortunate Fields in the 1920s. The school brought dogs with different blood lines into the program from all over the world. Few of them were related to each other at all, so they provided a broad genetic pool. The record-keeping was computerized, but on the first primitive computer it might take six, eight, or more hours to run the comparative data. Marian Jerszyk would start a computer program just before closing shop for the day, let it run all night, and retrieve the results the next morning. Today's computers can run the same program in a few seconds.

The breeding program focused first on sound hips and second on temperament. Both were important, but hip dysplasia was a particular problem. Its genetic component was complex, but with the help of Dr. Leighton's data bank, it was sharply reduced as a reason for rejection among German shepherds and Labrador retrievers. By the spring of 1994 hip dysplasia had been reduced from 30 to 5 percent in shepherds and from 18 percent to near zero in Labrador retrievers.

With Seeing Eye funding, Dr. Gail Smith at the University of Pennsylvania pioneered a new radiograph technique. The new X-ray method enabled loose hips to be identified at sixteen weeks of age. This program did not eliminate hip dysplasia, but it reduced its incidence and severity, so that it no longer interfered with the dogs' working lives. As active dogs retire, the school can examine their hips and see how effectively the radiographic technique predicted their working future. In addition to being given physical exams with sophisticated technologies, dogs chosen for breeding were carefully screened with six weeks of actual training to make sure they possessed the right qualities as guides before they were accepted for breeding.

The Seeing Eye was progressing toward the creation of a breed within a breed or, more precisely, two breeds within two breeds—German shepherds and Labrador retrievers especially adapted for guide work. One enthusiast pronounced them "specifically designed to guide. They're smaller and capable of handling all the complications of modern life and traffic." This claim would prove somewhat exaggerated, but it was true that the breeding program had gone a long way toward producing smaller, softer, and gentler dogs with the proper temperament and sound hips.

A blue-ribbon panel of consulting geneticists from Cornell, the University of Pennsylvania, and the University of Massachusetts spent several days at The Seeing Eye in 1994. It applauded the school's achievements in producing sound hips and proper temperament, but focused attention on litter size and effective work longevity. Obviously, litters of eight or ten are far more cost-effective than litters of two or three, and a guide dog who works for ten years is more valuable than one who lasts only six. But before these goals could be realized, the program would have to recover from some previous setbacks.

For two summers in a row, outbreaks of parvovirus infection at the breeding station wiped out whole litters. Parvo is an especially hardy virus. Each year it thrives in the outside world from spring until the first killing frost. Dog walkers, maintenance workers, garbage men, or other visitors could easily bring in parvovirus and other infections. A consulting team headed by Cornell's Dr. Leland Carmichael advised that to avoid new parvo outbreaks, the breeding station would have to quarantine its vulnerable inhabitants from potential sources of infection. Reluctantly, Walker's walkers were disbanded. All other visitors were required to wear outer booties. The area surrounding the kennel was treated with dilute bleach solution every day. Before entering the kennels or touching puppies, staff and visitors had to change their clothes and scrub their hands. "It is quite amusing," Doug Roberts said, laughing, "the ballet you have to go through, to change your shoes and put on outer booties and then inside kennel booties." It may be amusing, but it works!

As a partial replacement for the walking program, the breeding station has installed a large fenced yard, and periodically the dogs have obedience sessions, play time, and throw-the-ball time with members of the staff who have taken suitable precautions against the spread of virus.

Newborn puppies stay in the breeding farm kennels for six or seven weeks. By that time the maternal antibodies with which they were born are decreasing, and puppy-raisers are asked not to let them socialize with other dogs until they are about thirteen weeks old. By that time, they will have received two vaccinations that could not have been given while the antibodies with which the pups were born are still active.

In April 1991, The Seeing Eye took a major step. It appointed Dr. Dolores Holle to the newly created position of Director of Canine Health Management. She had received her B.S. from the College of St. Elizabeth, had done graduate work at the University of Minnesota, and had earned her doctorate in veterinary medicine from the University of Pennsylvania in 1981. Dolores Holle would prove herself an invaluable addition to the executive staff, but as important as her individual qualifications was the establishment of her position. At long last, the school had recognized that a veterinarian with a private practice could not give its dogs the attention they deserved. Ironically, some trustees asked Dr. Holle whether she would have enough work to keep her from getting bored. Little did they know!

The office being new, Dr. Holle had no support staff to speak of when she arrived, no departmental secretary, no one to enter health records into the rapidly developing data bank. There was a barely adequate kennel staff but no staff for the clinic—and this was at the time when the instructors were expanding the number of dogs in training from 90 to 120.

Today the clinic has two full-time assistants, and members of the kennel crew rotate in the clinic, so that it is staffed at all times. Another full-time veterinarian, Dr. Mary

Stankovics, was added, but this was scarcely enough. During the parvo epidemic in the summer of 1993, both doctors had to work twelve-hour days and cover the clinic around the clock.

The prevention of contagion in the kennels was one challenge for health maintenance. Deadlines were another. There had to be the right number and variety of healthy dogs ready for each arriving class, and it was essential to monitor the health of those right behind them in the training pipeline. "You're always playing beat-the-clock to provide healthy dogs for each class," Dr. Holle said, "but when you spot a problem, especially of a different sort, you need to ascertain if it is a heritable disorder."

The sophisticated computerization that Joseph Funke introduced throughout the school permeated every aspect of dog care, from the breeding farm and the puppy-raising program to the problems of graduates in the field. The genetic profile of each dog, along with its health and temperament records as a puppy, during training with an instructor, in class with a student, and in the field with its graduate partner, are all collected in the school's data bank. In the past, when a graduate phoned in to consult about some problem, the director of Programs might need to consult files from the training folder, the puppy-raising folder, the Student Services folder, the medical folder, or all four. Retrieving these files and leafing through them was an unwieldy and time-consuming process. Now, Doug Roberts or his staff can review any aspect of a dog's or graduate's history with a few strokes on the computer keyboard.

Computerization could calculate the odds that a dog would develop or be a carrier of progressive retinal atrophy, an eye problem to which many Labrador retrievers are subject. Scientific estimates were that 32 percent of the Labrador population world-wide carried the gene for P.R.A. A late-onset disease that might not show up until a dog is four or five, it could easily be misdiagnosed as an age-related problem. When the first case was discovered in 1992, the school contacted all owners of Labrador guide dogs and offered to pay for eye examinations. As a result, 23 Labs were diagnosed with P.R.A., and Dr. Holle established a program of ophthalmic examination. For a time, this involved trucking six Labrador retrievers to Cornell University every two weeks for an E.R.G., an electro-retinogram. A member of the kennel staff had to leave at four in the morning to get back at seven that night. Now the school has its own E.R.G. equipment, so examinations can be done in-house.

Dogs must be anesthetized for E.R.G.s and many other procedures, and the adoption of new and safer anesthetics was another technical advance, making possible more complete medical examinations. Over the years, the clinic has acquired increasingly sophisticated equipment, ultrasound for pregnancy determination and cardiac or kidney evaluation, an endoscope for stomach, small intestine, vaginal, or urethral examination, and a defibrillator for cardiac arrhythmia. When the school has approached the manufacturers of such expensive equipment, the mention of The Seeing Eye has had a magical effect. The Seeing Eye name has also facilitated invaluable cooperation from consulting veterinary specialists across the country.

There has been regular interaction between the training and canine health programs. If a dog urinated on a route in training, there were questions. Was this a behavioral or a medical problem? A variety of sophisticated diagnostic procedures were available. The concern was not only the health of the particular dog, but also the genetic implications of its problem for the breeding program.

The canine health program also interacts with puppy-raising. The Washington Valley clinic does not directly treat the more than 600 puppies currently being reared by puppy-raisers, but it keeps track of their health records. The Seeing Eye pays veterinary costs for the puppies, and their invoices are returned to The Seeing Eye. Unusual symptoms are brought to Dr. Holle's attention, and in such cases telephone consultations with the puppy's veterinarians are helpful.

With more than 600 puppies in the program and only 300 to 320 students per year, the "rejection" rate has risen to nearly 50 percent, but only because the standards for selection are growing more stringent. The dogs selected for training go into the Walker Kirby Canine Center. The rest are kept in a still newer facility, a 44,000-square-foot kennel capable of housing 160 dogs of various categories.

A puppy ward with a separate ventilating system lodges pups waiting for allocation to puppy-raising families. Another wing houses "adoptables," dogs who, having failed the selection process, will be given to adopting families. Separate areas are assigned to newly arrived dogs not yet classified, graduate dogs retired because of age or infirmity, test dogs being worked to see whether they possess the right temperament for breeding, and a few holdovers, dogs not paired with students in a previous class. Many of these, especially the adoptables, are in a dog-walking program. Two staff members assisted by two volunteers work on matching "failed" dogs to their adopting families.

The housing for all these dogs constitutes only one part of the most recent and perhaps the most impressive building project the school has yet undertaken. This is the new state-of-the-art canine health clinic and kennel underwritten by the extraordinary generosity of Vincent Stabile and his sister, Toni. Mr. Stabile provided a total of six million dollars for the construction, by far the largest donation in Seeing Eye history, while his sister added $150,000 for maintenance of the building. The Stabile Canine Health Center combines a fully equipped veterinary facility with the aforementioned kennel. The clinic includes two examination rooms, a laboratory, separate suites for surgery, endoscopy, dentistry, and electro-retinography, a pharmacy, a medical records room, and a glass-fronted isolation ward. The surgery and recovery area has twelve "beds." There are separate offices for the various directors and managers. The adjoining kennel includes all the special features of the Walker Kirby Canine Center.

To complement these extraordinary improvements in the facilities, Dr. Holle has expanded the role of the kennel staff to primary caretakers. They check stool for signs of problems, draw blood to check on heartworm, and take temperatures. They bathe the dogs, brush their teeth, clean their ears, clip their nails, and monitor their health and happiness.

Despite all its preoccupation with the breeding, rearing, and health of its dogs, The Seeing Eye has not forgotten the human half of the human-dog equation. The school is deeply concerned with the changing character of the population using guide dogs. For one thing, the causes of blindness have changed. Since the end of the Vietnam War there have been no war blind, and mandatory helmets for motorcycle riders and seat belts and air bags in cars had lowered the number of accidents that resulting in blindness in young people. The incidence of retrolental fibroplasia and diabetic retinopathy remain about the same. Macular degeneration afflicts an older population, as do the later stages of retinitis pigmentosa. The blind population has been aging, and so has The Seeing Eye's graduate body. Today, Student Services reports that several graduates in their eighties are applying for dogs, including one of eighty-eight. At ninety-two, Mary Coles was still walking her dog daily on Martha's Vineyard.

In response to the need for gentler and softer dogs for these older students, The Seeing Eye had begun to cross Labradors with golden retrievers. When Doug Roberts attended the International Federation of Guide Dog Schools in England, he was impressed by the success English schools had enjoyed with these crossbred dogs. The offspring of goldens crossed with yellow Labs all look like yellow Labs, but with the right match, Doug says, "you eliminate the silliness of the golden and the high energy level of the Lab. You get a gentler, steadier and less distractable guide endowed with hybrid vigor and resistance to some health problems." These dogs are especially suitable for aging students.

There may soon be special small classes for two or three senior citizens at a time. They would last only two weeks, involving less challenging routes and a less rigorous schedule. No awakening at 5:00 a.m. to take the dogs into the park!

Aging students are not the only reason for modifying the instruction program. A whole variety of changes in the traffic and terrain of modern America have posed problems that did not exist ten years ago. New four-cylinder cars are so silent that they are difficult to hear. Even far noisier motors can be drowned out by the rising level of background noise. Leaf blowers, power mowers, snow blowers, garbage compactors, and helicopters have made once peaceful suburban streets as noisy as metropolitan business districts. Pausing at a traffic signal, students find it difficult, sometimes impossible, to detect the flow of traffic. The extended rounding of ramped or blended curbs makes it easy for even experienced graduates to lose direction and unwittingly command their dogs to diagonal across a busy intersection.

Some traffic signals are automated to expedite vehicular flow without regard for pedestrians. A green light enabling a car on a side street to turn into a main artery may last only a few seconds, not long enough for a pedestrian to cross. A further complication is the problem of right on red. The pedestrian is supposed to have the right of way at a crosswalk, but motorists tend to forget this, focusing all their attention on the automobile traffic to their left and turning right at their first opportunity, possibly without seeing the guide dog team in the crosswalk. All this means that trainers must increase their dogs' awareness of cars. They expose them to more traffic and more complicated traffic patterns. This in turn elevates the dogs' level of stress. The gentler dogs needed for older students are more easily stressed and can become frightened of cars instead of learning how to deal with them.

For these reasons and more, the school made a change it had long been deliberating. It extended the length of the training period from three months to four. Every other guide dog school in the country had already extended its training period, and early in 1995 a new program for dealing with progressive retinal atrophy involved withholding Labrador retrievers from training for four months. As a result, class sizes were averaging eighteen rather than twenty-four students each. This offered maneuvering room to readjust the schedule and organize five teams of four instructors, each training their dogs for four months.

The extension allows senior instructors the travel time needed to visit and assess applicants so that they can be better matched to dogs in training. Up to now, such visits were possible only for applicants about whom there were some serious doubts, such as their true need for a dog, too much vision, too little hearing, psychiatric history, or diabetic neuropathy. These home visits have reduced waiting time for the applicants, but the real advantage of the longer training period is for the dogs.

Doug Roberts explains: "You cannot train a dog to have a different temperament. A high energy field trial retriever pumped up with eagerness to charge into the swamp and bring back the bird is inappropriate for guide dog work." The gentler representatives of "a breed within a breed" are more easily stressed, but the extra month of training allows the instructor to ease up on a dog who is feeling too much pressure until it regains its confidence. In this way dogs have been enabled to overcome incipient anxieties that would have disqualified them under the old schedule.

The Seeing Eye encourages its graduates to avoid escalators. They are frightening to dogs and can cause injuries. Students are taught how to minimize their hazards by keeping toenails clipped and making certain that there is plenty of forward leeway to allow the dog to skip off at the end of the ride. Subway platforms are a serious hazard. Several guide dog owners have fallen on tracks in New York and Washington, and a graduate of one school was killed. When there is a single-edged platform, sighted passengers tend to line up next to the wall, leaving a relatively narrow passage for a dog and master. If the master happens to be on the outside, a small step away from the dog can result in a fall. To avoid such missteps, The Seeing Eye provides station platform work and uses the Summit railroad station, which presents a longer and more menacing drop than the one in Morristown. Another addition is mall work. Because they have no clear traffic patterns, the wide-open spaces of malls and their vast parking lots are confusing. Masters cannot give dogs helpful directions. There are no clear lines of movement, and confusion increases stress.

Even with the additional challenges of recent years, the school has been increasing its percentage of successful pairings. The improvement has been due not only to extended training and scientific breeding, but also to the puppy-raising program. The average success rate in training for school-bred dogs over a three-year period was 71 percent. The success rate for puppies purchased from other breeders but brought up in puppy-raising families was 69 percent, nearly the same. By contrast, the success rate for adult dogs purchased over this same period was only 29 percent. Clearly, the canine "Headstart" program provided by puppy-raisers has been of crucial importance in providing successful guides. To further reduce the stress of training, the school has extended the puppy-raisers' custody from fourteen to sixteen and, ultimately, to eighteen months. The greater maturity of the dogs beginning training helps them to cope with the strain.

The explosion of puppies provided by scientific breeding and improved personnel at the Mendham farm has prompted an expansion of this program. There are seven members of the puppy placement staff, all women, whom Doug Roberts calls "the unsung heroines of The Seeing

Eye." Each of them is responsible for approximately one hundred puppy-raising families, who may call at all hours of the night or on weekends. The staff members have crossed New Jersey, eastern Pennsylvania, and northern Delaware giving talks to puppy-raisers, school assemblies, to PTA meetings, and to Elks, Lions, and Rotary clubs, building membership and public awareness.

As field representative, David Loux covers the entire country. He meets with agencies, rehabilitation centers, and schools, renewing old friendships and recruiting new students. As host to the graduate students in orientation and mobility who visit The Seeing Eye annually, he maintains important contacts with mobility instructors. Recently, he has been abetted by another blind graduate, Jay Stiteley. Sometimes together, sometimes alternately, the two keep workers for the blind aware of Seeing Eye programs. A high-technology guru, Jay Stiteley also conducts seminars on the use of adaptive technology for the blind and visually impaired.

Progress on all these fronts has not made the school complacent. Judy Deuschle, who succeeded Paula Pursley as director of Student Services, states frankly, "The Seeing Eye no longer dominates the field, and the better schools produce quality dogs. We are competing for a relatively small population. In 1996, there were some 8,000 graduates from ten established schools across the country. So what do you do to make yourself different, to make people want to come to The Seeing Eye instead of another school? What we feel sets us apart is our steadfast adherence to our basic philosophy: treating people with dignity and respect."

That includes the material comforts and health care the school provides: a resident nurse available for students twenty-four hours a day, special diets, spacious bedroom and recreation room facilities, the outside walks, gazebo, and patio, the laundry and exercise rooms, the array of computers in the Storer Technology Center, and the instruction in their use available from Dave Loux and Jay Stiteley.

But Judy means something more: "I tell the students that even though the training is demanding and stressful at times, we do whatever we can to ensure that the rest of their experience at The Seeing Eye is as pleasant and homey as possible. Whatever we can do for them, we will."

She is assisted by Michele Drolet, a Seeing Eye graduate, as a counselor to students. Michele has a readily accessible office, and she joins the students for midmorning coffee daily. On the first Thursday of every class, there is a session for returning graduates who wish to attend. Discussing their grief for their dogs with others who are feeling the same loss promotes acceptance. For those who have retired their dogs, it is helpful to learn that there is a waiting list of people wanting to adopt retired dogs.

There are many causes of stress for students. Every dog has its individual personality, and adjusting to a second dog can be as disconcerting as adjusting to a second spouse. Student Services seeks to alleviate as much stress as possible, so students can focus their full attention on learning to work with their dogs.

Almost all the interconnected programs described in this chapter—the breeding, computerization, puppy-raising, medical care, health maintenance, new challenges to guide work, and the consequent changes in training technique—have been related directly or indirectly to the dogs. But there have been important administrative changes as well. The long experience with fund-raising that had made Dennis Murphy an effective replacement for Stuart Grout in 1989 was no longer needed five years later. In September of 1995, he was replaced by Kenneth Rosenthal, a graduate of Amherst and Yale Law School, who had been a founding official of Hampshire College and its secretary-treasurer, responsible for business operations. Later he served as vice president for various commercial companies.

Ken is The Seeing Eye's president and chief executive. The other executives are now styled directors rather than vice presidents. Their newest member is Richard "Bud"

Liptak, director of Grounds and Buildings and project manager for the Stabile Canine Health Center. The work of the
directors is interrelated, and the remarkable progress of recent years is owing less to their individual talents than to
their ability to work as a team. They and their staffs are
devoted to The Seeing Eye's mission and are more interested in team success than in personal achievement.

In the context of this chapter, it is worth mentioning
that Ken Rosenthal's first appointment was the hiring of Dr.
Eldin Leighton as full-time director of Canine Genetics. The
newest advance in this area will become public shortly before the publication of this book. The Mendham breeding
station has gradually been surrounded by suburban residents who object to barking dogs. The kennels are not suitable for a germ-free environment, and the septic and oil
tanks are in violation of recently adopted state environ-
mental codes. For these reasons The Seeing Eye has purchased 254 acres in Chester, New Jersey, where it plans to
build a state-of-the-art breeding facility.

The Seeing Eye will continue its effort to breed ever
more suitable guide dogs, and perhaps I can best illustrate
the fruits of its program to date from my own experience.
Like all of my earlier dogs Pasha is a German shepherd, but
she does not have the high energy of my first dog. Minnie
walked at fully four miles an hour. More than once we completed a three-and-a-half-mile walk in the Litchfield Hills
in forty-six minutes. With Pasha, it takes an hour and ten
minutes. At the age of seventy-seven I could not handle
Minnie today.

Minnie was so frightened of thunderstorms that long
before my ears could detect the sound of distant thunder
she would crouch trembling by my knees. They do not
bother Pasha. At an especially loud clap of thunder, she
peers out the picture window to see what's up. She is full
of fun at play time, but lies patiently on the floor during
long meetings. She is curious and looks into every open

door when walking down a hallway, but she is not easily distracted. She is always eager to dive into her harness.

This past winter, we were walking along a snowy road when I heard a huge rumbling snowplow bearing down behind us. Pasha glanced over her shoulder but continued unconcerned. It thundered past and, some fifty yards ahead, turned right into the road that would take us home and stopped. Pasha walked on until we reached the intersection, then stopped and watched. She was not frightened by the huge, noisy engine. She was just waiting to see what it would do next. After a moment, it backed into the road, turned right, and went back the way it had come. With the path cleared, Pasha crossed the road and headed for home. There was nothing spectacular in all this, but it was a clear demonstration of self-confidence, judgment, and good sense—the working temperament of The Seeing Eye's breed within a breed.

22
My Dog Is a Shepherd

From her apartment window in midtown Manhattan, Toni Stabile had a clear view of the street below, and on one occasion she had seen a blind man with a cane take a painful and humiliating fall. In contrast, she regularly observed a Seeing Eye graduate whose Labrador retriever guided him to and from work. Both man and dog moved quickly and confidently. Both seemed always to be smiling. The contrast with the other blind man, hesitant and frowning, made a strong impression.

Her admiration for the pair from The Seeing Eye prompted Toni Stabile to suggest to her brother that they visit the school, and that visit led to the building of the Vincent Stabile Canine Health Center. I mention the graduate and his dog here as only one example of the thousands of partnerships the school has established over the years. They have included individuals of every description following a variety of careers in all parts of the country.

Dr. Shirley Chapman with her Vandy was a professor of political science at East Tennessee State when she was elected mayor of Johnson City. She wrote, "We were burning the deed or bond to city hall, which was paid off July 1. When Vandy saw fire, she immediately left the sit position and tried to pull me away from it. When I refused to move, she lunged for the burning paper now in a metal tray, grabbed it and put out the fire before a fireman next to the tray could stop her. She was not going to let me be around fire. The whole crowd cheered her, and the newspaper told the story on page one."

Joe Klatt was a real estate broker in California. According to his pedometer, he and Peggy clocked 2,200 miles on the streets of La Jolla in the same year that they sold $4.3 million worth of real estate. On the opposite coast, Robert Gerard, an assistant commissioner of mental health, used his Chantell to travel, not the sidewalks of New York, but its intricate subway and bus system. All Seeing Eye graduates have flown with their dogs, but Jim Storer, a veteran of twenty-five years in the radio business in Cleveland, reckons he and his guides have flown more than a million miles. His Angel may have been the first to fly a Concorde jet.

Other graduates have used their guides in more primitive settings. With a Labrador named Dinah, Paul Ponchillia, a Ph.D. in plant pathology, taught at Michigan State where his wife, Susan, was also a professor. The three took wilderness vacations during the summer, and one of them was to Auyuittuq on Baffin Island, the only national park above the Arctic Circle, where one-hundred-mile-per-hour winds are common. One day they hiked over ten miles of treeless tundra surrounded by glacial mountains and icy streams, "walking over rocks that were three feet around. Dinah was really good at picking the best way. A lot of times she saw a path and would go her own way instead of following Susan."

Michael May took his Totie not to the Arctic, but to Equatorial Africa as a member of the Experiment in International Living in Ghana. Dogs were so rare there, he reported, that "walking with a dog in Ghana would be like walking down Broadway with a lion on a string." The natives were so wary of dogs that, when flagging a bus, May used to hide Totie, and when they boarded together, everyone else jumped off.

May's subsequent career included a graduate degree in International Relations from Johns Hopkins, a stint with the CIA as a political analyst on Africa, and electronics research in Silicon Valley. He became a champion downhill skier, winning three gold medals at the 1982 World Games in Switzerland. Instead of having his sighted guide behind him, May had his guide just two or three feet in front. "I listen to the skis. As he makes a left, his skis cut into the snow and make a certain sound. I also listen to his voice. We ski very close together. Often we bump." May has been clocked at 54 miles per hour. Another graduate skier, Urban Miyares, has been clocked at 63 miles per hour. There may well be others with faster records, but I have been unable to keep track of all the graduates' activities.

For sheer physical and mental endurance, no one has yet matched the feat of Bill Irwin and Orient, who walked the entire twelve-hundred-mile length of the Appalachian Trail from Georgia to Maine in 1990. Of the sighted hikers who have walked the complete trail, most have done it in segments over a period of years. Irwin and Orient did it in one stretch between March and November. Irwin's autobiographical account, *Blind Courage*, describes taking literally thousands of falls, losing toenails, persevering through sweltering heat, drenching rain, and biting cold. A born-again Christian, Irwin undertook the Appalachian Trail as a sort of religious pilgrimage, a witness to his faith. The motivations of most graduates have been less exalted.

David Chappell was attending the university in Calgary, Canada, and was satisfied with the mobility of cane travel until he emerged from a night class one winter to find six inches of snow on the ground and an air temperature of twenty below. At the university, with people around, Chappell had managed to catch his bus, but when he was let off in a deserted residential area, he discovered why snow is called blind man's fog. He could not locate the sidewalks and managed to get home only by flagging down a passing car. He decided that it was time to get a dog.

Snow was not the problem for a Florida woman whose story was reported by Lukas Franck, an instructor who visits graduates having difficulties.[1] "It was a few days after a

---

[1] Instructors paying home visits to graduates have discovered that

local flood, and our graduate was out for a walk with her Seeing Eye dog. She came to a corner where she usually crossed and gave the forward command. The dog refused. She listened. No cars were coming, so she repeated the command. The dog whipped her around and started for home. The woman knew this was unusual, so she followed the dog as she was trained to do." After she got home, her husband drove to the spot to have a look. "There were two alligators, each five feet long, on the other side of the street." The clear moral was a rule that every instructor has repeated countless times to students in training: "Follow your dog!"

Follow your dog! Volumes of meaning and emotion lie behind those three words. Give your dog your trust. It will keep you safe. But partnership is a two-way street. You must earn your dog's trust. Apparently disparate comments by two quite different graduates are pertinent here. Davis Duty, who has had a distinguished career as a lawyer and jurist, credited much of his later success to what he discovered at seventeen, learning to adjust to his first dog. "I grew up in a lot of ways, because I had to assume responsibility for the dog as well as the responsibility for independence." Assuming the responsibility for a guide dog is demanding, especially for an adolescent. It is not only a matter of feeding, airing, brushing, and working the dog with the appropriate rewards and corrections. Like a parent for its child, a Seeing Eye master must be there for his dog twenty-four hours a day. It is a maturing experience. Duty learned to depend on his dog, taught his dog to depend on him, and used their mutual dependence to gain independence. Assuming the responsibility for his dog, Davis Duty grew up.

----

dogs may somehow recognize their presence and refuse to exhibit the behavior the instructor is there to correct. To hide from the dogs, they follow at some distance, observing from behind trees, parked cars, or the corners of buildings, stalking the graduates in so suspicious a manner that they have been stopped for questioning by alert police officers.

Karen Sands, an assistant district attorney in Albuquerque, New Mexico, put it quite differently: "The liberty and freedom the dogs provide are so preferable to any other means of travel, I'll never be without a dog again as long as I live. They're gorgeous and wonderful animals that provide a graceful way to be blind." The grace of the partnership is more than a matter of physical coordination. It is the reflection of a profound mutual trust based on the root meaning of grace. They are graceful because they are thankful, full of gratitude for each other.

I must bring this history to an end, and if I am to define what seems to me The Seeing Eye's essential quality I would have to focus on its selflessness. That selflessness is combined with scientific method, rigorous attention to detail, iron discipline, and hard work, but the selflessness is basic.

In the fall of 1957, I roomed with a diabetic bricklayer from Chicago. He had little formal education. Instead of "you" he invariably said "youse," but he was as courageous as anyone I have ever met. His diabetes was far advanced, and the exertion of walking affected his gait. He fell frequently. Asked how a trip had gone, he would answer cheerfully, "Me and Spot only fell tree times dis trip."

Another student who was familiar with diabetes confided that my roommate could not have more than six months to live. I am certain that George Werntz, Ibby Hutchinson, and the other members of the executive staff knew his medical history and prognosis, but people who have experienced the continuing miracle of guide dogs and humans year after year learn to believe in miracles. This man wanted a dog. He had the guts to train with a dog. He must be given the chance. Against all odds, The Seeing Eye gave. My roommate gave. His dog, Spot, gave. And he went back to Chicago with Spot. What happened then was not quite a miracle. He was not cured of diabetes, but he lived another three and a half years with the independence and dignity Spot gave him.

Willi Ebeling had his failings, but his great quality was a constantly renewing awareness of the miracle of the dogs. I recall a visit to the old headquarters on Whippany Road shortly before Uncle Willi was to retire. He was at least seventy and had been at the school for a quarter of a century, but he was in high excitement about an incident that had taken place the day before. A dog that had been with its new master for three days had misbehaved in the dining room. When the instructor corrected it, it growled at him. My wife and I looked blank, not understanding, and Uncle Willi explained:

"After only three days, mind you, the dog takes over the new master." His voice was vibrant with excitement. "Only three days. And when the instructor comes to give a correction, he growls. He says, 'This is my guy here. If there's any correction, he does it. Not you.' "

Years later, Ned Myrose told me of his experience with what must have been the same dog. He chose a Dalmatian named Nosey to pair with a Marine veteran.

"Three days after I gave him the dog, every time I got near him, Nosey would growl. That was not all. When he and his master stopped for a down curb, Nosey would lift his leg and wet on him. Good thing he was a marine instead of an old maid. He thought it was funny."

As soon as they left the school, Nosey's growling and his unorthodox urination both ceased. Ned Myrose said the probable explanation was that Nosey had undergone an uncertain puppyhood, being shunted from one owner to another. When he was paired with the marine, he had found the master he wanted and turned on Myrose, fearing that he would try to separate them. Once he arrived at his blind master's home, he had no more fear and showed no more hostility. The wetting had a similar cause. Urinating is the way a dog claims possession. He was telling his master "You belong to me." Away from The Seeing Eye, when he no longer feared separation, he had no need to assert possession. In a curious way then, both the growling and the urination had been expressions of Nosey's love.

In the course of nearly seventy years, some variation of this miracle of love has been repeated some 12,000 times. Blind men and women, young and old, have come from all parts of the United States and Canada, from many walks of life and ethnic origins. Some have suffered from poor orientation. Others have been frail or fearful. But if they had the courage to trust their dogs and the capacity to win their dogs' love, even the most unlikely left The Seeing Eye confident of their ability to lead a new life. Perhaps no one said it better than Larry Liggin:

> My dog is a shepherd, just what I want. She maketh me to rise early every morning. She leadeth me beside garbage cans and parking meters, and she restoreth my freedom. She guideth me in the paths of safety for my life's sake. Yea, though I walk through the thunder of the railroad station and among the mongrels of Flagler Street, I will fear no evil, for she is with me. The creak of her harness and the jingle of her collar, they comfort me. She prepareth a way for me in the presence of all confusion. She covereth my hand with affectionate licks and nibbles, and my love for her runneth over. Surely, with affection and correction, I shall follow her all the days of her life, and she will dwell in my heart forever.

Index

About the Author

Peter Brock Putnam went blind in 1941 shortly before his twenty-first birthday when, following a long depression, he attempted suicide. The gunshot that spared his life took his sight, but the challenge of blindness was just what he needed. He was paired with his first Seeing Eye dog in the fall and became the first blind undergraduate at Princeton early in 1942. Following graduation with honors, he married and entered graduate school, receiving his Ph.D. in history in 1950. He taught history at Princeton until 1955, when he left to become a writer. He has published six books: *Seven Britons in Imperial Russia, 1698–1812*; *"Keep Your Head Up, Mr. Putnam!"*; *Cast Off the Darkness*; *The Triumph of The Seeing Eye*; *Peter, the Revolutionary Tsar*; and *Love in the Lead*.

Dr. Putnam is a past or present member of a number of boards of nonprofit organizations, including those of The Seeing Eye, the Lucerna Fund, the Memorial Society Fund, and Recording for the Blind & Dyslexic, of which he was national chairman. He says of it, "The Seeing Eye offers freedom of movement in space. RFB&D offers freedom of movement in print for students who cannot read texts on account of visual, perceptual, or physical handicaps." He currently lives and writes in Princeton with his wife of more than fifty years.